ELDERLY WOMEN IN MEGAPOLIS

About the Author

Archana Kaushik Panda, a faculty in Social Work, University of Delhi, earned her Ph.D. from Jamia Millia Islamia, New Delhi. Her professional interests are many and varied, including gerontology, women, children, HIV/AIDS and Panchayati Raj.

Dr. Panda has participated in a good number of seminars and conferences, and has published several research papers and articles in journals as well as newspapers of repute. She has contributed to the development and upgradation of course material on 'Rural Development and Social Work' for Indira Gandhi National Open University, New Delhi.

ELDERLY WOMEN IN MEGAPOLIS

Status and Adjustment

Archana Kaushik Panda

CONCEPT PUBLISHING COMPANY, NEW DELHI-110059

The Indian Council of Social Research gave the financial support towards the publicaion of this work. However, the responsibility for the contents of the book—facts, opinions, conclusions, etc—is entirely that of the author and not of the ICSSR

ICSSR Consultant: **Prof. K.D. Gangrade**

ISBN 81-8069-200-0

First Published 2005

Published and Printed by
Ashok Kumar Mittal
Concept Publishing Company
A/15-16, Commercial Block, Mohan Garden
New Delhi-110 059 (INDIA)

Phones : 25351460, 25351794
Fax : 091-11-25357103
Email : publishing@conceptpub.com

To my supporting parents
loving husband &
darling son Anand

PREFACE

Though old age is considered to be a part of the life-cycle, certain emerging trends relating to the population of the elderly have been a cause of concern. Earlier on, the number and proportion of the elderly in society used to be rather low. In modern times, with medical and technological advancement, these have gone up substantially, all over the world. There are countries like Sweden and England where almost a third of the population is of aged persons. In contrast, developing countries have but smaller proportions. None the less, it is growing fast. India has, at present, 77 million elderly people and by 2025 this is likely to go up to 177 million. Another important demographic fact that attracts the attention of gerontologists and social researchers is: 'aging is feminized'. Globally, elderly women are outnumbering their male counterparts.

Apart from this numerical dimension, change in the socio-cultural milieu has contributed significantly to the marginalization of the elderly people. Joint family system, which used to act as a social safety-net for the aged, has given way to nuclear family. Value system too is undergoing rapid changes, which do not always favour 'grey years'. Community is losing its grip to act as a means of social control, especially in urban areas. The aged, from active contributors to the family economy and social life, have become passive receptors of care and support. Unconditional love and respect that used to be showered upon them have now become dependent upon their performance and achievement in life, failing which they are considered a spent-force.

How do the aged cope with this new social situation? What is the situation of an aged woman whose situation is considered to be even more disadvantageous than her male counterpart? How an elderly female handles health related issues when she enters into old age with life-long experience of gender bias, malnutrition, early marriage, repeated and multiple pregnancies, gynæcological ailments combined with general deterioration of physical strength and sensory capabilities? How is her mental health influenced when she no longer finds herself in the coveted roles of parenting and home manager? Do life-long economic dependency and lack of vocational skills bring a sense of insecurity in her in old age? Does she feel satisfied with life when she looks back and takes stock of her life's achievements and failures? How does she deal with urban lifestyles like limited living space, impersonality, fast pace of life, cut-throat competition, women's entry into the job market, etc.?

These are some of the many issues that call for priority attention and perhaps systematic study. The present work is a modest attempt in this direction. It seeks to understand the adjustment of elderly women to age-related changes in the urban milieu. The study looks at the health and well-being issues among aged women. It also pays attention to the role played by elderly women in their family and neighbourhood and the respect and recognition they receive. Stated differently, it is an attempt to find out the factors that enhance harmonious adjustment of senior ladies with their social environment. It also deals with sense of security among aged women. Finally, it suggests ways and means to enhance well-being among elderly women.

I do hope that this book is going to help the people engaged in the care and welfare of elderly in the creation of an enabling and encouraging environment where aged women would lead their life with contentment, happiness and dignity.

Archana Kaushik Panda

ACKNOWLEDGEMENTS

The present work has seen the light of the day as a large number of professionals and organizations have extended to me ungrudgingly help and cooperation. Mentioning all of them is nearly an impossible task. However, a prominent few among them may well not be missed out.

I am extremely grateful to my supervisor, Prof. M. Z. Khan, for being so supportive and patient during all the stages of the implementation of the present work. His depth of knowledge and his attention even to minor details have been instrumental in inculcating and developing a kind of research attitude in me for which I will remain in debt to him throughout my life. His guidance, encouragement and affection gave me the strength to bring the present work to a satisfactory head. Mrs. Khan has been equally compassionate and loving. During long hours of sitting at her residence, she would ensure congenial atmosphere with all her hospitality and motherly affection. I thank her for all her gestures of love and understanding.

Present work would have been difficult to complete without the help and cooperation of my respondents. In spite of their preoccupation and, sometimes, ill-health they have spared their valuable time and freely discussed their feelings and emotions. I earnestly thank all of them. Cooperation of the secretaries of Resident Welfare Associations and many residents of Pushp Vihar, New Delhi, is also acknowledged.

Further, I thank my mummy and papa who have remained a source of constant encouragement and support without which it would have been impossible to pursue the work. They have enabled me to pursue my research goals, motivating me all the time, especially when I would feel low. In fact, their contribution can never be expressed fully in words. I am grateful to my brothers, Amit and Atul, for their unflinching support. I wish all the researchers have younger brothers like them. They always have time to undertake mundane works, say, photocopying of material, providing me transport, and depositing university dues—to mention a few.

I must thank my husband for his love and support. I feel pleased and proud to have a life-partner who has always understood and empathized with my research constraints and achievements. He has constantly encouraged me to aspire and achieve higher goals in life.

I owe a special debt to my *dadi-ma,* grandmother, for sharing with me her dreams and aspirations. In fact, the stimulus to undertake the present work had come from her only. I also miss the presence of my *dadaji, nanaji* and *naniji,* who are no longer physically on the scene but who, when around, had always emphasized that their granddaughter should attain high professional goals. I appreciate the encouragement and support given by all my relatives, especially my in-laws. I also thank my friend Beena for her invaluable support and encouragement.

I express my thanks to Indian Council for Social Science Research, New Delhi, for extending the much-needed support for the publication of the work. Indeed, this will go a long way in sharing my ideas with a wider audience.

While on this, I must place on record my thanks to Mr. Ashok Kumar Mittal, Chairman and Managing Director and other staff-members of the Concept Publishing Company, New Delhi, for bringing out the work in print and for endowing it with rich production values.

Archana Kaushik Panda

CONTENTS

Preface vii

Acknowledgements ix

List of Tables xii

List of Diagrams xv

1. Introduction 1
2. Demographic, Social and Economic Background of the Elderly Women 39
3. Pattern of Social Adjustment 75
4. Health, Well-being and Social Adjustment 111
5. Social Acceptance of the Elderly Females 146
6. Sense of Security and Adjustment 182
7. Conclusion 211

Appendix 233

References 243

Index 264

LIST OF TABLES

1.1	Elderly population: Size, growth rate and proportion for different regions	8
1.2	Growth of elderly population by sex in India, 1901-2001	10
1.3	Percentage distribution of population aged 60 plus by work status, sex and residence in India, 1991	12
1.4	Dependency ratios and indices of ageing in India, 1951-2001	13
1.5	Percentage distribution of the aged population by sex, residence and level of education, India, 1991	14
2.1	Population of Delhi by sex and age-group	44
2.2	Age and sex-wise distribution of the elderly in India, 1981-1991	47
2.3	Association between marital status and death fear among the elderly respondents	51
2.4	Religion-wise distribution of population of India, Delhi and Pushp Vihar	54
2.5	Association between caste affiliation and educational status of the respondents	58
2.6	Occupational patterns of the respondents and their husband	73
3.1	Association between attitudinal adjustment and feeling of loneliness among the respondents	87
3.2	Association between Conflict adjustment and self-rating of the respondents of their life	94
3.3	Association between need adjustment and feeling of security-insecurity among elderly women	100
3.4	Association between need adjustment and consultation on family matters	101

3.5 Association between role adjustment and respondents' rating of their fulfilment of expectations from life 105
3.6 Association between overall social adjustment and self-evaluation of health among the respondents 110
4.1 Percentage distribution of the elderly females over the activities of daily-living in the three age-groups 120
4.2 Association between health condition of the respondents and their marital status 126
4.3 Association between overall health condition and overall social adjustment among the respondents 127
4.4 Association between overall health condition of the respondents and their feeling of loneliness 130
4.5 Respondents' rating of their past, present and future life 132
4.6 Association between optimism-pessimism and overall social adjustment among aged females 136
4.7 Association between overall social adjustment and respondents' rating of their past, present and future life 141
5.1 Most commonly shared activities by elderly respondents with their husband 152
5.2 Most common household activities performed by the respondents in their household 157
5.3 Association between willingness-unwillingness among the respondents in doing household work and their adjustment 160
5.4 Most commonly performed activities by grandmothers during care of their infant grandchildren 161
5.5 Association between willingness-unwillingness among the respondents in doing household work and their adjustment 164
5.6 Commonly performed activities by grandmothers with their grandchildren 165
5.7 Commonly performed activities by the respondents with their friends 170

5.8	Association between consultation on family matters and social adjustment of the respondents	174
6.1	Association between the past income patterns of the respondents and their religious affiliation	191
6.2	Association between expenses on religious activities and religious affiliation of the respondents	198
6.3	Association between feeling of security-insecurity among the elderly respondents and their marital status	201
6.4	Association between the feeling of security-insecurity and having bank account among the respondents	203
6.5	Association between the feeling of security-insecurity and loneliness among the respondents	205
6.6	Association between economic security-insecurity among respondents and their consultation in family matters	209
6.7	Association between security-insecurity and overall life-satisfaction among the aged respondents	210

LIST OF DIAGRAMS

2.1	Marital status and loneliness	52
2.2	Educational status and religion of the respondents	55
2.3	Type of family of respondents	64
2.4	Educational status and age of the respondents	70
3.1	Attitudinal adjustment and decision-making	88
3.2	Conflict adjustment and life-satisfaction	95
3.3	Role adjustment and unwillingness to do household chores	106
3.4	Frequency distribution of respondents over social adjustment	109
4.1	Overall health condition and age	125
4.2	Overall health condition and respondents' rating of life	133
4.3	Life-satisfaction and marital status	144
5.1	Social adjustment and activities shared with grandchildren	166
5.2	Common activities shared with friends	168
5.3	Social adjustment and acceptance by family members	178-180
6.1	Respondents' sense of security to buy/arrange certain things	200
6.2	Security-insecurity and optimism-pessimism	206
6.3	Sense of security and social adjustment	208

1

INTRODUCTION

Older persons occupy a unique place in society. Earlier, they used to be in the forefront of family and community affairs and decision-making. They would invariably head the family and their likes and dislikes would be imbibed by the rest of family members. Similarly, they used to occupy a place of prominence in the community. Often their word would be a law. At any rate, their word in the matters of customs and traditions would be about the final. Agricultural economy, patriarchal social structure and joint family system would sustain and reinforce their importance.

However, the social situation has undergone a radical change. The process of industrialization has overshadowed agricultural economy and joint family households have given way to nuclear family system. What is more, intellectual liberalization and democratic institution and process have become an integral part of contemporary life-style. Merits and demerits apart these social changes have had a profound influence on the situation of older persons. Often times, they are found to have been socially marginalized—be it the household or the community. In this regard, the situation of elderly women attracts a pointed attention.

Since the beginning, women had a social status less than equal to that of men. In many cultures, they were taken to be physically weak and intellectually imperfect, requiring the protection of father in infancy and childhood, of husband during their adulthood, and of sons, in their old age. Ironically enough, in modern times, social changes seem to have aggravated this situation for senior ladies. Their participation in education, remunerative work and community affairs is patently and woefully low. In most rural and urban areas, elderly women have to content with yet another exigency; migration. More often than not, adult and able-bodied persons migrate to industrial-urban centres for work, leaving behind elderly women, say, to their own devices. Are elderly persons or aged women, in particular, to be left to fend for themselves or, else, we need to evolve appropriate and effective social intervention policies and programmes? Before proceeding further, let us have a close look on the phenomenon of ageing.

Old age is a natural part of the life-cycle. It is considered as the closing period in the life-span. Many believe that it is an incremental phase of the life-cycle while others associate it with health problems or disease. This debate aside, ageing is a universal phenomenon. However, at the collective level, old age poses a challenge to policy makers in developing as well as developed countries. In modern times, this challenge is further accentuated, interestingly enough, by the rapid growth of science and technology. Better nutrition, sanitation and health facilities have decreased mortality rates and increased expectancy of life. Denoting a demographic transition, it has radically altered age-structure of the population. As a result, the population is moving towards a rectangular survival curve, in which fewer persons die from disease and most live until the very near end of the maximum life-span. And, thus, many countries are found face-to-face with what is popularly termed as 'greying of the nation'.

It follows that the proportion of the elderly in the general population is steadily growing. At present, developed countries have undergone change to become aged societies. There are some countries like Sweden and the United Kingdom whose about a third of the population is of persons aged 60 years or more. In Scandinavian countries and Japan, the expectancy of life at birth is over 75 years. Almost all European countries and many others including the USA are also very close to this demographic trend. The phenomenon of ageing and the issues related to it are not primarily confined to developed countries alone. These are emerging concerns in developing nations also, may be having a smaller ramification. Thus, from a 'world of children', the status a century back, it is rapidly becoming a 'world of old people'. May it be noted that demographic transition has come about only in the closing decades of the preceding century.

In this context, India is no exception. At the time of Independence, the undivided India had a population of a little over 350 million. Expectancy of life at birth was just 32 years, the female longevity being even less. Within a span of mere five decades, the demographic situation has markedly changed. India's population has gone up manifolds and life-expectancy has almost doubled. With the number of the elderly on an increase at a rate faster than the general population, the greying of India has become more visible than ever. At present, India has about 76 million elderly and in about two decades the number will go up to a mind boggling 150 million or more. Are our policy concerns aligned to the issue of ageing and aged persons?

It is often held that, increasing age imposes several limitations on the elderly, making their adjustment somewhat difficult. It, then, becomes too easy to see elderly persons as mere passive receptors of care. And, since contemporary society values youth, preconceived notions about old age are widespread with varying intensity. Often elderly people are taken as a liability, incapable of contributing anything to the society. It is not rare to come across young people who regard old age as a handicap or an incurable disease. Such myths often make ageing and the aged a subject of pity. Reportedly, many younger people in the USA use such uncomplimentary terms as 'wrinklies' and 'crumblies' while referring to old persons. These and similar negative stereotyping of aged persons tend to lead to situations in which their segregation or even alienation becomes inevitable. They become socially marginalized or disadvantaged.

Myths and stereotypes apart, senescence or ageing calls for a dispassionate appraisal and rethinking. Gerontologists and social scientists are engaged in understanding the causative factors that tend to make the elderly a vulnerable group. Globally, measures have been taken to improve their situation.

The United Nations, in 1982, organized the World Assembly on Ageing in Vienna as a forum to launch an International Action Programme for the Aged. It aims at guaranteeing economic and social security to older persons as well as providing them with opportunities to contribute to national development. The Assembly, among other measures, sponsored the idea of 'active ageing' as an important strategy for the adjustment of the aged in the society. The United Nations, in 1991, has laid down a set of five principles as guidelines for ushering an aged society as—independence, participation, care, fulfilment and dignity of older people. It implies that, we are not only concerned with increasing the longevity but also intend to 'add life to years'. Doubtless, this requires concerted and coordinated efforts in such sectors as health, human development and welfare. This is what is forcefully reverberated by Kofi Annan, Secretary-General, the United Nations: "Today, with the ageing of individuals and populations in developed and developing countries alike, we face a two-fold challenge, first in the promotion of life long individual development, so that individuals reach old age with life skills, vocational skills, good health and good family and social networks. Second is the creation of an enabling and encouraging environment in which individuals of all ages can participate actively and receive care and support when needed" (Address on the occasion of the Seventh International Day of Older Persons, October 1, 1997).

Stated differently, the elderly are emerging, as a special population group with differential needs and problems. This makes for a challenge, harmonious adjustment of the elderly in the family, community and society. It underlines a need to understand the concept of ageing before we look into the challenges the elderly are facing.

Concept of Ageing

To a layman, ageing of a person is characterized by a range of changes like greying of hair, wrinkling of skin, stooping of the gait, fading of eyesight and hearing, curtailment of independence in functioning, and imposition of retirement or superannuation by society (Khan, 1997). In fact, ageing is a process of growing old, regardless of chronological age. It begins at conception and eventually ends with death. According to Birren and Renner, "Ageing refers to the regular changes that occur in mature and genetically representative organisms living under representative environmental conditions as they advance in chronological age" (1977). However, terms 'ageing' and 'old-age' are, often, used interchangeably.

"Human ageing can be understood", observes Bromley, "as a complex, cumulative, time-related, psycho-biological process of deterioration occupying the post-developmental phase (growth) of life" (1974). Strehler (1976) proposes four criteria of ageing: (1) it is universal, it occurs in all members of the population (unlike diseases); (2) it is 'progressive', a continuous process; (3) it is intrinsic to the organism; and (4) it is degenerative (as opposed to developmental or maturational changes).

Birren, *et al.*, further describe ageing as "a process of change involving all aspects of the organism. Its consequences range from altered structures and functions of the component tissues of the body, to an altered relationship of the organism, to its physical and social environment. Ageing is a progression of adult changes, characteristic of the species and which should occur in all individuals, if they live long enough" (1963). Butler and Lewis view old age as "a multiple determined experience that depends on an intricate balance of physical, emotional and social forces anyone of which can upset or involve others" (1977).

Given this, ageing could be viewed from three major but overlapping perspectives – biological, psychological and social. All these dimensions of ageing collectively play an important role in adjustment of the elderly with their environment.

Biological age is an estimate of individual's present position with respect to his potential life-span. It is closely related to chronological age but the two are not identical. In determining the biological age of an individual, genetic factors, undoubtedly, play an important role (Shock, 1960; Verzar, 1963). Further, psychological age refers to the adaptive capacities of an individual in comparison to the average. It also includes subjective reactions of the individual to changes brought about due to biological and social aspects of ageing. How well an elderly comes to terms with ageing and accepts the changes related to old age, would largely depend upon a number of inter-related factors like personality characteristics, socio-economic background, life-events, etc. (Birren, 1960). On the other hand, social age refers to societal expectations of how people should behave at a particular chronological age (Tibbitts, 1960).

It is often felt that chronological age is a poor criterion in marking off old-age. There is not a single point at which a person becomes old. Individual differences in terms of effects of ageing can be seen easily. Some individuals are physically old at 40 years and some young at 60 years as denoted by their agility or physical abilities. Similarly, at 75 years, some individuals are young and spry while others are old and frail. Persons have different rates of ageing that do not necessarily correspond to their chronological age. In part, this can be explained by many individual characteristics as well as environmental factors such as heredity, sex, race, environment, family pattern, education, occupational status, etc. Comparison of the elderly in Western countries, with that in most of the Third World countries confirms this. Reportedly, majority of women, in developing countries, have suffered throughout their life from poor health, malnutrition, low literacy and indifferent social status. In their old age, these conditions further worsen. This apart, it is difficult to identify a cut-off point where middle age ends and old age begins. Is there a gender difference in ageing?

Indeed, cultural aspects have an important bearing on when a woman takes herself as old or is perceived by others as old. A few criteria, in this regard, could be brought under the focus. One way of looking at ageing in women is in terms of biological changes that seem to herald onset of ageing. Menopause indicates that a woman's reproductive function has come to an end. This physiological truth is more obvious in females than in males. In societies where women's reproductive function is overvalued, a post-menopausal woman is considered old, even asexual. Equating menopause with loss of vitality, sexuality and femininity makes this event a marker of ageing (Prakash, 1994).

Next, a woman is considered old when her eldest son marries and brings home his wife (D' Souza, 1982). At this stage, there will be major changes in her roles and status. She is supposed to hand over her household responsibilities to the bride. This is symbolically seen in the custom of handing over the keys to the new *bahu* (daughter-in-law). In India, in terms of 'social age' women are considered old at a younger age than men. This is collaborated by Prakash (1994) in her research finding—females consider themselves old at median age of 50 years while their male counterparts feel that their old age comes at 60 years and above.

Certain social security schemes have, among others, gender as criterion for providing old age benefits. To exemplify, in Kerala, while the cut-off age for Old Age Pension for males is 60 years and above, for females it is 55 years or more (see Khan and Bagley, 1989). While paying attention to the situation of the elderly equally important are their social, psychological and health incidents. Still, for demographic and statistical purposes chronological age appears to be most acceptable. Further, in different nations, in their statistical systems, different cut-off points for the aged are used, depending on official national ages of retirement and life-expectancies. It makes cross-cultural comparisons difficult. Many developed nations maintain cut-off for old age as 65 years. In India, the age of 60 years has been adopted by the National Policy for Older Persons, 1999, for the purpose of classifying a person as old.

Demographic Trends

Worldwide, old age is fast occupying centre-stage of national policies. The reason being the proportion as well as absolute numbers of the elderly, in the general population, is increasing at a fast rate. In the next few decades, most rapidly ageing countries like Sweden, Japan, Germany, Italy, etc., will have 40 per cent or more of their population of older persons (UNDP, 1999). Every year, around 9 million older persons are being added to the world's population. As a result, there is now a new period after superannuation commonly known as 'third age'. It is projected that, there may be, in next 50 years, more grandparents than grandchildren, in these developed nations.

Among the more developed regions, Sweden has the largest proportion of the elderly (34.9 per cent) followed by the United Kingdom (32 per cent) and France (29.2 per cent). In juxtaposition, among the less developed regions, Nigeria has the smallest proportion (5.6 per cent), followed by India (6.9 per cent) and Egypt (7.9 per cent). Sooner or later, these developing nations will experience a decline in their rate of natural population growth similar to what has already occurred in developed countries. As this process accelerates, age structures will change and the elderly will be an increasingly larger proportion of each country's total population.

Table 1.1 : Elderly population: Size, growth rate and proportion for different regions

	1970	*1980*	*1990*	*2000*	*2025*
World					
Size (million)	307.8	381.8	487.9	612.3.	1201.2
Annual growth rate (per cent)	2.1	2.3	2.4	2.8	2.7
Per cent to total population	8.3	8.6	9.2	9.8	14.8
More developed regions					
Size (million)	148.9	173.5	205.7	235.7	342.7
Annual growth rate (per cent)	2.3	1.5	1.7	1.4	1.5
Per cent to total population	14.2	15.3	17.1	18.7	25.3
Less developed regions					
Size (million)	158.9	208.4	282.1	376.6	858.5
Annual growth rate (per cent)	2.0	2.7	3.0	2.8	3.3
Per cent to total population	6.0	6.3	6.9	7.6	12.1

Source: World Population Prospects 2002, United Nations, New York, 2000.

Table 1.1 presents the percentage of elderly population to the general population in the world, more developed regions (Northern America, Europe, USSR, Australia, New Zealand) and less developed regions (Africa, East and South Asia, Malaysia and Micronesia Polynesia). It may be noted that though proportion of elderly population to the general population in the more developed regions is much higher (18.7 per cent) than less developed regions (7.6 per cent), annual growth rate in the latter region (2.8 per cent) is just double the more developed regions (1.4 per cent) for the year 2000. It means that the gap in the number and proportion of the elderly between less developed and more developed regions is narrowing.

Indian Situation

Since first half of the last century, the aged population, in India, barely constituted 5.5 per cent (20 million) of general population. In 1991, this proportion rose to 6.7 per cent (56.7 million). Currently, aged population in India is projected to be 76 million. The global population of the elderly is likely to be around 612 million (9.8 per cent). As per the United Nations classification, India has progressed from a mature society (i.e. elderly population between 4-7 per cent of the total population) to an ageing society (i.e. elderly population more than 7 per cent) by the Twenty-First century (United Nations, 1997).

Table 1.2 brings out detailed information on the elderly population in India from 1901 to 2001. It clearly shows that proportion of elderly females is higher than their male counterparts. Is it because they have added longevity?

Life Expectancy

Advances in medical sciences, like development of vaccinations against many diseases responsible for high infant and child mortality rates and invention of sulfa-drugs that save lives from pneumonia and other killer diseases, have resulted in increase in life-expectancy, throughout the world including developing countries. It is largely responsible for the expansion of the elderly segment in general population. In India, in 1901, life-expectancy, of males, at birth, was merely 22.5 years and that of females was 23.3 years. In 1951, it rose to 32.4 years in males and 31.7 years in females. Census (1991) showed that Indian males had a life-expectancy at birth of 59 years and females that of 59.7 years. Human Development Report (2001) shows, at present, life-expectancy at birth is 62.9 years. Thus, globally, life-expectancy is increasing, though with varying rates in different parts of the World. Do developmental initiatives in standard of living, hygiene, medicine and the like, would enable the elderly to live a full biological life-span with better quality?

TABLE 1.2 : Growth of elderly population by sex in India, 1901-2001

Year	*Persons*		*Males*		*Females*	
	Number	*Per cent*	*Number*	*Per cent*	*Number*	*Per cent*
1901	12.06	5.06	5.50	4.55	6.56	5.59
1911	13.17	5.22	6.18	4.81	6.99	5.65
1921	13.48	5.37	6.48	5.04	7.00	5.70
1931	14.21	5.09	6.49	4.86	7.27	5.35
1941	18.04	5.66	8.89	5.43	9.15	5.91
1951	19.61	5.43	9.67	5.21	9.94	5.66
1961	24.71	5.63	12.36	5.46	12.35	5.80
1971	32.70	5.97	16.87	5.94	15.83	5.99
1981	43.98	6.42	22.49	6.35	21.49	6.50
1991	55.30	6.55	28.23	6.45	27.07	6.66
2001	75.93	7.70	38.22	7.55	37.71	7.86

Source: Ageing in India: Paper No. 2 of 1997: Registrar General and Census Commissioner, India.

Sex Ratio

Existence of prejudices and discriminations against females, in India, can be seen through sex ratio. Census 2001 reveals 933 females per 1000 males. Female fœticide, infanticide, their lesser share in health, nutrition, education and development aspects have resulted in lower sex ratio in India. Ironically enough, beyond the age of 60 years, women outnumber their male counterparts. In 1991, there were 6.5 per cent of elderly in the total population, out of which 6.4 per cent were males and 6.6 per cent females. Projections for 2001 indicate women's proportion to be 7.8 per cent in contrast to 7.5 per cent of men. By age 70 years, there are nearly 6 women for every five men and by age of 80 plus, the ratio has moved to approximately 4:1 (Sharma, 1992). Looking into the marital status, incidence of widowhood is much higher among aged females. Currently, compared to 19 per cent of widowers, there are 64 per cent of widows. Higher life-expectancy for females at 60 plus and women marrying older men has resulted in large number of elderly widows. These demographic figures denote that ageing is, primarily, becoming an experience of females. Are our social intervention programmes for older persons gender sensitive?

Work Participation

It is observed that rapid technical changes and their introduction in modes of production, often, make the aged less relevant. Skills and capacities of the elderly, by and large, do not match with present day job market. Moreover, compulsory retirement around 60 years exacerbate their problems. Situation of aged females is much more grave, who have, most often, throughout their life, remained economically dependent on their family. A deeper look into the work status shows that, in 1991, in 60 plus age group, in urban areas, 42 per cent males and 5.4 per cent females were main workers whereas 57 per cent males and 94 per cent females were non-workers. Corresponding figures of elderly non-workers for rural areas were 35 per cent and 81 per cent respectively. Table 1.3 gives percentage distribution of aged population by work status, sex and residence in 1991. As the aged, in urban areas, more frequently, avail benefits of retirement including pension, work-participation rate was higher among rural elderly, both males and females. It would be interesting to note that even in 60 plus population of non-workers, many (1.16 per cent males and 0.62 per cent females) reported themselves as seeking work. The absolute numbers of elderly seeking work are 1.35 lakh males and 1.42 lakh females.

Table 1.3: Percentage distribution of population aged 60 plus by work status, sex and residence in India, 1991

Residence	*Sex*	*Main workers*	*Marginal workers*	*Non-workers*	*Seeking work*
Total	Total	36.25	2.89	60.87	0.80
	Male	59.52	0.01	39.47	1.16
	Female	11.24	4.90	83.86	0.62
Rural	Total	39.59	3.50	56.90	0.76
	Male	64.21	1.14	34.64	1.07
	Female	12.90	6.06	81.04	0.61
Urban	Total	24.31	0.68	75.01	0.92
	Male	42.43	0.51	57.07	1.36
	Female	5.43	0.87	93.70	0.65

Source: Ageing in India: Paper No. 2 of 1992: Registrar General and Census Commissioner, India.

Lower work participation rate, among the elderly, has increased their dependency ratio (proportion of the population aged 60 and above to that of the working age population in the age group 15-59 years). Elderly dependency ratio has risen from 9.8 in 1951 to 12.3 in 1991. Contrarily, child dependency ratio and total dependency ratio rose till 1971 and, thereafter, have fallen due to decline in fertility rates (Registrar General, India, 1997).

Another indicator called index of ageing expresses ratio of elderly (60 plus) to children (0-14 years) in the population. In 1951, it was 14.3 elderly per 100 children. In 1991, the corresponding figure rose to 18.4. Dependency ratio and indices of ageing, from 1951-2001, are reflected in Table 1.4. A sharp rise in index of ageing, in 2001, poses a threat to scarce national resources in our country. It also puts burden, on the working age group (15-59 years) and the State, in meeting their basic and civic needs.

Table 1.4 : Dependency ratios and indices of ageing in India, 1951-2001

		Dependency ratio		
Year	*Child*	*Elderly*	*Total*	*Index of ageing*
1951	68.49	9.80	78.29	14.31
1961	76.97	10.56	87.53	13.72
1971	80.82	11.47	92.29	14.20
1981	73.64	11.92	85.56	16.18
1991	61.43	11.31	72.75	18.42
2001	50.94	12.59	63.53	24.72

Source: Sharma, S.P (1994).

Literacy

In post-independence period, India has re-doubled its efforts to raise the educational level of its citizens. Census 2001 records literacy rate as 65.3 per cent as against 52.2 per cent in 1991. Though literacy rate, in the country, is gradually increasing, educational status of the elderly is still unsatisfactory. In 1981, only about 35 per cent of the elderly males were literate as compared to 47 per cent of general male population. Among women the scenario is even worse. A quarter of the female population was literate in 1981, but only about 8 per cent of elderly women.

Percentage distribution of elderly population by sex, residence and level of education in India in the year 1991 are shown in Table 1.5. It reveals that, according to 1991 census, almost three-fourths (73 per cent) of the 60 plus population was illiterate out of which 87 per cent were females. The position of aged women was much worse than that of men in this regard. Out of the 27 per cent literate, 4.91 per cent of aged men were matriculates and 2.09 per cent graduate and above, the corresponding proportion of women were only 0.85 per cent and 0.29 per cent respectively.

Table 1.5 : Percentage distribution of the aged population by sex, residence and level of education, India, 1991

	Total			*Rural*			*Urban*		
	Total	*Male*	*Female*	*Total*	*Male*	*Female*	*Total*	*Male*	*Female*
Illiterate	72.8	59.4	87.3	78.9	66.3	92.5	51.3	34.0	69.2
Literate	27.1	40.6	12.7	21.1	33.6	7.5	48.7	65.9	30.8
Primary	9.9	14.2	5.4	8.4	13.0	3.4	15.4	18.3	12.4
Middle	4.5	6.9	1.9	3.2	5.5	0.8	9.0	12.1	5.8
Secondary	2.9	4.9	0.8	1.3	2.4	0.2	8.7	14.0	3.2
Higher Secondary	0.6	0.9	0.2	0.2	0.4	0.0	1.8	3.0	0.6
Graduation and above	1.2	2.1	0.3	0.3	0.6	0.0	4.4	7.6	1.1

Source: Registrar General, India, 1997, Census of India 1991.

As would be expected, the educational level of women was far worse in rural areas compared to urban areas. As many as 92.5 per cent of the rural women were illiterate corresponding to 69.2 per cent of those in urban areas. Reasons for this pervasive gender difference could be traced mainly to socio-cultural milieu. In the past, low levels of education did not work against the aged, as they do in the contemporary society. Does such an educational background render the elderly, especially women, vulnerable in the changing society?

Above mentioned scenario of demographic aspects of ageing indicates that though in Twentieth century the aged remained as an almost invisible group in the Indian family, Twenty First century is going to make them a highly visible group with a life-style of its own and with differential needs and challenges. For better understanding of senior citizens, let us look into the bio-psychological aspects of ageing.

Bio-psychological Aspects

In every stage of human life-cycle individuals undergo certain changes in their biological and psychological spheres. This is true with old age also. Ageing brings change in the capacities, perception, learning, problem solving, feelings, emotions, skills and social behaviours of persons (Birren, 1959). In old age, there is a reduction in functional capacity of organs of the body, gradual tissue degradation, and cellular atrophy resulting in increased susceptibility to diseases and impairment of the body organs (Khan, 1997). With advancing age, due to physical deterioration and decrease in vitality, elderly people exhibit greater vulnerability to diseases. Considering the bio-chemistry of the body, reduction in anabolic or 'building-up' reactions and increase in catabolic or 'breaking-down' reactions characterize old age.

Changes at the cellular, tissue and organic level, in old age, lead to many deformities and diseases. Deterioration in capacity of sensory organs results in ailments like cataract, glucoma, retinal disorders, hearing defects, denture, etc. It may hamper activities of daily living among the elderly making them more prone to accidents and fractures. In old age, sense of taste and smell diminish resulting in appetite loss and reduction in food consumption, which may further lead to many deficiency disorders. Parbhu (1997) informs that gastric acidity decreases in large percentage of elderly leading to impaired absorption of many nutrients. Next, diseases like fibrosis, gout, rheumatism, arthritis, osteoporosis, spondalitis often pose locomotion problems among senior people. Such health problems also tend to influence the psychological well-being and social life of the elderly.

Many degenerative ailments like arteriosclerosis, cerebro-vascular diseases, hypertension, diabetes are prominently found among elderly. Respiratory diseases, such as chronic bronchitis and asthma, disturb the elderly, particularly, those in urban areas. Also, the ageing body fails to supply enough oxygen to brain cells due to which there is increase in reaction time (Birren, *et al.*, 1980). Such changes make the elderly introvert and more rigid in their attitudes, impairing their social functioning. This demonstrates the inter-relationship between physiological and psychological changes.

Elderly usually face a higher risk of developing mental as well as physical morbidity. Their vulnerability to mental problems is due to ageing of the brain, physical problems, socio-economic factors, cerebral pathology, emotional attitude and the family structure (Joshi and Sengupta, 2000). Depression and dementia often accompany ageing. Gupta and Vohra (1987) find a range of functional disorders, among elderly respondents, as depression, dementia, acute psychological reactions, hypomania, obsessive-compulsive neurosis and hysteria. Further, many elderly display problems like forgetfulness and dementia. Often, while physical impairments are recognized and treated, mental health problems go unnoticed. Hall (1922) claims that old age, like adolescence, has unique psychological processes, which probably exhibit a higher degree of variability than do the functions of youth. Do these psycho-physical changes pose hurdles in harmonious adjustment of the aged with their environment?

A close look on the health condition of aged females shows that they are at a disadvantageous position than elderly males. Apart from the age related diseases, as mentioned earlier, they also suffer from gynæcological problems. Added to this, their childhood and adulthood, more often than not, is denoted by malnutrition, deficiency disorders, multiple pregnancies, which have a negative influence on their health in old age. This is commonly seen in developing nations. Further, females are more prone to osteoporosis, particularly after menopause, which makes their bones quite fragile (Ganesh, 1997).

Foregoing discussion brings out that biological and psychological factors play crucial role in human ageing. Therefore, adjusting to decreasing physical strength, psychological capacities and changing social roles become important developmental tasks for the aged. Also, learning to make adjustment with loneliness due to separation from and/or death of significant others and preparation for one's own death are other developmental tasks for this stage

(Havighurst, 1973). In this regard, Butler and Lewis (1977) claim that although fear of death is obvious, older people tend to fear it less than the youngers and often are more concerned about the death of those they love.

These bio-psychological considerations cut across generations. These are there and will be there. What stands out is the changing socio-cultural milieu.

Socio-cultural Milieu

Strangely enough, several socio-cultural factors that pose hurdles in harmonious adjustment of the aged can be best understood in the background of the past traditions. In ancient and medieval India, it used to be predominantly an agrarian society. In this society, many socio-cultural factors enabled the aged to adjust successfully with their family and community, much of it was due to the institution of joint family. In the joint family, the couple with their married sons, daughters-in-law and grandchildren live under one roof, share meals cooked in a common kitchen and pool their income to be appropriated by the *'karta'* as per the needs of individual members. Usually the *karta* would be the eldest male in the household. According to Kakkar (1981) there used to be some kind of division of work specifying roles and relationships between and among family members. These hierarchy of roles would be legitimated by tradition, generation after generation. Regardless of personal talents or achievements, a member's relative position in the hierarchy of joint family, his obligations to those 'above' him and his expectations to those 'below' him used to be immutable, life long. Ordering principles behind this hierarchical system used to be age and sex. Elders have more formal authority than younger persons, and men have greater authority than women. A woman's authority would usually depend on her husband's position in the household. Among others, joint family assured social security of all including orphans, widows, handicapped and the aged.

Likewise, the elderly were the custodians of rituals and religious ceremonies. What to do, when and how, would often be a matter of their direct or indirect concurrence. Their presence or intervention would often contribute to the resolution of conflicts—both inside and outside the household. Having experience, the elderly played a significant part in the socialization of the young. Their status, in those days, was ascribed. They enjoyed status, security, authority, honour, prestige, power and privileges. The joint family system was considered as the best 'social safety net' in the society. It provided a safe haven for the elderly, meeting their social, emotional, and financial needs.

Another important social institution, that reinforced the ability of the family to provide caring environment for the aged was the community. This social institution, commonly known as *biradary*, caste, kin-group or sect defined and laid down moral sanctions on the family and acted as pressure group in promoting the care of the aged. It may be noted that such in-built social systems are, perhaps, the most effective and economical social security. But do these social institutions regard male and female aged at-par in assigning status and authority in family and community?

Speaking of feminine identity, Kakkar (1982) observes that the dominant psychosocial realities of a woman's life can be condensed into three—'daughter to her parents, wife to her husband and mother to her children'. Though affection denotes a girl's early childhood, the socialization process, among others, lays emphasis on how to be a 'good wife and daughter-in-law'. Towards this, ideals of submissiveness, self-denial, self-effacement and self-sacrifice, the *Sita-Savitri* image, devotion to husband are sought to be internalized. Their role is circumscribed, mainly, by the four walls of the house and is reinforced in myriad of ways.

Traditional culture has discouraged females from assertive social engagements outside the domain of the house and related interactions. Generally speaking, females—more so, those in the older age groups—have typically been socialized to remain in the private sphere of the household. They would participate in larger social gatherings, mainly, at the time of performing certain kin obligations. Sen (1994) points out, "the roots of vulnerability in later life have, often, related to a lifetime of gender-based economic, social, and cultural inequalities where social roles combined with differential opportunity structures available to men and women have their effect".

However, it may not be inferred that the females, particularly the elderly ones, are marginalized in the family, community and society. The authority and status of a woman, in joint family group, somewhat increases with age. As a newly wed daughter-in-law she may have to be docile and submissive but with increasing age her status also improves, particularly after giving birth to a son. And as mother-in-law she exercises full authority over her daughter(s)-in-law. Also, she yields significant influence not only on her husband but also on her grown up sons. She has a considerable say in matters related to females of the household. More often than not, she oversees household activities like cooking, washing, cleaning and taking care of children, ailing and the elderly. In fact, the elderly woman occupies an important niche in the power structure of the family group.

Indeed, the elderly woman's position is that of a privileged one in the family. Still, the factors that influence her socialization do mould her personality in ways that perpetuate female subordination. These factors, more often than not, seem to pose hurdles in her adjustment in the present socio-cultural milieu.

In view of the recent social changes, due to modernization, urbanization, migration, increasing entry of women in work force, increasing intergenerational distance and decreasing family cohesiveness, caring of the elderly is fast becoming a problem (Desai, 1983; Ramamurti and Jamuna, 1986; Ramamurti *et al.*, 1992b). Mishra (1996) observes that, since the knowledge and experience of the aged people are not considered necessary for the proper functioning of the rapidly changing new society, they are sidelined and their needs are neglected. If so, then, do urban characteristics like impersonality, fast pace of life challenge smooth adjustment of the aged in family, community and society?

Urban features like high occupational and income disparities, intense competition in almost every sphere of socio-economic activity, lack of we feeling, among others, have brought changes in the ascribed status and authority of the elderly. Technological advancement in most aspects of life, in general, and economic, in particular, has challenged the utility of knowledge and skills of older people. Since technology needs young, so there is compulsory retirement around the age of 60 years (Desai, 1998). It seems, earning capacity, being the major criterion for achieving status, older persons are considered non-productive dependents after retirement. It implies that dependence of the elderly on younger members has resulted in the loss of their traditional authority and status.

Further, nuclear family set-up is becoming the order of the day for reasons more than one. Most towns and cities have high-density neighbourhood or, say, apartment houses noted for limited living space. With privacy and studies of children given priority, lack of proper accommodation along with high rentals, probably affects the capacity of the family to care for their elderly. Next, traditionally, the role of care giving is assumed, more or less, by women. Now-a-days, women folk are, mostly, involved in outside economic activities. Seldom do they have sufficient time even for domestic work, what to say of care giving to the elderly. On the other hand, aged persons, particularly those at 70 plus, need constant care. Financial stringency is another reason as to why middle and lower income group families face problems in maintaining their elderly. It indicates that it would not take long to see that urban life-styles have further aggravated the situation of the elderly. Is the gender difference significant in determining role and status to the aged in urban areas? Do aged women have an edge over their male counterparts in adjusting to 'new roles' in the family or community of urban character?

Kamalamma and Selsa (2000) have studied the problems of elderly women of urban Kerala. They observe that 60 per cent of the women are unable to cope with daily routine. Most of them look after the kids and mind the house especially during the absence of grown up family members. More than a third of the elderly women state taking responsibility of house-keeping. At times, they also spend some time on television viewing.

However, the main problem of most females, reportedly, is of loneliness for want of company. Further, Kapur (1997) reports that there exists some tension, in many families, where daughter-in-law and son are not able to give enough time to their elderly due to their job commitments. The aged females, in turn, feel neglected, unwanted and frustrated. Urban neighbourhood or community also does not seem to provide for their recreational and interactional needs. These conditions appear to make the elderly, particularly aged females, noticeably alienated. Do aged women have no control over their social environment? Does old age bring only frustration and despair to them?

Social Adjustment of Elderly

The above discussion may imply that present socio-cultural milieu poses hurdles in the adjustment of the aged with their environment. It indicates that changed circumstances are responsible for most problems of the aged. Factors like their marital status, socio-economic position, health condition, capacity to undertake activities of daily living and familial and social support all seem to influence adjustment of the aged. Similarly, superannuation from economic roles and deterioration in health switch their roles from self-sufficiency to dependence on grown up children.

However, many researchers pay attention to the other side of the coin. They report that the environmental factors are not the sole determinants for adjustment or mal-adjustment of the aged in family and community. These elderly themselves have several physical, social and psychological peculiarities that hinder their fuller adjustment within the family and community settings (Khan, 1997). They have a set of perceptions, attitudes and philosophy of life, which may not be always in consonance with the changed social environment (Herzog, *et al.*, 1982; Ramamurti and Jamuna, 1993, Chadha, *et al.*, 1996).

It follows that these factors may have some influence on the adjustment of the aged, but the ability of the elderly to adjust, an intrinsic factor, plays a bigger role. Ability to adjust harmoniously includes adaptation to changed circumstances, flexibility, positive attitudes and cheerful disposition and the like. The nature and extent of social adjustment of the aged may vary according to their personality make-up and the family and community environment.

Stated differently, the adjustment of the elderly with their environment depends upon their perception of social reality. In fact, this is the case with every person. All tend to preserve a state of social homeostasis and efforts made in this direction are termed as adjustment response. It is an essential, complex, and continuous process of life. Individuals keep on learning means of better adjustment with their environment throughout their life. According to Heyns (1957) the process of adjustment has two aspects. One, it refers to the entire sequence from the time a need, tension, drive or motive is aroused, the behaviour starts seeking effective solution until the need is satisfied, the tension reduced, and the drive extinguished or the motive fulfiled. Two, it also includes coping with frustration, conflicts and pressures arising out of unsatisfied needs and unfulfilled goals. In the process of adjustment with the environment, positive responses get reinforced and generalized and while the negative ones are reduced and extinguished. With time, all tend to develop a pattern of adjustment, which becomes a dominant part of their personality. At times, it becomes difficult to modify or alter this pattern. Often, this is the case with aged persons. The elderly tend to have crystallized personality patterns that are not so easy to change. However, it may not be concluded that the aged cannot change themselves according to their environmental demands. The aged do have the capacity to adapt themselves to the changing socio-cultural scenario of the society.

This capacity to adapt is mainly responsible for the adjustment-maladjustment of aged in their family. The adaptation comes from 'acceptance' of changed circumstances. A person is angry, frustrated and unhappy when things move against expectations. For example, over expectations from the family members to serve the elderly or to give enough time to them may lead to maladjustment. On the other hand, if they accept that now the family members have other priorities than to give time to them they may reconcile with the situation. This may result in better adjustment of elderly women with their family (see Kapur, 1997).

Reportedly, adjustment in old age is significantly related to acceptance of ageing changes at physical, social and emotional levels (Ramamurti and Jamuna, 1992). However, preconceived notions about ageing and the aged may also retard the process of adjustment. The elderly, who have fears that old age takes away roles and status they have had life long, obliterates brighter aspects of senescence. This may hinder their capacity to enjoy their grey-years. On the other side, acceptance of these changes as inevitable and as normal age related changes by old people would go a long way in having a harmonious adjustment (Jamuna, 1989a). However, it seems, external factors like poor economic viability and social prejudices against females, in general, and widows, in particular, poses greater disadvantage to women than men. This gives rise to several prickly issues. Do elderly women, particularly those in urban areas, face special problems in adjustment?

Review of Literature

Grading and differentiation based upon age and sex are two of the most common referents used in differentiating among human beings (Palmore, 1969). It is often held that, in later years of life, women are less likely to maintain independent living arrangements, more likely to be living without the companionship and support of spouse and typically suffering from lowered incomes. Keeping in mind the forgoing discussion and issues relating to elderly women, an attempt may be made to look into the existing literature. This is proposed to be done mainly in four areas:

Physical health and adjustment

Apparently health status is a contingent condition that greatly facilitates process of adjustment. Mishra (1987) reports that proper health status and overall activeness are positively associated with adjustment along with other variables. Prakash (1989) observes that problems of mobility increases with age—12 per cent respondents in 66-75 years age group, 40 per cent in 76-85 years and 60 per cent in 86 plus years age face varied locomotion problems. Also, two-thirds of aged females are confined to homes due to sensory and locomotion problems. She further reports chronic illness and impairment among all women in 86 plus age-group. In their study Olteanu *et al.* (1994) maintain that autonomy and staying active are important for the aged. Ramamurti and Jamuna (1992) emphasize on 'life-satisfaction', which, in turn, is dependent upon self-perception of health, self-acceptance of ageing changes, self-rating of capability in daily living, activity level and perceived functional disability. Khan (1997) reports that, in urban areas, 70 per cent of the elderly are assessed as hale and hearty, 13 per cent as weak and 18 per cent as ailing.

While studying the health and attitude towards health among elderly, Reddy (1996) observes that, by and large, the aged people do not have much knowledge about various age-related diseases. This, in turn, influences their health attitudes and practices. On this dimension, rural elderly are relatively worse off in health awareness than their urban counterparts. This underlines a need of awareness-generation programmes. In a longitudinal study, Minkler *et al.* (1993) make an interesting observation—the aged, in better health, have greater amount of contacts with family than those in poorer health. The former also have more feelings of closeness to family members.

It would be, thus, seen that physical health and mental health have much in common but the linkage between health and adjustment needs to be further studied in different social contexts.

Economic security and adjustment

Economic security is considered to be an important variable influencing the well-being of senior citizens. Many researchers have focused their attention on this aspect. Sati (1987), in his study on retired males, reports that 46 per cent of the elderly respondents are re-employed and nearly 35 per cent are in need of employment. However, life-satisfaction, in old age, is not necessarily linked with occupation or income. Dhillon and Chhabra (1989) highlight the differences in coping strategies of elderly belonging to lower, middle and higher income groups which include: seeking interpersonal help, fatalism, escapism, action, optimism and control. Prakash (1989) pays attention to economic dependence-independence among aged women. Only 17 per cent women have a share in their spouse's property. Also, 90 per cent do not have any independent income or property. Paintal (1991) maintains that reduced sense of economic security is not exclusively associated with poor adjustment. Ageing *per se* seems to affect sense of economic-security even among those who are well adjusted. For this, there are several primordial and temporal reasons. "Women experience greater stress", comments Lopata (1978), "on the account of financial matters. Traditionally, division of labour has specified managing and worrying about money as the duty of husband. Consequently, women, especially those in older age group and in middle classes, are frequently lacking in knowledge regarding financial matters".

It follows from the above discussion that economic dependence among aged women, particularly in a developing country like India, is clearly high. This apart, its bearing on their social adjustment has not attracted adequate research attention.

Mental health and adjustment

The magnitude of mental morbidity, in India, among the aged population, is nearly 4 million, claims Bose (2000). This is a serious cause of concern when seen in the context of woefully low psychiatric services. Das (1994) observes certain mental signs of old age among older people as loss in concentration or attention, loss of recent memory, development of religious sentiments, frustrations, depression, weakening of reflexes, etc. Grewal (1991) finds that older people having failed to achieve their goals earlier in life, become bitter, disappointed, and cynical. They blame others for their failures and remain depressed and unhappy. Patel (1997), in his study, finds chief mental problems, among the aged, as mental tension (88 per cent), fear of death (74.5 per cent), feeling of dependency (71 per cent), anxiety (70 per cent), loneliness (62.5 per cent), helplessness (60 per cent), depression (52.5 per cent) and feeling of uselessness (52 per cent). Feinson (1987) finds that older females have greater psychological impairment than their male counterparts. Khan (1997), considering 'sleep' as an indicator of mental health, points out that 9 per cent elderly of high-income group families have insufficient sleep as compared to 41 per cent in lower income group. On the level of anxiety, 61 per cent of elderly score low, 25 per cent average and 4 per cent high. Women are reported to have anxiety more than men. About 41 per cent aged respondents are pessimistic, 38 per cent balanced and 22 per cent optimistic. Daniel (1995) brings out that those retirees who stay cognitively active and also those who feel themselves younger recall significantly more materials than those who are cognitively inactive.

These researches reveal that mental health problems of older people are many and of various nature. These ailments, unfortunately, do not receive proper attention of family and, often, go unnoticed and untreated. The linkage between social adjustment and mental health, however, needs to be examined closely.

Social relationships and adjustment

Social relationships play crucial role in the self-concept of an individual. And harmonious adjustment is hypothesized to be a necessary condition for positive social relationships. Rao (1994) has done a study on elderly in rural areas of Visakhapatnam. He finds that older people do not have the kind of authority and respect the aged in traditional society are supposed to possess. Their advice and opinion are not sought after eagerly. Their views are considered outdated. Further, the position of elderly females is vulnerable because of the sanctions of patriarchal social structure. Kumar (1991) brings out that health and economic status of the aged influence interpersonal relationship between old and young generations. Reportedly, the aged maintain their status and interpersonal relationship, if (i) their spouse is alive, (ii) they are physically fit, (iii) they have valuable material and property under their control, and (iv) they adjust to changing family environment. Peretti and Tero (1991) report that 87 per cent of the respondents mark 'coping with loneliness' as most important factor in development and maintenance of a close friendship. Sociability is yet another most frequent (84 per cent) trait. Khan (1997) observes that for the elderly the most liked person in the household are—grandchildren (51 per cent), children (37 per cent), spouse (11 per cent) and daughter-in-law/son-in-law (1 per cent). Among the most empathetic family members sons and daughters figure prominently (42 per cent), followed by spouse (33 per cent), grandchildren (16 per cent) and daughters-in-law and sons-in-law (5 per cent). Study by Chadha, Willigen and Kedia (1996) shows that social involvement in old age depends upon a number of factors including marital status, income level, individual resource control and health status. In the study, social networks are conceptualized in terms of the size and nature of a person's web of interactions. Results show that there is little difference in mean network size of age strata from 55 years to 74 years. After 75 years, there is significant and cumulative decline in social engagements. Also, women's networks are about 18 per cent smaller than those of men. Individuals with poor health have significantly smaller social networks. Widowed have smaller social networks than married. No significant difference in social engagements on the basis of income level of the respondents was observed. Another study in semi-urban areas of Chittoor district, Andhra Pradesh show that satisfaction with role activity, positive husband-wife communication, positive self-image and satisfaction in life are important factors contributing to adjustment (Jamuna, 1994).

Existing literature suggests that interpersonal relationships in the life of the elderly directly correspond with their level of social adjustment. However, this dimension needs to be further explored.

The foregoing literature survey brings out that much research attention has been paid to the elderly and the problems they face in their day-to-day life. Similarly, issues of adjustment-maladjustment have also not escaped the attention. However, insufficient attention has been paid to gender variations in the level of adjustment. So is the matter with the possible linkage between adjustment and health, economic security and interpersonal relationship.

Critical Issues

Khan and Bagley (1989) maintain that senior people may not exactly make for a social problem, yet they do have a situation, which signifies an area of social need. Demographic trends confirm the same. India, currently, has approximately 76 million elderly. It is more than the total population of Australia. By the fourth decade of this century, the aged population may be crossing 100 million. It suggests that almost every family is getting involved in the issues relating to care and support of the elderly. As discussed earlier, age dependency ratio is shooting up rapidly taxing the economy of the household. This challenge is not confined only at the family or community level. The state also needs to look into the welfare of the aged citizens and do balancing of scarce resources between younger and older generation. Caring and adjustment of the aged is a multi-dimensional aspect, which needs the attention of social researchers.

World-wide, attention is now being focused on elderly females. Due to higher female life-expectancy at the age above sixty years, they will far outnumber their male counterparts in the next few decades. It has been estimated that elderly women above 60 years in age would constitute 14.1 per cent of the total population of India by 2025 (United Nations, 1989). This speaks of the immensity of the problem. A higher incidence of widowhood (54 per cent), illiteracy (87 per cent), malnutrition, high economic dependency project the vulnerability of elderly females (Census, 1991). In this context, a gender specific outlook needs to be studied, especially, on the adjustment of aged females. Literature survey highlights the inadequacies in the existing data on women, particularly older women. In fact, research on the elderly, in India, has picked up only in recent years. Aged women, with their unique place in the family and society and with specific needs and challenges, also merit the attention of social researchers. Reviews of research on the elderly have focused on this lacuna. Not withstanding this general drawback, some studies are available dealing with several aspects of the life of elderly women. These studies have helped in gaining some insight into the needs and problems of aged women in India and to compare various aspects of their life with their contemporary cohorts in other nations. Still, there is need to carry out researches on well-being of the elderly women particularly those living in urban set-up (Bali, 1995).

Some of the urban characteristics like impersonality, fast pace of life are likely to influence the adjustment of aged females. Lack of proper housing accommodation, women going out for economic activities are expected to pose problems in family's capacity and/or willingness to take care of their elderly. This urban environment, definitely, have some role to play in the adjustment of elderly women. It needs to be studied systematically.

Further, decreasing physical strength and increasing susceptibility to diseases and impairment of body organs is often associated with old-age. How do the elderly cope with these physical changes? Are these differential coping patterns associated with their social adjustment? These issues need to be explored.

Next, according to 1991 census, workforce participation rate among females of age 60 plus is 5.4 per cent (main workers). Elderly women, more often, do not have the ownership of property. It follows that economic dependency ratio among aged females is high. The correlation between economic security and adjustment of elderly females is far from being clear.

Old age brings in gradual diminution of social roles for the elderly. Differences in these psychosocial factors, in relation to gender, needs clarity. Also, their adjustment patterns are likely to differ markedly. These need to be studied systematically.

Multi-disciplinary approach is needed to study various aspects of elderly including their adjustment-maladjustment in an urban context. This study, from social work perspective, is likely to give an insight into the adjustment patterns and problems of aged females and a foresight in suggesting suitable interventions for enhancing their social functioning.

Present Work

The study addresses aged women in an urban setting. Elderly females have attracted much research attention on account of several reasons, some of which have been discussed earlier. Increased life-expectancy has ensured high proportion of elderly females among the aged as well as in general population. Socio-cultural factors that weigh against females in patriarchal social structure persist during old age, too. Also, age-related degenerative changes at the physical and mental levels seem to affect adjustment of aged women. Added to this, features characterizing urban living appear to enhance loneliness and alienation among them. Against this backdrop, an attempt is made to understand the adjustment of the aged women in family and neighbourhood. Towards this, the present study sets out the following objectives:

1. to study the demographic status and socio-economic background of aged women in a metropolis;
2. to ascertain the level of social adjustment among them;
3. to study the health status of older women in relation to their adjustment in the family and neighbourhood;
4. to examine the linkage between their social adjustment and their acceptance by family and neighbourhood;
5. to analyze social adjustment among aged females in terms of their sense of security; and
6. to find out the relation between social adjustment and life-satisfaction among them.

Certain key terms, used in the study, may well be dealt with:

Aged Woman: A female who has attained the chronological age of 60 years or more.

Social Adjustment: It is an ongoing process, which facilitates one to adopt oneself to social environment. It supports and facilitates an aged woman in initiating and maintaining harmonious and mutually satisfying interactions and relationships with her significant others.

Health: The World Health Organization (1945) defines health as 'a state of complete physical, mental and social well-being, and not merely an absence of disease or infirmity'. For the purpose of the study, observable indicators of a healthy aged woman would be her optimal sensory capabilities, fewer ailments and relative independence in activities of daily living. Stated differently, a healthy aged woman would have the convenience to perform her daily life-activities independently and the effectiveness with which she would cope with the age-related changes.

Well-being: It is a state of being healthy, happy and free from want. In the present study, an aged female would be presumed to be in a state of well-being, if she has sound sleep, freedom from worries and tensions, loneliness, death fear and has optimism and high rating of life.

Social Acceptance: It is the recognition and appreciation of the roles and status of an elderly woman by her family members and neighbours. When grandchildren, family members, neighbours and friends actively interact with an aged female, involve her in day-to-day decision making and approach her for sharing problems and feelings, she is presumed to be socially accepted.

Economic Security: It is the feeling of assurance an aged woman has that, irrespective of her economic dependence-independence, her kith and kin would take care of her needs and wants.

Life-satisfaction: The feeling of contentment and happiness the aged woman has, especially, from her past-life. An elderly female who is enthusiastic, active, having a sense of purpose and positive acceptance of age-related changes would be considered satisfied with life.

Research Design

It goes without saying that a research design with proper formulation of problem, careful sampling procedure, appropriate tools for data collection and data analysis has a profound bearing on the outcome of research. Should we focus on relatively homogenous neighbourhood and should we interact with elderly women and gather information in the light of study objectives, we would be able to unravel those gerontological dimensions, which we are looking for. As the study is descriptive in approach, all the successive stages are oriented accordingly.

The study intends to examine social adjustment of aged women in the family and neighbourhood of an urban area. Towards this, information could be gathered from family members, neighbours or elderly women themselves. Aged females would be the best option to get accurate information about them. The study is essentially confined to aged females living in the family—whether natural or adopted.

Sampling

The present study focuses on the National Capital Territory of Delhi. Being the capital of India, Delhi is a hub of political activity. Its population is estimated to be 13.8 million (Census, 2001). During 1991-2001, the decadal growth rate in Delhi was 46.3 per cent. Indeed, all of it is not on account of natural growth. Migration from different parts of the country to Delhi plays a vital role. The metropolis has a population density of 9,294 persons per square kilometre, which is the highest in India. To a great extent, the city is also characterized by impersonality, cut-throat competition almost in every walk of life, high income differentiation, fast pace of life, etc. Furthermore, the metropolitan population is often noted for marked economic, cultural and social disparities posing, among others, umpteen methodological problems.

Delhi has many prosperous and posh colonies like Jor Bagh, Paschim Vihar and Adarsh Nagar; but it also has deprived residential colonies like Jahangir Puri, Dakshin Puri, Seema Puri and Seelampur. All said and done, these are disparate neighbourhoods. On the other hand, it also has residential areas, having largely middle-income group families. The example may be cited of Pushp Vihar, Janak Puri, Preet Vihar and Rohini. They have large number of middle-income group housing, built and maintained by Central Public Works Department (CPWD) or Delhi Development Authority (DDA). They house, in the main, lower-income group and middle-income group families. These colonies come much closer to the requirement of homogeneity. For the purpose of the study, a large neighbourhood has been a requirement, as it would yield a large sample. Keeping these issues in view, information on residential colonies from CPWD and DDA offices has been collected. Besides, a large number of residential colonies have been visited to ascertain their suitability. As Pushp Vihar, Saket meets most of the research requirements, it has been selected as the study area. Pushp Vihar is one of the biggest colonies built and maintained by CPWD in South Delhi. In official parlance, buildings in Pushp Vihar are 'government-quarters' allotted to serving government officials, although, a few 'smart' allottees have also taken to sub-letting. Pushp Vihar, taken together, has about 6000 residential flats and about 20,000 persons live in them.

Next, the researcher approached District Election Office to acquire voters' list pertaining to Pushp Vihar with a view to securing information about the occupants especially about elderly females. However, this organization could not oblige as, at that time, municipal elections were round the corner. Subsequently, the sitting Municipal Councillor was approached who did have the needed voters' list. The elected representative was more cooperative and helpful and he allowed the researcher to photocopy the list. From the list, elderly women's names and addresses were noted down. All told, 727 aged women have been living in Pushp Vihar. Looking at the study objectives, a sample size of 350 aged women appeared to be satisfactory. However, a 'reserve' was also needed so as to offset 'casualties'. Given these considerations, a sample of 400 aged women has been selected using 'random number tables'.

Tools of Data Collection

Tools used by researchers for collecting data on elderly and on adjustment have been looked into (Ramamurti, 1972; Mishra, 1996; Khan, 1997). Although, the study is addressed to middle-class family groups, possibility of having illiterate respondents cannot be ruled out. The elderly respondents, themselves, might not fill-in information supplied in 'mailed-questionnaire'. Further, respondents are likely to have limited time, they could hardly be expected to spare unduly large time for research-purposes. So, non-participant observations could not be used for studying adjustment of aged females. Moreover, there are subtle dimensions, often times, requiring 'probe questions' which could be satisfactorily dealt with in interview-settings. Next, often times, family members have certain 'reservations' against seeking information by a stranger from their elderly relatives. Rapport building, before interviews, could tackle these issues effectively. Also, any relevant supplementary information would be gathered during interviews in order to develop some case records. In addition, chances of non-responses due to factors like language problem, low eyesight, poor health, lack of interest, etc., would have been reduced to a great extent during interviews. Keeping these considerations in view, the researcher has planned to use Interview Technique for gathering information from the elderly females.

In order to have uniformity, comparability and generalization, the present study has opted for paying due attention to study objectives and the key issues arising from them. Towards this, a structured interview schedule, covering such dimensions as identifying information, family background, economic condition, economic security, health and well-being, social acceptance and social adjustment, has been developed. It has about 73 main items (excluding a few items by way of interviewer's observations). The schedule also includes items on Social Adjustment Scale. Initial draft was thoroughly edited and reviewed by several experienced researchers. Subsequently, it was translated into Hindi version. It was, then, pre-tested on 50 aged women in Police Colony, Hauz Khas, New Delhi. In the light of pre-testing, the interview schedule, both Hindi and

English versions, was modified in terms of contents, thrust and communication. It was planned that interview would be conducted in Hindi but the interview schedule would be in English, the working language of the researcher. Given this, 410 copies of English version of the interview schedule were printed.

Data Collection

The present study has relied upon both secondary and primary data. Secondary data have been gathered from many libraries in Delhi, which mainly includes Indian Council of Social Science Research, Jawaharlal Nehru University, Jamia Millia Islamia University, National Council of Educational Research and Training, Delhi University, Helpage India, Age-Care India, etc. Also, information has been gathered from various Ministries and government departments. Getting census data, especially that of 2001 have been a tedious job. Many visits have been paid to Census offices at the central and district levels. Added to this, data through internet have also been gathered. However, gathering secondary data have been relatively an easy task than primary data collection.

During primary data collection, the researcher has paid many visits to Pushp Vihar colony in order to gain familiarity with the structural and functional aspects of the study area. The main concern was getting access to the community. Pushp Vihar has several Resident Welfare Associations (RWAs) whose executive heads are called 'secretaries'. Researcher met these secretaries and requested for their co-operation in contacting aged women in the neighbourhood. Formal letters were mailed from Department of Social Work, Jamia Millia Islamia University, to the secretaries of RWAs. In turn, they circulated a letter to the residents for extending necessary help to the researcher. This has been an exercise, which has gone a long a way in securing the help and confidence of the residents.

During collection of data, the researcher has paid visits house by house. Most interviews have been done in the late afternoons, evenings and on holidays when the respondents have been relatively free to talk. Many times, after their own interviews, quite a lot of respondents have helped the researcher to approach to other aged women of their locality. During interviews, a number of respondents have shared their life-experiences and feelings, apart from the issues covered in the schedule. However, sometimes, it has been a 'knotty issue' to be alone with the aged woman as family members would prefer to listen to the conversation. At times, they would interject and speak on behalf of the respondent inhibiting her own natural responses (such interviews/answers were not included in the analysis). Interviews taken in parks and *mandirs* avoided such problems. In some cases, it was hard for the researcher to convince the family members of the prospective respondents about the purpose and confidentiality of interviews. Also, perhaps, in suspicion, many family members did not allow the researcher to talk to their elderly relative even after showing permission letter from RWA. All things considered, the respondents and their family, except in a few cases, have given the researcher full help and cooperation. Collection of primary data has taken six months.

Taken together, 350 interviews were completed from Pushp Vihar and Saket. As would be expected, several interviews could not be conducted due to such reasons as: (a) unwillingness shown by some prospective respondents; (b) apprehension by family members (news of murders, robbery in the adjacent areas of Pushp Vihar, also strengthened their fears); (c) incomplete interviews due to unavoidable reasons; (d) communication problem: some females belonging to Orissa, West Bengal and South India did not understand Hindi or English; (f) poor health did not permit some aged women to give interviews; (g) according to voters' list, many aged women could not be identified due to: (i) change of address and non-availability of new address, (ii) some had gone back to their villages for more than 6 months and (iii) death of prospective respondents.

Analysis and Report

In the light of study objectives, primary and secondary data, thus collected, were organized and processed. Processing of secondary data did not pose much of a problem. They were classified, tabulated and presented diagrammatically at required places in the report. On the other hand, processing of primary data involved many steps. Since the researcher herself has collected data, any inconsistency was cross-checked at the time of interview itself. Still, completed interview schedules were re-checked for any errors in recording. Next, responses in interview schedules were coded on basis of a code-book prepared at planning stage. It had about 150 variables, including 4 composite variables. The coded data have been fed into SPSS spread-sheet. Then, frequency and mean tables were developed. In these tables, distribution and statistical values were examined and a number of cross-tables were taken out with a view to ascertaining inter-linkages between variables. However, only those cross-tables have been focalized, which have contingency coefficient value of at least 0.19 or better. Also, in respect of composite variables, correlation matrix has been developed to see whether the constituting variables hang well with each other; and the variables showing insignificant association have been eliminated. In appropriate cases, the data have been subjected to further analysis. Responses of some open-ended questions were listed out and analyzed separately. Furthermore, some fifteen case-records were developed, using mainly interview information and interviewer's observations. These case-records are likely to provide some qualitative insight into the situation of the elderly females.

At the planning stage itself, a detailed chapter scheme was prepared. This has been modified at the successive stages of the implementation of the work. In the present form, the report is divided into seven chapters. Chapter 1 – Introduction – includes building up of research argument, and incorporates literature survey and research methodological details. Chapter 2 highlights personal, familial, educational and economic background of the elderly females. Chapter 3 discusses factors influencing social adjustment of aged females. Their health and well-being have been analyzed in Chapter 4. The issues related to social acceptance of elderly women have been dealt in Chapter 5. Chapter 6 focalizes economic insecurity-security of the aged females. Last section, that is, Chapter 7 summarizes findings and presents main conclusions.

What does the researcher hope to achieve from the present endeavour is best expressed by the words of a study respondent, *"Beta! Main dua karti hun, khuda se"* she said, *"Ki teri yeh padhai mujh jaise buzurgon ki zindgi ko behtar banane main kaam aye"* (I pray to God Almighty that may your study improve the life of old people like me). Hopefully, this study fulfils the expectations of the respondents and provides an insight into the situation of aged women and paves way for their better social adjustment.

2

DEMOGRAPHIC, SOCIAL AND ECONOMIC BACKGROUND OF THE ELDERLY WOMEN

While ageing is universal, the mounting proportion of the elderly in the general population is relatively a recent phenomenon. The trend seems to be steady all over the preceding century. In the past, though people lived long to their old age, their number and proportion in the total population would seldom be so high. This demographic transition has been brought about by the improvement in nutrition, basic health-care and the control of many infectious diseases as well as decline in birth and infant mortality rates and increase in life-expectancy. At present, the world's elderly population is nearly 600 million and by the year 2025, it is expected to rise to 1,100 million (United Nations, 1999). Recently, most developing countries of Asia, Africa and Latin America are fast heading towards a 'grey world'. In a way, both China and India have elderly population, which exceeds the total population of a large number of countries. Further, the situation obtaining in many countries has it that elderly women outnumber elderly men. Added to this, the fastest growing group of the aged population is the 'old-old' (80 years and above). In 2000, there were 70 million 'old-old' and their population is expected to increase to more than five times in the next five decades. This demographic change has drawn the attention of the world-community to social, economic and political issues coming up due to the phenomenon of ageing on a massive scale. This change can be viewed both as a challenge as well as an opportunity to explore measures for the optimum utilization of wisdom and expertise of elderly people.

Population Growth

The demographic transition commonly known as 'greying of nations' can no longer be taken as 'just another statistical projection'. It calls for a response to the needs of millions of elderly persons whose number is increasing at a fast rate. Wallace (1999) describes this phenomenon as 'age-quake'. "If we understand the implications of ageing, age-quake will not descend on us unexpectedly like an earth-quake with death and destruction all around", observes Wallace, "instead, we will be prepared to face a world converging on the elderly". Indeed, presence of a large number of the elderly is going to influence the structure and function of the society. This demographic change confronts each country with a range of challenges. In developed countries, challenges mainly concern intergenerational relationship and social security systems. Their endeavour is to ensure increased life-expectancy with better quality of life for their citizens. Ramachandran (1994) observes that, in developed countries, to one person eligible for social security, only three persons are contributing to social security. It is likely that this ratio may reduce further. This throws an additional burden on the earning population of the country.

The United Nations (1999) projects that, by the year 2025, a major share (72 per cent) of the elderly population would be residing in developing countries. These developing nations are, often, characterized by poor economic conditions, lack of adequate health-care, education and social welfare systems. So, for these countries maintaining elderly population would be difficult as there are hardly enough resources to meet the needs of its young population. The cost of social insurance and social assistance for the senior citizens can be quite taxing for nations with scarce resources. Further, the trend of feminization of ageing is also clearly visible in developing nations. There would be 604 million elderly females in the World by the year 2025, out of which 70 per cent would be in these developing countries. Added to this, Africa and Asia have an especially high proportion of widows (De Alvarez, 1991). Against this backdrop, the situation of elderly females, in developing nations, gives a discouraging picture. Illiteracy, poverty, social and economic dependency deprive, these elderly women, of the skills and personal resources to cope with the changing physical, social and economic conditions. These challenges differ from country to country depending upon their economic growth, infrastructure for education, health care and social service and other socio-cultural parameters. "The solution of these challenges", observes Lassonde, "will determine social cohesion, the place of the elderly in public-life, and the dignity and degree of well-being, that societies will be able to ensure for a growing proportion of their elderly population" (1997).

Attention may, now, be drawn to the present demographic picture in India. India occupies about 2.4 per cent (32,87,263 square kilometres) of the world area and inhabits nearly 16 per cent of the world population. There has been four-folds increase in India's population in the last 100 years. As on 1st March 2001, the country has the population of 1,027 million. According to census 2001, birth rate, in the country, is 26.1 per 1000 persons and death rate is 8.7 per 1000 persons. Infant mortality rate is 70 per 1000 live births. India has recorded the population growth rate as 17.4 per 1000 persons. Statistics show that with improved nutrition and health care services, the expectation of life at birth has gone up significantly. The average life-expectancy at birth for males is 62.3 years and for females 65.3 years (Census, 1991). Thus, now every person born in India is expected to cross the official figure of old age, that is, 60 years.

The 1991 census shows that the population, in the age category of 0-14 years, was 36.77 per cent, while the elderly population counted 6.16 per cent. In 2001, the proportion of children, in the total population, has fallen to 35.4 per cent and the proportion of the elderly has gone up to 7.2 per cent. The demographers further predict that, by the middle of the present century, children (0-14 years) would be the smallest category in the Indian population. Size of the elderly population will expand as will the middle age-group (*Source:* TOI, July 3, 2000, Monday). Further, the proportion of grandchildren and grandparents in India are going to be almost equal in 2081. At that time the children, in the age-group 0-14 years, would be 20.3 per cent while the elderly population is projected to be 21.12 per cent (United Nations, 1989).

India represents wide diversities in terms of religion, caste, language, culture, per capita income, health, educational and nutritional status and other socio-cultural characteristics. As a logical corollary, the needs and problems of the aged would differ from state to state. Also, social welfare schemes like Old Age Pension vary in different regions of the country. Many states face difficulties in providing for the aged population as they often lack wherewithal to meet even the basic needs of their general population. Similarly, educational and health-care facilities and poverty, in different parts of the country, seem to have a significant influence on the number and proportion of the elderly. A look into the regional variations shows that, in 1991, Kerala has the highest proportion of elderly persons (8.8 per cent), followed by Himachal Pradesh (8.1 per cent), Punjab (7.8 per cent) and Haryana (7.7 per cent). Among the regions having lowest proportion of senior citizens, Assam (5.3 per cent) followed by West Bengal (6.1 per cent), Bihar (6.3 per cent) and Rajasthan (6.3 per cent) top the list. The National Capital of India, Delhi, has 4.7 per cent of the elderly in its population and, therefore, is a 'young-city'.

Elderly in Urban Setting

The place of living, socio-cultural, political and economic characteristics and other similar factors influence the well-being of the aged. Likewise, rural-urban characteristics also play a salient role. Needless to add, urban family groups markedly differ from rural family groups. These differences are noticeable in terms of structure, size, mode of production and consumption, interpersonal relations, etc. Generally speaking, members of these groups differ from each other in terms of capabilities, resource-generation and social likes and dislikes. Equally important is the consideration of impersonality, almost inherent in urban environment, in contrast to cohesion and bonding in rural community (Khan and Kaushik, 1999).

Commercialization, industrialization and political changes have accelerated the pace of urbanization. India has been no exception to this. The urban component, in its population, has been steadily growing decade after decade. In 1991, almost one-fourth of India's population was classified as urban. In 2001, the corresponding figure has risen to 28.1 per cent. Also, the proportion of elderly men, living in rural areas, tends to increase with age. In contrast, greater proportions of elderly women are living in urban areas. The reason may be that elderly women are more vulnerable to chronic illnesses and widowhood, and urban residence may provide specialized health and social services (Vijayanunni, 1997). The trend, from the above data, of gradual increase in the proportion of the elderly females in urban areas, puts forth the challenge to the urban governance to meet the needs of senior citizens. At this point, a few details about Delhi may be provided.

Delhi being the political capital of India occupies a unique position on the globe. This cosmopolitan city possesses an amalgamation of various cultures of people with different religion, caste, class, race, languages and socio-economic background from different parts of the world. It is spread over an area of about 1483 square kilometres. The National Capital Territory of Delhi is administratively divided into three areas — New Delhi Municipal Council, Delhi Cantonment Board and Municipal Corporation of Delhi. Accounting for 1.11 per cent of the country's total population, Delhi has a population density of 9,294 persons per square kilometres.

From a mere 9 lakh persons in 1941, Delhi's population has grown to 94.2 lakhs in 1991. Population of Delhi has increased to 1,37,82,976 persons in 2001. The capital has recorded birth rate of 20.3 per 1000 and death rate of 4.8 per 1000. Infant mortality rate is 31 per 1000 live births and sex ratio is 821 females per 1000 males. Delhi has a high literacy rate of 81.8 per cent, with 87.3 per cent male and 75 per cent female literates (see *India: Book of the Year,* 2002). Table 2.1 shows the population structure of Delhi. According to 1991 census, Delhi has 34.7 per cent children and 4.7 per cent aged, in its population. Thus, theoretically, 60.6 per cent of the population earn for the dependent population of 39.4 per cent (Children and the aged). Further during 1981-91, the decadal growth rate has been 51.4, which has declined to 46.3 in 2001.

Table 2.1 : Population of Delhi by sex and age-group

Age-group (Years)	*Male*	*Female*	*Total*	*Per cent to total population*
0-14	1725337	1548145	3273482	34.7
15-19	518268	396603	914871	9.7
20-24	538191	444675	982866	10.4
25-29	517180	439608	956788	10.2
30-39	810088	627947	1438035	15.3
40-49	502230	365501	867731	9.2
50-59	283533	220616	504149	5.3
60+	236969	202551	439520	4.7
Age not stated	23716	19486	43202	0.5
Total	5155512	4265132	9420644	100.0

Source: Delhi Statistical Hand Book, 2000.

Now, we need to understand some of the characteristics of Delhi, peculiar to urban areas, that influence the well-being of those in the golden age-group. Delhi has high quality of medicare, educational facilities and work-opportunities. However, high growth rate of population might make these facilities inadequate. Fast pace of life, intense competition in almost every sphere of socio-economic activity, diversity of occupations, income-disparities, rapid and intense communications and impersonality are some of the ubiquitous features of life in Delhi. Further, like most towns and cities, the capital, too, has high density neighbourhoods or, say, apartment houses noted for limited living space. This may be creating tension for many couples to provide adequate space to their children for studies and privacy and for their elderly relatives.

More often than not, both husband and wife go to work to make ends meet or to maintain or raise standard of living. As a consequence the care of the dependent elderly often suffers. Also, political institutions and processes have undermined the cohesion, which, earlier on, used to denote family groups. In turn, social norms, traditions and mores have undergone a change or loosened their hold on individuals and groups. It would not, thus, take long to see that life-styles of Delhi and, in general, of urban areas have further aggravated the situation of the elderly, unless some creative measures are tried out.

Next, Delhi tops in crime rates in India. Now-a-days crimes against elderly are on rise. With migration of children abroad, many elderly are left behind alone to fend for themselves. Such persons easily fall prey to the anti-social elements that do not hesitate even to end the life of the aged for the sake of some money. Such rising rate of crime against senior citizens is a matter of concern for all of us.

After examining the larger context, that is, the city as a whole, now let us appraise the immediate environment of the elderly females under study. The colony of Pushp Vihar was constructed in 1984. It has five sectors, 1, 3, 4, 5, and 7. Sectors 2 and 6 are still to be constructed. Every sector has its own Resident Welfare Associations that are found to be quite active. Well planned, it has CGHS dispensaries, five Government schools, two public schools and one shopping complex in each sector, making the goods of daily-use easily available. Many elderly females have made the task of buying vegetables and milk from the nearby market their daily routine. It is also well connected through roads from other parts of the city with good bus service and other means of transportation. Offices of Mahanagar Telephone Nigam Limited, Delhi Vidhut Board and Central Public Works Department are with in the vicinity. There are many playgrounds and recreational centres. It has four temples, and one church within the colony. Attending *satsang* and *kirtan* in these places of worship, is also a regular activity of many aged women.

Personal Background

Studying the issues related to aged people, exclusively at the macro-level, would be considered as shortsightedness. It may be argued that the characteristics and problems of the elderly are almost similar in all societies or at least within a community, which might not be true. Old age and related issues are significantly diverse. People age differently because they have their own unique hereditary endowments, different socio-economic and educational background and differential patterns of living with diverse life-experiences. These differences increase with age and predispose individuals to react differently to similar situations. Therefore, it may be our narrow view to classify a person as typically old or any trait as typical of old age. Attention, now, may be paid to the personal characteristics like age, marital status, educational background, occupational status, and type of family of the respondents in the study.

Age Distribution

Chronological age is a significant indicator of allocation of roles and responsibilities in any society. Age is an important variable on the basis of which all societies make assumptions about the appropriate behaviours and levels of functioning of people. Individuals have rights, roles, opportunities and responsibilities assigned or denied on the basis of their age. In the ancient and medieval era, respect was ascribed to any and every person higher in age. And hence, grey hair would bring a unique authority and power to a person in family and community. However, the law of change has altered this situation too. One respondent of Pushp Vihar expresses it as, *"Hamen aajkal voh izzat nahin milti jo hum apne bade buzurgon ko diya karte the"* (now-a-days we don't get that respect which we used to give to our elders and elderly). Let us take a look into how various factors of well-being are related to age.

Senior citizens can be classified into various sub-groups on the basis of their age. These are 'young-old' (i.e. 60 to 69 years) 'middle-old' (i.e. 70 to 79 years), 'old-old' (i.e. 80 to 89 years) and 'oldest-old' (90 years and above). Table 2.2 gives the percentage distribution of persons aged 60 years and above by sex, age and residence, India, 1981-91. According to 1991 census, there are 62.8 per cent elderly in 'young-old' category. This sub-group is often considered to be quite fit and healthy. The 'middle-old' sub-group is approximately 26 per cent. Those in 'old-old' category may frequently require a lot of support from family, community, health care services, etc. This group constitutes 9 per cent of the total aged population. 'Oldest-old' sub-group, who is approximately 2 per cent of the aged population, is likely to show greater dependency. Many elderly, at this stage, become passive receptors of care and support. It is important to note that there is a slight increase in 'old-old' (1.2 per cent) and 'oldest-old' (1.5 per cent) categories of the elderly. This indicates that, in future, maximum growth is recorded in latter and not in the former two categories of the elderly.

Table 2.2 : Age and sex-wise distribution of the elderly in India, 1981-1991

Year	*Age*	*Total*			*Rural*			*Urban*		
	(Years)	*Total*	*Male*	*Female*	*Total*	*Male*	*Female*	*Total*	*Male*	*Female*
1991	60-69	62.8	62.7	62.9	62.7	62.4	63.1	63.1	63.6	62.3
	70-79	25.9	26.0	25.8	26.0	26.1	25.8	25.7	25.6	25.7
	80-89	9.1	9.2	8.9	9.1	9.3	8.8	8.9	8.7	9.2
	90-99	1.9	1.9	1.9	1.9	1.9	1.9	1.9	1.7	2.1
	100+	0.3	0.3	0.3	0.2	0.2	0.3	0.4	0.3	0.4
1981	60-69	64.1	64.4	63.8	64.3	64.2	64.0	64.1	65.1	63.1
	70-79	26.3	26.3	26.3	26.4	26.1	26.3	26.0	25.8	26.3
	80-89	7.8	7.8	7.9	7.8	7.7	7.8	8.1	7.6	8.5
	90-99	1.4	1.3	1.5	1.4	1.3	1.4	1.5	1.2	1.7
	100+	0.3	0.3	0.3	0.3	0.3	0.3	0.3	0.2	0.4

Note: Excludes figures for Assam in 1981 and Jammu and Kashmir in 1991.

Source: Census of India.

It appears as if chronological age not only influences the physical strength and agility of humans but also their psychological and social well-being. Neugarten (1971) observes that as people grow old, sex-role reversal occurs—while men become passive, withdrawn and reserved, women's need for dominance and affiliation becomes stronger. Also, aged males accept their changing social and emotional needs more easily than elderly females. Ageing brings negative changes in self-concept and life-satisfaction, increase in emotionality and rise in frustration tolerance (Abrams, 1991). Dhillon and D'Souza (1992) find that age significantly effects resignation and aggression, mode of coping with frustration, social maturity and emotional adjustment and need for affiliation. These studies show that advancing age has some influence on factors like emotional adjustment, social maturity, flexibility, need patterns, frustration tolerance and coping strategies of an individual.

In Pushp Vihar, the age of the respondents ranges between 60 to 96 years. Mode is 60 years, mean is approximately 66 years and median is 65 years. Three age categories have been evolved to facilitate further analysis. These include 35.4 per cent respondents in the age-group of 60 to 62 years, 34.6 per cent in 63 to 67 years category and 30 per cent in 68 to 98 years. This distribution is largely homogeneous (standard deviation = 6.70) and is leptokurtic (Kurtosis = 4.04), which means that the concentration of frequency is more in younger age group, that is, 60 to 62 years.

In the study, 164 respondents are currently married. The mean age of the respondents' husband is approximately 69 years. As in the earlier case, the husbands of the elderly women are divided into three age groups. Data show that 36.6 per cent of the husbands are in the age-group of 61 to 66 years, 37.8 per cent in 67 to 70 years and 25.6 per cent in 71 to 98 years.

Does advancing age affect the health and well-being of the aged females? Old age, apparently, affects the physical health and strength of a person. Data show that among the 'young-old' respondents (60 to 67 years), only 16 per cent have reported decline in hearing capacity. With increasing age hearing capacity worsens. Among older aged females (68 to 96 years) 68.2 per cent have deteriorated hearing capacity. Similarly, among younger respondents (60 to 67 years) only 14.4 per cent suffer from trembling. On the other hand, in the age category of 68 to 96 years, 70.6 per cent respondents tremble.

In the same way, digestive problems get doubled up as we move from the age-group of 60 to 62 years to 68 to 96 years. Also, 95 per cent of the respondents, in 60 to 67 years age category, can get up and sit at their own. In juxtaposition, 71.4 per cent respondents, in the age-group of 68 to 96 years, are autonomous in getting up and sitting. In activities of daily living, say, taking medicines at their own, elderly females who require help are three times more in the age-group of 68 to 96 years when compared with those in the 60 to 62 years. Further, some indicators of psychological well-being like loneliness and death-fear, show no significant association with age of the elderly females. It can, then, be inferred that with increase in age, sensory capacities and health status of the elderly females deteriorate but some psychological factors seem to be independent of advancing age. Age may influence other variables like educational status, occupational status, mental health, etc., which are dealt with a little later.

Marital Status

Indian cultural tradition has it that a woman is dependent, first on her father, subsequently on her husband and lastly on her son. In adult life, she is expected to find her identity through her husband. Thus, marital status plays a crucial role in the life of a female. Remaining spinster mitigates with the social norm and, therefore, often brings obscurity to the woman. Thirty-eighth round of National Sample Survey (NSS) brings out that, in 1987, only 0.7 per cent aged females in rural areas and 1.1 per cent in urban areas were in the category of 'never married' (see Biswas, 1994). Further, in patriarchal society, after marriage, a female goes to live with her husband's family. There, being dependent—socially as well as economically, a female's status is guided by that of her husband. She enjoys status and authority according to the position of her husband in the family and society. A change in her marital status, say, due to divorce, separation and widowhood, touches off several socio-cultural changes in a female's life. For example, widowhood not only brings bereavement but also an associated loss of status, discrimination, loss of economic power and lowering of self-esteem. In addition, widowhood is often accompanied by tacit handicaps and even restrictions in her domestic and social spheres. In certain cultural groups, a widow is considered inauspicious in social and religious activities. As a result, she is given a differential and unequal treatment. She is treated as an object of collective discrimination (Jamuna, 1995). In the same connection, a divorced and deserted female is looked upon with disdain (Saroja and Badiger, 1999). On the other hand, the NSS survey shows that, in 1987, among the aged, females suffer from widowhood or separation almost three times more than their male counterparts.

Many researchers have looked into the impact of widowhood on a female. Ramamurti (1989) observes that loss of husband, in later years, leaves her high and dry and dependent on her children. In some cases she finds herself almost deserted. Thomas, Digiulio and Sheehan (1988) bring out that loss of husband not only creates a psychological vacuum but also brings loss of status and lowering of self-concept among females. What is the situation in the present study? The loss of husband makes a female susceptible financially, emotionally and socially. "*Jab tak aadmi jinda hota hai,* Kalawati (name changed), a resident of Pushp Vihar, bemoans, "*hum tabhi tak maalkin hote hain, baad main to sirf bache-kuche din katne hote hain*" (we feel we are mistress till our husband is alive, after that we somehow manage to spend remaining days of our life). Still another respondent feels, "*Bina aadmi ke budhapa katna aik shrap hai* (In old age it is a curse to live without husband). In the absence of husband they may feel helpless, unattended and isolated.

In the study, 46.9 per cent respondents are married, 50.9 per cent widows, 2 per cent separated and 0.3 per cent divorced. Since the proportion of separated and divorced aged women in the study is very small, these categories have been merged with that of widow. Further, in consonance with the results of National Sample Survey, 38th and 42nd rounds (Biswas, 1994), findings of the present study show that, with age, chances of widowhood increases. In the age-group of 60 to 62 years, 37 per cent respondents are widowed. The corresponding proportion, in the category of 63 to 67 years, is 49.6 per cent. In the age-group of 68 to 96 years, 76.2 per cent respondents are widowed, almost double of the first category.

Analysis shows that married respondents rate their present and future life as happy or very happy, almost twice more than widow or separated. Similar are the observations of Chadha, *et al.* (1992) that married older people are found to be low on hopelessness and high on life-satisfaction as compared to their widow/widower counterparts. Data further show that the number of elderly females often having fear of death is three times more in the category of widowed or separated than their married counterparts. Table 2.3 highlights the association between marital status and death fear. That this relationship is strong is indicated by relevant statistics (rank correlation = +0.47; product-moment correlation = +0.40).

Table 2.3 : Association between marital status and death fear among the elderly respondents

	Fear of Death			
Marital status	*No*	*Rarely*	*Sometimes*	*Often*
Married	63.8	6.9	9.4	20.0
Widow/separated	8.4	12.4	19.1	60.1

As would be expected, marital status also influences respondents' self-comparison of their health status. Married respondents (26.8 per cent), more often, perceive their health as good or very good than widows (18.9 per cent). Likewise, further analysis shows that married respondents possess an optimistic attitude towards life more than others. Among those who perceive their future as 'bright', 70 per cent are married and only 30 per cent are widowed or separated. Those who view 'vague' future ahead, 50 per cent are married and 60 per cent widow. Also, 69.6 per cent of widow elderly women consider their future as hopeless as compared to 30.4 per cent of married females. Similar findings are reported by Jamuna and Reddy (1991) that widows have a considerably more negative self-concept than non-widows.

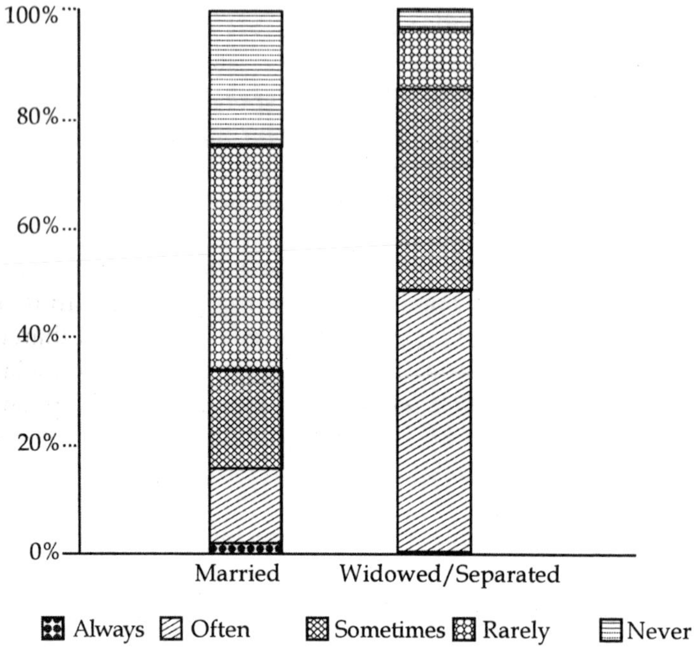

Diagram 2.1 : Marital Status and Loneliness

Diagram 2.1 gives a comparative view of feeling of loneliness among widowed and married respondents. It shows that among the respondents who often feel lonely, the proportion of widows (48.4 per cent) is more than three times higher than their married counterparts (14.6 per cent). Similarly, 40.9 per cent married and 11.3 per cent widow respondents rarely feel lonely. So, fewer married respondents feel lonely as compared to widows. Lopata (1979) also observes that loneliness is the most common problem faced by the widows.

Dress of people, many times, gives an indication of their status. Since elderly females are, more often than not, dependent on their family, condition of their dress also denotes their integration in the family. While conducting interviews, the researcher has observed the condition of the dress the respondents were wearing. It was seen that, among the respondents, those who were in fresh dress, 64.5 per cent were married and 35.5 per cent widow. Those who were putting on worn out dress, 41.4 per cent were married and 58.6 per cent widow. Further, 80 per cent of widow respondents were wearing mended clothes as compared to only 20 per cent of married respondents. There appears to be a significant association between marital status of the respondents and their living arrangements. Observation data show that 66.7 per cent of married respondents live in exclusive room compared to only 33.3 per cent of widow respondents. Those living in shared room 58.5 per cent were married and 41.5 per cent widow. Among those respondents living in *barsati,* 23.8 per cent were married and 76.2 per cent were widows. This brings out an unmistakable difference in the living condition and, perhaps, the status between married and widow aged women.

Religious Affiliations

Religion, according to MacIver (1937), is the relation between man and some higher power. It has two main dimensions—spiritual and ritual. Spiritual dimension gives a person internal strength to deal with crises in life. Wolff (1959) reports that religious beliefs, prayer and faith in god, all help the aged to overcome problems like loneliness, grief and unhappiness. Courtenay *et al.* (1992) consider religiosity as a coping mechanism, which is more frequently found among the 'old-old'. The other dimension of religion is ritual, which concerns worship and such events as marriage, child-birth and death. In these the aged often have a definitive role. They counsel and guide other family members in the observance of these rituals. In doing so, their integration in the family and community also goes up. It provides the elderly as much satisfaction as diversion from routine and monotony (Gangrade, 1989).

In India, Hindus form the largest religious group followed by Muslims, Sikhs and Christians. Table 2.4 provides comparative view of religion-wise distribution of persons in India, Delhi and Pushp Vihar. The study results largely confirm to aggregate trends, with one exception. Sikhs are somewhat over-represented in the sample. The proportion of respondents professing other faiths like Buddhism, Jainism, also is significantly higher in the study area.

Table 2.4 : Religion-wise distribution of population of India, Delhi and Pushp Vihar

Religion	*India*	*Delhi*	*Pushp Vihar*
Hindu	80	82	74.9
Sikh	2	4.0	10.3
Muslim	14	11.7	3.4
Christian	2.4	0.9	6.3
Others	1.6	1.3	5.1

Source: Census of India 2001.

Religion appears to have special significance to the elderly. Courtenay *et al.* (1992) claim that faith in religion, in old age, is the key to a happy life as it helps in the reduction of the fear of death. Added to this, religious organizations perform many functions in the life of the elderly, say, providing companionship and counselling (McDonald, 1973). These studies suggest that religiosity plays a crucial role in the well-being of an aged. However, the present study shows that there is statistically no significant association between factors of psychological well-being like optimism, life-satisfaction, sleep, worry and tension, loneliness, etc., and religious affiliation of the elderly females. Similarly, respondent's decision-making in the family and respect received from significant others also are independent of religious affiliation. Apparently, while religiosity is an important component, religious affiliation does not seem to influence the well-being of the elderly females.

As discussed earlier, religion, among others, is a factor that enables the aged to integrate in the society during ritual-performances. These differ from religion to religion. As a consequence, they provide differential opportunities to the elderly to take up the role of decision-maker or guide in performance of rituals, say, during marriage of grandchildren and child-birth. Present study shows that, among the respondents having their granddaughters-in-law (52 respondents), most of the Hindu aged females (78 per cent) are consulted in the marriage ceremony of their grandchildren. Only 50 per cent of the Christian respondents have been consulted and no Muslim respondent has been consulted on this issue in their household. Almost one-third of the Sikh respondents are consulted in their grandchildren's marriage. Among Hindus, elderly females play a significant role during ritual performance at the time of marriage and child-birth. This may be the reason for higher proportion of Hindu respondents being involved in decision-making during the marriage of their grandchildren.

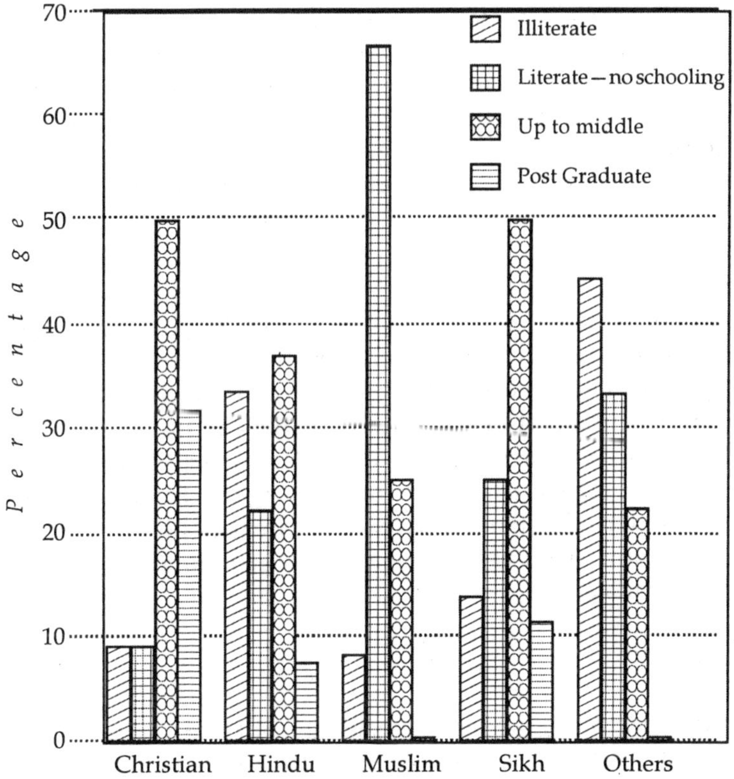

Diagram 2.2 : Educational Status and Religion of the Respondents

Does religious affiliation have any role in providing opportunities for education to females? Diagram 2.2 brings out several interesting details. In the category of illiterate elderly respondents, the proportion of Muslim women is the smallest (8.3 per cent). This does not confirm to the aggregate data trends. This position is partly explained by subsequent categories. Among those elderly women who are literate but who have not done any schooling, the proportion of Muslims is highest (66.7 per cent). However, their proportion is markedly lower when it comes to schooling or higher education. In terms of education up to middle or eighth standard, both Christians and Sikhs, have a largest proportion (50 per cent in each case), followed by Hindus. The difference further becomes noticeable when attention is paid to college or higher education. The proportion of Christians is highest (31.8 per cent), followed by Sikhs (11.1 per cent) and Hindus (7.3 per cent). It may be noted that no Muslim elderly woman figures in this category. Taken together, in the present sample, the situation of schooling and education is not very encouraging. While only 46.6 per cent of the respondents have been to school or college, others are either illiterate or have had informal education.

Next, it would be relevant to examine religious affiliation in relation to the past occupational status of the respondents. Analysis shows that all Muslim respondents have remained housewife or, say, non-workers and none of them has been involved in any economically gainful activity. So is the case with 95 per cent of Hindus. Among Sikhs and Christians the situation is a shade better. About 86 per cent of the Sikhs and 60 per cent of the Christians are in this category. Thus, it may be inferred that Christian elderly women are better off in terms of education as well as participation in economically gainful opportunities.

Caste

Caste-system is a unique characteristic of Hindu society. This age-old institution has stratified the society into four *varnas*—Brahmin, Kashtriya, Vaishya and Shudra. As in the present form, it is rigidly hereditary. Brahmin, Kashtriya and Vaishya are often grouped as 'upper-caste' and Shudra as 'lower caste'. The caste-system imposes certain restrictions on its members in the matter of occupation as well as social intercourse. As a consequence, persons belonging to upper caste have traditionally better educational and economic opportunities than those belonging to lower caste. After Independence, Government of India has tried to improve the situation of these underprivileged sections, officially termed as—Scheduled Castes (SC), Scheduled Tribes (ST) and Other Backward Classes (OBC)—through several affirmative actions. For example, children belonging to SC and ST are provided stipend/ scholarships during their school and college education. In public sector job openings, they enjoy 'reservations'. During last 50 years, among other changes, in caste norms, occupation has tended to become independent of caste affiliation. Khan and Qamar (1996) observe that more than a half of their SC respondents (53 per cent) are engaged in salaried jobs while only 18 per cent are in daily wage work. As far as social intercourse is concerned, urbanization and industrialization, among others, have blurred caste distinctions. In a study in Delhi, two-thirds of the SC respondents have visited their upper caste neighbours, in their marriage ceremonies during the last one year (Khan and Qamar, 1996). Does education and occupational status of elderly females vary with their caste background?

In the present study sample, 37.8 per cent are Brahmin, 15.6 per cent Kshatriya, 27.1 per cent Vaishya and 19.5 per cent belong to SC, ST, or OBC. Keeping, this in view, we will look into the educational status of the respondents. Table 2.5 reveals noticeable dimensions. One-third of the respondents are illiterate. Confirming to the aggregate data trends, the proportion of the SC, ST or OBC respondents is highest (43.2 per cent) in the group of illiterates. In the same category, the proportion of Brahmins (21.6 per cent) is just a-half of the former group. Vaishya and Kshatriya have nearly equal proportion, but lesser than SC, ST or OBC and Brahmin. In the subsequent category of 'literate but no schooling' proportion of Brahmin respondents (44.8 per cent) is almost double the next highest group—Vaishya (22.4 per cent). Representation of SC, ST or OBC in this category is the lowest. In the next category of education up to eighth standard, proportion of Brahmin respondents is the highest (44.3 per cent), followed by Vaishya (38.1 per cent) and again proportion of SC, ST or OBC respondents is the lowest (5.2 per cent). Looking into the education up to post-graduation, Brahmin respondents (57.9 per cent) are much ahead of others. Vaishya respondents occupy the second rank, followed by Kshatriya. None of the respondent belonging to SC, ST or OBC figures in this category. It is thus apparent that Brahmin respondents are clearly better off in terms of educational attainments while SC, ST or OBC respondents are on the lowest rung. May be among the upcoming generations, these caste differences may not be so marked.

Table 2.5 : Association between caste affiliation and educational status of the respondents

Caste Group	*Illiterate*	*Literate but no schooling*	*Education up to middle*	*Post-graduate*
Brahmins	21.6	44.8	44.3	57.9
Kshatriya	17.0	19.0	12.4	15.8
Vaishya	18.2	22.4	38.1	26.3
SC, ST or OBC	43.2	13.8	5.2	0.0
Total	33.6	22.1	37.0	7.3

Researchers have also paid attention on the relation between caste and occupational status. Prasad (1990) reports that, in the work-force, lower castes are largely confined to traditional occupations, hard labour and so-assumed menial jobs. Their proportion progressively decreases in office jobs, skilled work, administrative posts and professional work. Reservation in jobs has certainly had some impact but unevenly. It must be restated that females have an added disadvantage, in any caste, in our patriarchal society. Attention may be focused on the present occupational status of the respondents belonging to different castes.

Data gathered in the present study show that 95.4 per cent of the respondents (including pensioners) are non-workers or only housewife. Given this, attention may be diverted to their husbands. Those who were engaged into agriculture, Brahmin males have the highest proportion (33.3 per cent), followed by Vaishya (26.7 per cent), Kshatriya (3.8 per cent) and SC, ST or OBC (17.8 per cent). In the category of those involved in self-employment, Brahmin and SC, ST or OBC males show highest proportion (33.1 per cent each), followed by Kshatriya and Vaishya (16.7 per cent each). In trading, Brahmin males have a proportion of 51.5 per cent, followed by Vaishya (27.3 per cent), Kshatriya (15.2 per cent) and SC, ST or OBC (6.1 per cent). Lastly, among respondents' husbands engaged in salaried work (Government or PSU) those belonging to Brahmin, have a proportion of 38.8 per cent, followed by Vaishya (31.3 per cent), SC, ST or OBC (20.1 per cent) and Kshatriya (9.7 per cent). Data in the present study show that caste has no marked influence on the occupational status of the respondents or their husbands. This is also indicated by relevant statistics (product-moment correlation = +0.02).

Attention may be paid to the treatment received by the respondents of different castes from the members of their household, as observed by the researcher. Among the Brahmin respondents, 89.5 per cent received affectionate treatment while 10.5 per cent got indifference from their family members. Among Kshatriya respondents, corresponding figures are 95.8 per cent and 4.2 per cent respectively. Likewise, 82.5 per cent Vaishya respondents got affectionate treatment and the rest faced indifference. Lastly, among the respondents belonging to SC, ST or OBC, 70.6 per cent were treated affectionately, 17.6 per cent with indifference and only 2 (11.8 per cent) disdainfully. There is a mild trend that in the upper caste households, members are a little more deferential towards the elderly.

Do elderly females belonging to upper caste enjoy greater decision-making power in their family? Analysis shows that, in the matter of marriage of their grandchildren, 85.7 per cent Brahmin, 83.3 per cent SC, ST or OBC, 77 per cent Kshatriya and 62.5 per cent Vaishya respondents are consulted. While buying things for household, 75 per cent Kshatriya, 68.3 per cent Vaishya, 66.7 per cent of Brahmins and 33.3 per cent of SC, ST or OBC respondents are consulted. This gives the impression that caste is not significantly related to the status of elderly females in their family.

Mother-Tongue

Mother-tongue is not only a means of communication but also an indicator of cultural background and even psycho-social make-up. The dynamics of mother-tongue, many times, allows persons to relate to their fellow countrymen easily. On the other hand, at times, it poses hurdles while interacting with persons belonging to other lingual groups. In the present study, the researcher was not able to interview four elderly females because of language-problem. Further, these gentle old females remain confined only to their household, as they could not communicate with the neighbourers. This has also kept them away from such activities as attending *satsangs*, chatting with neighbours, shopping, etc., which several senior females living in Pushp Vihar often take to.

In the study sample, more than a-half (51.7 per cent) of the respondents speak Hindi as their mother tongue. This is followed by the group speaking Punjabi (21.1 per cent). Another 27.1 per cent respondents speak other languages like Urdu, Bengali, Tamil, Telugu, Gujarati, etc. Among the Hindus, almost 65 per cent speak Hindi, 15 per cent Punjabi and 20 per cent other languages. Muslim respondents primarily speak Urdu. Also, Sikhs (95 per cent), with a few exceptions, speak Punjabi. Similarly, 77.3 per cent Christians speak languages like Tamil, Kannada, etc., 18.2 per cent Hindi and 4.5 per cent Punjabi. It follows that in the present study group, we have many-India, language-wise.

Period of Stay in Delhi

Do the elderly who come to stay in Delhi at a later stage in their life face problems in adjusting with the fast pace of Delhi-life?

Following is the case-study of an aged female, who comes to visit her son in Delhi and finds it difficult to cope with the city life-style.

Indifferent Delhi

Ramkali (the name has been changed to protect the privacy of the respondent), 72 years old, is a religious lady. She was born and brought up in a small town of Haryana. She was married at an early age of 15 years. All her seven children are married and well settled. Her eldest son, a government-employee, lives and works in Delhi. After the death of her husband, she was staying in the ancestral house with her three sons. Her daughters-in-law and grandchildren picked up quarrels on slightest opportunity. She had a separate room where she cooked for herself and did all her activities of daily-living independently. Husband's pension was more than enough for her limited needs.

Now, she is with her son in Delhi on an occasional visit. Here, her daughter-in-law and three grandchildren give her lots of love and respect. A few neighbourhood women are even jealous of her happy life. But, she abhors the fast life of Delhi and indifference of the neighbours, where nobody has time for others. Absence of a small town-life including routine temple going disturbs her. All the more, free mixing with the *sudras* makes the Brahmin lady uncomfortable. In Delhi, in spite of all comforts, she feels a vacuum in her life and wishes to go back to Haryana at the earliest. She would prefer to visit Delhi only once or twice a year. *"Mera to bilkul man nahin lagta"*, murmers Ramkali, *"Halanki beta-bahu bahut khayal rakhten hain phir bhi dilli mujhe nahin suhati"*(Delhi does not suit me, although my son and daughter-in-law care for me a lot).

The period of stay in Delhi may be crucial for getting accustomed to urban-life. Those living in Delhi for several years often show better adjustment to the urban-environment than those who are relatively new to the place. Some aged women may find it difficult to accept that the females of their household go out to work instead joining them in their leisure time. They feel lonely, unattended and unwanted. However, gradually the elderly women learn to cope with the urban life-style. Therefore, period of stay in Delhi is assumed to be an important variable to ascertain the integration of aged women in the family and neighbourhood.

In the present study, almost one-forth of the respondents are born and/or brought up in Delhi. Another 32.3 per cent respondents came to the city when they were between 15 to 49 years of age and 42.6 per cent when they were 50 years or above in age. Added to this, the range of the period of stay in the *moholla* is 190 months (approximately 16 years). Thirty-eight per cent respondents are staying in their present household or *moholla* for the past 1 to 4 years. Another 34 per cent respondents are staying there for the past 5-7 years and 27 per cent from 8-16 years. Mean, in this case, is 69.9 months, approximately 6 years. The data are heterogeneous (standard deviation = 40.398). Skewness (= +0.24) shows that the distribution of frequency is more towards the longer period of stay in *moholla*.

Family Background

Family is the bastion of human civilization. It is the foremost primary group. Apart from meeting basic survival needs, it also provides security—economic and emotional, love, care and support to its members, whether they are children, adults or the aged. Dandekar (1996) notes that according to many surveys old men and women, in India, are likely to live with their children more often than those in Western countries. In our country, the concept of welfare institutions for the aged such as residential homes are not very popular because family is assumed to be responsible to take care of their elderly. Chadha (1991) points out that the aged living with their family score much higher on life-satisfaction than their counterparts in institutions like old-age homes. The status of the aged, often, is judged by their family background and living-arrangements. Attention, therefore, may be focused on the family-composition of the aged respondents.

Family Composition

Like others, the elderly also need the support and security of family. Family-type determines, to some extent, the kind of support and care the elderly can get. In this regard, security and well-being of the aged, to a large extent, have been ensured by joint family groups (Gangrade, 1989). On the other hand, nuclear family groups, though becoming the trend of the day, are too person-centred to favour the situation of the elderly (Khan, 1997). These days, not only joint family but also many alternate forms of family have been taking care of the elderly. In the present study, respondents living with their husband, married or unmarried sons, and/or unmarried daughters, are considered to be in their 'natural family'. Alternatively, those aged women who are staying with their friend's or in-laws, or siblings' family are considered as living in 'adopted families'.

In the present study, six family set-ups have been identified. Joint family groups (i.e. respondent staying with her married sons) are the most popular having the proportion of 80.9 per cent. In joint families, elderly females have the opportunity to take up many roles like care-giving to grandchildren and home-management when the young females of the household are out for work. A slightly different family set-up has been observed where the respondents are living with their husband and unmarried children in one apartment and in the adjacent one her married son stays with his family. Here, though kitchens are separate, the members share two apartments as their one big household. The proportion of respondents living in such 'extended families' is only 0.9 per cent. In Pushp Vihar, 12 per cent of the respondents stay in nuclear family (i.e. respondents with her husband and/or unmarried children). Next, 3 per cent of the elderly females are staying with their son-in-law, daughter and their children. Another 2.6 per cent are living in the family of their relatives like brother-in-law or sister-in-law. Lastly, 0.6 per cent respondents are residing with their friends' family. For analysis purposes, these family set-ups have been grouped into three—joint, nuclear and adopted, having the proportions as 81.8 per cent, 12 per cent and 6.2 per cent respectively (see Diagram 2.3).

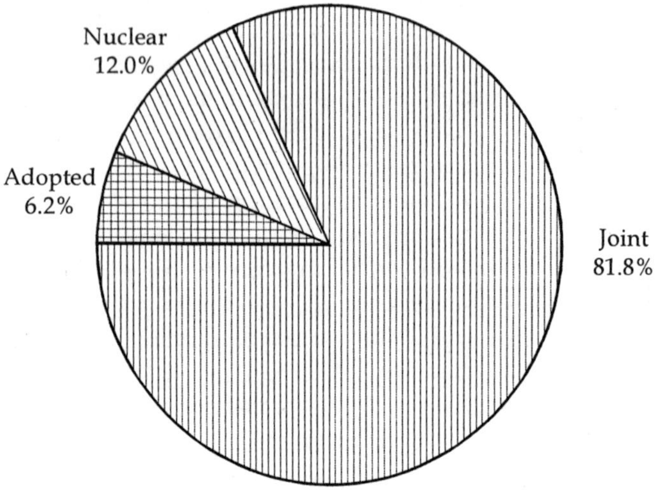

Diagram 2.3 : Type of Family of Respondents

Some elderly women are not fortunate enough to live in their 'natural family'. There are 22 aged females staying in adopted families. Reasons are—their only son staying abroad (5 cases), touring job of only son (4 cases), death of only son (1 case) and no son or no child (6 cases). And rest of the respondents did not cite any reason. Following is the case study of an aged female whose only son has out-migrated for better economic prospects, adding to the social, and psychological insecurities to her elderly mother.

Son! I need you, not money

Damayanti, 66 years is a widow. She is staying with her brother-in-law and his family. Her only son is in the United States. Two years ago, after death of her husband, her son accepted a job in America. Without considering her mother's plight, he flew away within a month for a bright career. Since then, Damayanti is staying in this family. Her son sends money regularly but bothers to phone her up only once in 5-6 months. Her married daughter can't go against her in-laws to keep her old mother with her. Damayanti's brother-in-law and his family are quite happy with the money that she contributes to the family for her maintenance. The respondent doesn't like staying there but is helpless. She misses her son too much. Daily, she silently weeps for her son. Her dreams of getting her son married and playing with her own grandchildren are crushed away. Though there is no obvious conflict between her and the family but still she doesn't feel 'home-like' environment. She knows clearly that she is respected only because she is a source of income to the family and it is the money that is forcing them to respect her.

Though elderly are forced to leave their natural families for some reasons, most often, their well-being is not ensured in the adopted families as seen in the case of Maya.

Missing own family

Maya is a 62 years old widow living with her friend Laxmi, and her family. She however, doesn't fail to feel the pain of loss of her own family. Her happy family consisted of her husband, only son, daughter-in-law and two little twin grandsons who had given her the best reward of life—grand-motherhood. She was a source of envy among her age-mates for having a loving and caring family. But this happiness was of short duration. A year back, her son, *bahu* and grandchildren had gone for a vacation in Kullu-Manali, where their car met with an accident and fell into a gorge deep down to about 700 feet. Within seconds all were dead. Her husband—a heart patient—couldn't absorb this horrible incident and died soon, leaving behind her wife Maya all alone on this earth. Homeless Maya couldn't have found herself in a better place than her friend Laxmi's house. Maya tries hard to cope up with her memories by engaging herself in the household chores. She plays with grandchildren of her friend, rest of her time she spends in *puja*. She admits that though her friend and her family are doing their best for her but she all the time feels the pinch in her heart that it is not her *own* family.

Below is another case study of an elderly woman, Prem, who is forced to part with her husband on account of financial and space constraint. Their two sons have divided the responsibility of their up-keep with one parent staying with one son without looking into the consequent emotional turmoil of their old parents.

Parting from husband

Prem is 68 years old married lady staying with one of her two sons in Pushp Vihar. Her daughter-in-law is working. She has to take care of her granddaughter and look after the household activities. Her husband stays with another son and his family is in Rohini. Two years back, they all were living together here, in Pushp Vihar as a joint family. Then, one day her sons declared to live separately and took the decision of dividing the unwanted responsibility of old parents on account of lack of adequate space and monetary constraint. It is very painful for Prem to live separately from her husband in old age when throughout their life they have always lived together. She doesn't express her frustrations overtly in front of her family as it will lead only to exchange of hot arguments with no solution. "We didn't separate our children because of financial stringency", distressed Prem expresses, "but in old age our children have forced us to part. I miss him too much. I don't know how he is being cared for". She thinks that her emotions have no value for her money-minded children. *"Jindgi bhar saath rahe"*, with tear filled eyes she murmers, *"Ab budhape main alag ho gaye (from husband) kyonki bacche hum dono ko aik saath nahin paal sakte. Yahan meri ahamiyat aik noukrani se bhi kam hai"*. (We stayed together for our whole life. Now, in old age, our children can't maintain us together. Here, my status is even less than a servant).

Size of the Household

No denying the fact that in large sized households elderly people get greater opportunity for interactions. In this regard, urban aged are often believed to be at disadvantageous position than their rural counterparts. In metropolitan cities like Delhi, flats or apartments have limited space, more often, inadequate for large sized families. The present study shows that 50.3 per cent respondents are having 2 to 5 members in their household. Another 28 per cent aged females have 6 members and 21.7 per cent respondents have household size as seven. Mode is 6 members in the household. However, there are on the average 5.5 to a household. The data are more or less homogeneous (standard deviation = 1.889).

In this connection, an assessment of the number of children of the respondents would be insightful. Children, particularly sons, are considered as a security in old age. Barge, *et al.* (1994) bring out that one of the important motive behind fertility-behaviour is old-age security. In the present study, one respondent has had no child. On the other hand, 40.9 per cent of the respondents have 1 to 3 children. Another 37.1 per cent have 4 children and the rest 21.7 per cent respondents have 5 to 7 children. Most common trend is having 4 children (mode = 4) while mean is 3.67. The group is homogeneous (standard deviation = 1.174).

Let us pay attention to the number of (grown up) children living with respondents in the household. In 6 per cent households, respondents live with their husband with no children around. Almost in 70.9 per cent households, respondents live with their one of the (grown up) children and in 18.3 per cent households aged females stay with their two (grown up) children. In 4.9 per cent households, respondents live with their 3 to 4 (grown up) children. Mode is one child in the household. Looking into the number of daughters-in-law, 9.4 per cent respondents do not have any *bahu*, 34 per cent respondents have one, 32.9 per cent have two and another 23.7 per cent have 3 to 6 daughters-in-law. Attention may be focused on the number of daughters-in-law living in the household with the respondents. Data depict that 19.4 per cent do not have any daughters-in-law in the household. Seventy per cent have one and 10.6 per cent respondents live with their 2 to 3 daughters-in-law in the single household. It may be noted that the size of the family is not statisticaliy related to such variables as religion and caste.

It is a common observation that grandchildren are close to their grandparents. Often they provide new roles to their grandmothers. In the present study, one grandmother says, "*Mera pota mujhe jindgi se mila hua sabse bada inaam hai*" (my grandson is the greatest gift life has offered me). Another one comments, "*Asal se sood pyara hota hai aise hi pote potiyan apne bacchon se bhi pyre hote hain*" (as interest is more dear than actual amount likewise grandchildren is more loving than own offspring). Data show that 17.7 per cent of the respondents have no grandchildren. Almost one-third (28.9 per cent) of the respondents have 1 to 2 grandchildren and 23.4 per cent 3 to 4 grandchildren. Another 30 per cent respondents have 5 to 14 grandchildren. Most common trend is having two grandchildren (mode = 2) and mean is 3.48. Looking into the number of respondents' grandchildren living in the same household, almost one-fourth (24.6 per cent) of respondents have no grandchildren, 14.3 per cent only one, 35.4 per cent two and 25.7 per cent respondents 3 to 7 grandchildren. One old respondent, blessed with a great-grandson utters, "*Maine padpote ka munh dekh liya, ab seedhe swarg jaungi marne ke baad*" (I have seen the face of my great-grandson, now I shall straight go to heaven after death).

It, thus, appears that the elderly females, in general, have fairly large family size (mode = 6) and have a substantial opportunity to interact with grandchildren (mode = 2). The impact, if any, of family size and presence of grandchildren would be dealt with a little later.

Educational Level

Education is taken to inculcate, among others, understanding, reasoning and self-reliance that play a crucial role in adjustment. Education is, often, believed to be the key factor for the empowerment. Kumar (1991) observes that educational attainment has considerable bearing on the financial condition as well as living standards. Aoki *et al.* (1996) point out that high social activity is related to high educational attainments. However, educational status of the elderly, in our country, gives a gloomy picture. More than two-thirds of the aged males and almost 90 per cent of aged females are illiterate (Bose, 1998). It may be restated that, in 1991, literacy rate among elderly males was merely 27 per cent and that among aged females it was all the more disheartening—just 13 per cent. It was far below the national average of 52.2 per cent. Though, Indian Constitution and legislation may provide equal status to males and females, social reality puts females at a disadvantageous position—educationally, economically and socially. Let us examine the educational status of the respondents and their husband in Pushp Vihar.

In this study, 29.7 per cent of respondents are illiterate, 23.7 per cent can read and write but have never gone to school. Another 38 per cent aged females have studied up to middle class. Only 8.6 per cent respondents have acquired education up to post-graduation. Mean years of schooling is 3.5. Further, analysis of the data shows a wide gap between the educational status of respondents and that of their husband. Only 4.6 per cent husbands are illiterate as compared to almost one-third of the respondents. Next, 9.4 per cent elderly males (husband) are literate but had no schooling, another 27.4 per cent have studied up to middle-school and rest 26 per cent have gained education up to tenth standard. Almost one-third (32.6 per cent) of the respondents' husband have studied up to post-graduation, which is four times higher than that of the respondents. In general, their husband have gone to school and are studied up to 11th standard. It suggests that aged females lag behind their husband in terms of educational attainments.

It may be restated that literacy rate among the elderly has always remained less than that of the general population. The incidence of higher rate of illiteracy may be due to poor schooling facilities during their childhood years as well as cultural constraints over education of females. Diagram 2.4 presents the respondent's educational status in different age-categories. It shows that highest proportion (19.1 per cent) of illiterates is in the category of 68 to 96 years. Illiteracy in this age-group is more than three times higher than in the age-group of 60 to 62 years (5.4 per cent). Respondents in the age-group of 63 to 67 years show highest proportion in the category of 'literate but no schooling', followed by oldest respondents (68 to 96 years). In the same way, the proportion of younger respondents, in the age-category of 60 to 62 years, is almost seven times higher in the acquisition of post-graduation degree than their older age-cohorts (68 to 96 years). That educational qualification improves as we move from oldest respondent category to the youngest ones, is strongly indicated by relevant statistics (rank correlation = –0.46).

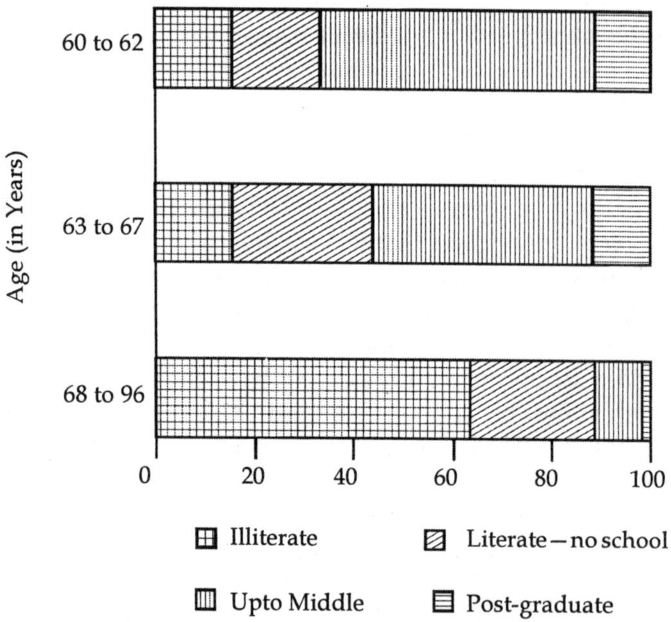

Diagram 2.4 : Educational Status and Age of the Respondents

Next, results bring out that there is no association between educational status of the respondents and indicators of psychological well-being like optimistic attitude, death-fear, loneliness, type of sleep, tension and anxiety, etc. Also, educational status of the respondents is not related to consultation in the family matters.

Above discussion shows that aged females in the group of 60 to 62 years are more educated than the older ones. What is the educational status of the young females in the household? Does the level of educational attainment of daughters-in-law influence the quality of interactions with the mother-in-law? Attention may be paid to the educational status of the daughters-in-law. A little less than one-third (30.3 per cent) daughters-in-law have studied up to 12th standard. Another 43.1 per cent have studied up to graduation and 83 per cent have acquired degree of post-graduation and above. The data, further, indicate a clear and strong association between educational status of mother-in-law and daughter-in-law. Relevant statistics (product-moment correlation = +0.46) put forth that educated elderly females tend to have daughters-in-law who have attained a higher educational qualification.

Occupational Status

Occupational status, many times, gives an indication of the economic position, self-confidence and life-style of an individual. Those working in government or public sector undertaking, have to retire at or around the age of 60 years. Conversely, for those working in unorganized sector, their personal health condition, often, influences their period of superannuation. Most of these jobs (like labour work, harvesting, hand-embroidery, etc.) need physical strength and sound sensory capacities. So, younger persons usually replace the elderly with poor strength, low eyesight or, say, locomotion problems. Attention may now be focused on the situation of the females. Those women who have remained as housewife are generally considered as non-workers as the economic value of their work, being invisible, remains often unacknowledged. Contrarily, the proportion of women engaged in some income generating activities is too low, 4.1 per cent in organized sector and 16 per cent in un-organized one (see Country paper for Beijing Conference, 1995). Does economic employment ensure financial security?

The aged retiring from organized sector often get social insurance in terms of pension, provident fund, etc. However, their proportion is quite low, just 11.6 per cent. On the other hand, the proportion of aged in informal sector is 88.3 per cent, more than seven times the proportion of their counterparts in formal sector (Reddy, 1996). Needless to add, unorganized sector does not provide any social security to the aged. Coming back to the situation of aged women, those who have been housewife are obviously dependent on their family for financial security. What is the position of those engaged in economic activities? Sahayam (1988) observes that the proportion of aged women working as agricultural labourers is almost one and a half times higher than their male counterparts. It appears that patriarchal social milieu, often, aggravates the life-long dependency in old age. Prakash (1996) finds that, though most females have had contributed significantly in the family occupation of agriculture, 90 per cent of the aged women are financially dependent on their family with no property ownership. In view of these considerations, attention may be diverted to the situation obtaining in Pushp Vihar.

Table 2:6 gives a comparative view of past and present occupational patterns among the respondents and their husband. The data, on the past occupational status, show that 92 per cent of the respondents have remained housewife only. Out of remaining 8 per cent respondents involved in economically gainful activities, 3.4 per cent were in private sector. Corresponding proportion in the case of their husband is 12 per cent, almost four times higher than their female counterparts. This difference in proportions further gets accentuated in the category of government employees. The proportion of males (44 per cent) is almost 13 times higher than females (3.4 per cent) in this category. Similarly, the ratio of males to females, in the case of involvement in trading, is 25 : 1. No female figures in the category of public sector undertaking in contrast to 4 per cent males. There is a clear and wide gap between the occupational levels among the respondents and their husband.

Table 2.6 : Occupational patterns of the respondents and their husband

Occupation	*Elderly female*		*Husband**	
	Past	*Present*	*Past*	*Present*
Non worker/housewife	92.0	84.6	0.0	7.7
Agriculture	0.0	0.0	16.0	1.4
Self-employment	0.6	0.6	8.9	1.7
Trading	0.6	0.6	15.1	6.9
Private service	3.4	0.3	12.0	5.4
Private service undertaking	0.0	0.0	4.0	0.9
Government service/pension	3.4	14.0	44.0	22.9

* Excluding the deceased.

Looking into the present occupational status, 14 per cent of the respondents are pensioners in contrast to 22.9 per cent of their male counterparts. Only 1.5 per cent respondents are currently involved in some economic activity in comparison to 16.3 per cent males. Proportion of housewife or non-workers is the highest (84.6 per cent). The drop in the proportion of housewife or non-workers, from the past to present occupational patterns, among the respondents, may be due to inclusion of those females who receive pension after their husband into the category of 'government service' (see Table 2.6).

Is there any association between educational status and past occupational pattern among elderly women? The data indicate that almost all illiterate respondents (99 per cent), except one, have been housewife or non-workers in the past. Those respondents, who are literate but have never been to school, 97.6 per cent have been housewife while 2.4 per cent have been workers. Those who have studied up to middle, 91.7 per cent have been housewife or non-workers. Further, among those who have studied up to post graduation, 46.7 per cent have been working previously. It shows a direct relationship between educational level and occupational status.

Now-a-days, young females are taking up economic roles outside the four walls of the household. In this study, 29 per cent of the respondents' daughters-in-law are employed. Almost 3/4th (71 per cent) of daughters-in-law are housewife. A close look into the occupational status of the daughters-in-law and the age of their mother-in-law would give some insight into the aspect of care-giving to the elderly. Data show that, 30.6 per cent of daughters-in-law, whose mothers-in-law are between 60 to 62 years, are employed. In 63 to 67 years category of age of elderly females, 41.3 per cent of daughters-in-law are employed, while in the category of 68 to 96 years, only 15.6 per cent of daughters-in-law are working, almost half the proportion in the first category (60 to 62 years). With advancing age, elderly people need greater care and support from the family due to declining body strength. This might be a reason of trend of decreasing occupational level among the daughters-in-law with increase in the age of their mother-in-law.

This demographic scenario gives the context in which we would be looking into the adjustment abilities and problems of the aged females of urban context.

3

PATTERN OF SOCIAL ADJUSTMENT

With the gradual conversion of human societies into grey-world, attention is being increasingly focused on the adjustment of senior citizens. At the physiological level, old age is, often, accompanied by lower energy level, reduced sensory capacities and restricted mobility. Also, mental agility does not remain the same as it used to be. Added to this, society also limits the roles played by persons in their old age. Retirement from employment and children coming of age and settling down in occupation in life are some of the events that apparently shrink their roles. Given these considerations, adjustment of senior citizens appears to be problematic in the family, community and society.

However, adjustment is a highly personal phenomenon. Age alone may not be a predictor of adjustment or mal-adjustment. An elderly, just because of age, cannot assume to be facing adjustment problems. Rather, interaction of many intrinsic and extrinsic factors influences adjustment of an individual. Many writers have shown that the individuals' thoughts and emotions have major influence over their adjustment patterns and even on their body's functioning (see Cannon, 1963; Everson and Cole, 1966). Chopra gives a little different perspective. "Biological age (in terms of critical life-signs and cellular processes) and psychological age (that is how old an individual feels s/he is) can be 'reprogrammed'. The body seems to age beyond our control only because we are collectively conditioned to believe so, because the mind influences every cell in the body. Human ageing is fluid and changeable. Ageing is much more dependent on the individual than was dreamt of in the past" (1993). It follows that the major responsibility of having a viable adjustment in the social milieu is on the person. External circumstances, according to Chopra (1993), have but a secondary role to play.

Before looking into the factors that seem to facilitate or inhibit adjustment of a person, let us first pay attention to the concept of adjustment.

Adjustment

In everyday life, the word 'adjustment' is frequently used. Some use it merely as the ability to adapt and some take it as happiness and freedom from personal problems. To others, it may mean an unhappy conformity to social demands and expectations. The Dictionary of Education defines 'adjustment' as "the process of finding and adopting modes of behaviour suitable to the environment". Here what is being emphasized is conformity to the environment. Similarly, Adam considers adjustment as "a continuous process by which a person varies his behaviour to produce a more harmonious relationship between himself and his environment" (1972). In this definition, balance, between personal needs and norms of societies, is considered crucial for adjustment. Chamber's Dictionary defines adjustment as "the outcome of the individual's efforts to deal with stress and meet his needs". This definition gives another aspect of adjustment, that is, coping with conflicts. Kumar gives a comprehensive definition of 'adjustment' as "a process, involving both mental and behavioural responses, by which an individual strives to cope successfully with inner needs, tensions, frustrations and conflicts and to effect a degree of harmony between these inner demands and those imposed on him by the objective world in which he lives"(1988). Fairchild (1966) also gives emphasis to the 'social' aspect of adjustment. He observes, "adjustment refers to those types of relationships, between personality, groups and cultural complexes, which are harmonious and naturally satisfactory to the personalities and groups involved".

Conceptually, there is no difference between the terms 'adjustment' and 'social adjustment' except that the latter emphasizes more on social relationships. Social adjustment is the adaptation of an individual to a social environment in the process of performing a social role with a view to maximizing gains or minimizing losses. Warren defines it as "the changes in habitual conduct or behaviour, which an individual must make in order to fit into the community in which he lives" (1962). The term—social adjustment—indicates the process by which an individual or a group reaches a state of social equilibrium.

Adjustment is a complex term. Foregoing discussion reveals two aspects of adjustment—first, as a process and second, a state, that is, the result of such a process. Adjustment, as a process, is a response to stimuli—external or internal (here, irrespective of the consequences of that response). The result of such a response is a state that may be favourable or unfavourable for the individual. Favourable responses help in establishment of harmonious relationships with environment. Unfavourable responses further ask for coping with frustrations and conflicts due to unfulfilled needs and unsatisfied demands. Adjustment, in itself is a neutral term. 'Well adjusted' and 'mal-adjusted' are among the various levels in the adjustment continuum. Most people fit in the middle range of this continuum. Also, it must be remembered that adjustment is relative, and not absolute in character. There is nothing like a perfectly adjusted person. At the most, it can be said that some individuals have the ability for harmonious adjustment. Then too, harmonious adjustment is not necessarily static or permanent. Rather, it is dynamic in character. A well-adjusted person, at one point of time, may start showing mal-adjustment. Also, nature of adjustment changes from person to person. An aged woman may be well-adjusted in the immediate family but may face difficulty in adjusting with neighbours. This follows that adjustment has several manifestations. An aged woman, quietly crying in her room on the harsh behaviour of her *bahu*, daughter-in-law, is adjusting. Another one, backbiting her *bahu* in front of relatives and friends, is also showing adjustment. Still, the other, exchanging hot arguments with her *bahu*, is also adjusting to the circumstances, in her own way.

What factors make the elderly adjust harmoniously? Do

they have some peculiar personality traits that make their adjustment difficult?

Social Adjustment and the Elderly

Certain viewpoints have been given by gerontologists on the adjustment of the aged in society. In ancient India, human life-cycle was divided into four *ashramas*. While *brahmacharya ashrama* (0 to 25 years) was devoted to acquisition of knowledge and skills, *grahstha ashram* (25 to 50 years) was associated with starting and enjoying family-life. *Vanaprastha* (50 to 75 years) is a period when a person starts detaching himself from his family. By then, his son starts his married life and he hands over his responsibilities to his son. Same is the expectation from the elderly female. She is supposed to give the charge of the household to her daughter-in-law. The last stage is *sanyasa ashram* when there is complete renouncement from worldly affairs. The inherent theme behind this ashram theory is acceptance of roles and responsibilities when the society needs so and handing them over to younger generation when society thinks that youngers are more capable of performing those roles. This detachment is not a negative thing. It demands a great deal of emotional and spiritual maturity. It means reducing the expectation levels and encouraging youngsters to take up the key roles and status, which the elderly have enjoyed for years (Dhillon, 1992).

On the similar thinking lines is the 'Disengagement theory' given by Cumming and Henry (1961). It proposes that ageing involves mutual withdrawal or disengagement between the elderly and the society. During the period of disengagement a person accepts a secondary position, transfers family responsibility to the younger members and reduces social participation. He disengages himself from worldly ambitions. Here, the emphasis is not on leaving things physically but change should be brought in the expectation.

Activity theory is often considered as antithesis of disengagement theory (Havighurst, 1963). It is also referred to as 'golden years' concept of ageing. It asserts that, in order to be happy in old age, individuals need to be active. It argues that if existing roles and relationships are lost it is important to replace them. Replacement to roles and relationships is necessary because when activity-level drops, there is corresponding drop in level of satisfaction. Ramamurti (1972) brings out that individuals who keep themselves physically and mentally active are prone to feel more satisfied than those who do not. In the same wavelength, is the continuity-theory (see Dhillon, 1992). It starts with the single premise that individuals will try to maintain, as long as possible, their preferred life-style.

Role theory (Mead, 1937) has a prominent place in gerontology. It is often held that, for various reasons, say, shrinkage of joint family system, involvement of younger generation in non-traditional economic activities and change in attitudes and value-system of youngers, the aged in the family are facing a 'role-less' status. Feelings of role-less and powerlessness often generate isolation and meaninglessness in their life. Thus, according to this theory, satisfaction with life will depend upon the extent to which the aged is able to replace their roles (see Shanas, 1961).

Social Exchange theory given by Rosow (1967) has special significance in understanding adjustment and role-relationship. As an economic concept, social exchange evokes cost-reward aspects of various interactions of an individual. Three propositions are given as: (1) more often a person rewards another for an activity, more often the other will emit this activity; (2) more valuable the reward, more often the activity will be emitted; but (3) at some point the frequency of reward leads to satiation and discontinuation of even rewarded behaviour. The theory suggests that an individual seeks those situations in which rewarding outcomes are most likely to be experienced. In viewing ageing as exchange, Dowd (1975) argues that, due to old age, certain skills and expertise of the people become outdated or lose their value. This decreases their bargaining power in social exchanges in relation to their social environment. Older person's disengagement is not mutually satisfying for the individual and society as claimed by disengagement theory.

Rather, in the exchange relationship, between older persons and society, the latter enjoys a distinct advantage.

Another important factor in the adjustment is the self-perception. Through life-experiences and socialization, individuals develop a perceptual framework through which they selectively perceive and interpret stimuli (see *Phenomenological theory*, Dhillon, 1992). Individuals can perceive the same phenomenon very differently. For example, aged may respond differently to phenomena such as retirement, health-change, or widowhood. Differences in their responses are not due to the phenomenon itself, but to the perception and interpretation of that phenomenon.

To sum up, these theories mention certain attributes that influence adjustment and integration of the aged in the family and neighbourhood. Acceptance of changes in roles, power and status is necessary for good adjustment. Reduced expectation lowers the tension and frustration. Also, staying active is essential in order to remain fit and healthy. Happy ageing is characterized by satisfaction with one's present life and a psychological state of happiness and content with existing conditions. Ramamurti (1970) frames six highly significant variables as predictors of life-satisfaction. They are self-acceptance of ageing changes, self-perception of health, self-rating of ability in activities of daily-living, belief in life after death and karma philosophy, satisfaction with familial and social interaction and self-rated behavioural flexibility. Are there any factors that facilitate or inhibit the adjustment abilities of the elderly?

Facilitators and Inhibitors of Social Adjustment

A close look into the development and dynamics of relationship would be of help in understanding various factors influencing adjustment. Relationship has an extremely important place in the life of people (Klinger, 1977). It is the source of joy and happiness. Sometimes, it also causes pain and suffering, when incongruent. Sustained interaction over a period of time leads to relationship-building. A relationship is formed when such interaction is rewarding to both the parties. Capella (1988) observes that, often, with time, partners in a relationship form 'mental creations' depending upon the views of themselves, their relationship-partner and the development of their relationship. Partners in a relationship develop certain expectations regarding the role and associated power between themselves. It is easier for either partner to consider the relationship and its associated aspects like role, expectation, power, etc., for granted and more or less permanent. Some of such relationships are seen between marriage partners and parent-child. Such taken-for-granted relationships often become part of one's life's routine, often, unnoticed and unconsciously. However, any change in the behaviour of either partner can alter the relationship-dynamics. Changes in relationship are inevitable for reasons, say, change in mood, attitudes, circumstances. Individuals become distressed and frustrated if their mental creations differ from reality and they do not adapt themselves to these changes. Such changes in or loss of relationship disrupts established patterns of behaviour and thereby lowers one's self-esteem (Duck, 1986).

This is also true with elderly people, who do have mental creations about their relationship with their husband, children and significant others. They have a set of expectations from them. And, gaps between mental creations and reality are not uncommon. At any rate, these situations become a source of distress for the aged. One respondent in Pushp Vihar puts it in this way, *"Kabhi mere bachche sara din mere aage-peeche ghoomte rahte the, har chote kaam ke liye mujse poochte the, aur aaj yehi bachche mere bina apne sab faisle le lete hain"* (there was a time when my children were always around me, taking advice for every small thing, and today they take all their decisions by themselves and I am ignored). Those who accept these changes in relationship as natural or inevitable tend to have better adjustment. *"Aaj ke samay main yadi hum apne vicharon aur manyataon ko thopenge to parivaar main bana ke nahin chal payenge"*, says one aged lady, *"Hamen hi badalna hoga"* (if we impose our thoughts and concepts in the family our adjustment will severely be jeopardized, so, we have to change ourselves according to the new circumstances). Therefore, flexibility and adaptability seem to contribute to harmonious relationship between the aged and others. It may be noted that acceptance of changes not only includes social relations but also deteriorating physical strength and accompanying change in mental agility.

Another important dimension in relationship is the communication-pattern. Khan (1997) observes that those aged who are amiable and forbearing, possess communication-skills and have warmth towards family members, continue to be important to the family. Among others, positive communication-skills include verbal or non-verbal expression of appreciation and recognition of care and support offered (or given) by significant others. There is a strong evidence that positive exchange provides a buffer between stressful event and emotional distress (House, 1981). On the other hand, in unsatisfactory or dysfunctional style of communication, focus is on stubbornness, criticism and disparagement. Rook (1990) brings out that negative social exchange exhibits stronger or more reliable association with well-being than does positive one. So, those individuals who exhibit negative communication-pattern, often, get the same in response. This, in turn, affects their well-being (Ewart, *et al.*, 1991).

Attitude towards life also seems to have an impact on social adjustment. In fact, Cousins (1979) has shown that it is our attitude and our thinking process that influences our life. This is also true in the case of elderly people (Mishra, 1987; Natrajan, 1987; Ramamurti and Jamuna, 1993a). Further, Havighurst (1961) observes that feeling of happiness and satisfaction with one's life, health, family, friends, work and finances, zest, positive self-concept and optimistic mood tone help in viable adjustment in old age. But, do gender differences bring differential experiences to people?

Many studies reflect gender difference in certain attributes influencing social adjustment. Barer (1995) finds that elderly females appear to be regressive and show withdrawal behaviour while aged males are more aggressive. Similarly, Cochran and Hale (1983) report that aged women rate higher on restlessness, aggressiveness, hostility and inferiority. Needless to add, in patriarchal societies, during socialization, values like dependence, tolerance and submissiveness are taught to females. Often they tend to develop feeling of inferiority and weakness. Contrarily, Machin and Davies (2000) observes that partially, due to her biological make-up, but, mainly, her roles as wife, mother and homemaker, the female is more emotionally mature than her male counterpart. In consonance, Dhillon (1992) brings out that the roles, most women play in their life, help them develop an ability to deal with most of the stresses that occur in old age. It appears that adjustment is a personal phenomenon. It is the individual's own discretion to view and interpret a situation and adapt positively for harmonious social interactions or react negatively to make the relationship bitter. This is exemplified by the wills of two elderly females who were interviewed during the course of the study. One of them remarks, "*Meri bahu bhi to meri beti hi hai na!*" (my daughter-in-law is also my daughter). The other one says, "*Bahu ke aane se beta paraya ho jata hai*" (with the arrival of daughter-in-law my son no more belongs to me).

Domains of Social Adjustment Scale

Having gained some insight into the facilitators and inhibitors of harmonious adjustment, attention may be diverted to assess the level of adjustment among aged females. It may be restated that social adjustment is often taken to be an ongoing process, which facilitates one to adopt oneself to social environment. It supports and facilitates an aged woman in initiating and maintaining harmonious and mutually satisfying relationships with her significant others. In the process of adjusting to the social environment, a variety of psychological attributes like personality traits, communication and coping skills, experience, learning, etc., interplay to form a perception. Aged women respond to a stimulus from their social environment on the basis of this perception.

Perception, or stated differently, attitude plays a crucial role in our life. Thurstone defines an attitude as "the degree of positive or negative affect associated with some psychological object" (1947). By a psychological object, Thurstone (1947) means any symbol, phrase, slogan, person, institution, ideal or idea towards which people can differ with respect to positive or negative affect. Mostly, our behaviour is guided or directed by our attitudes. They influence our perception towards a stimulus and, in turn, guide our behaviour. It may be reiterated that qualities like adaptation to changed situations, positive communication pattern, optimism, healthy outlook towards life, initiative to take up roles, realistic expectation are, among others, essential components of the ability to adjust harmoniously. On the other hand, attributes like rigidity, possessiveness, jealousy, boredom, seclusion, confrontation and avoiding taking new roles and responsibilities often lead to mal-adjustment.

In order to measure an aged female's ability to adjust effectively, summated rating scale, also known as Likert scale has been used in the study. Though it is primarily used to measure attitudes but several researchers have used it as a tool to study various dimensions of adjustment (see www.psychtests.com; and www.queendom.com). Many researchers also have used the scale for studying different aspects of ageing and the aged like attitude towards older people, their employment, etc., (Mishra, 1987; Randhawa, 1991; Linda, 2000).

As far as elderly are concerned four theme areas are important—attitudinal adjustment, conflict adjustment, need adjustment and role adjustment. The summation of the four sub-theme areas would be overall social adjustment. In this connection, the researcher gathered statements on 'adjustment' from library work, newspapers, and research journals and other similar sources. These statements were carefully reviewed and edited (Edwards, 1969). From a range of 368 statements, 87 were selected. These statements have been assigned five-point response categories—'Strongly agree', 'Agree', 'Uncertain', 'Disagree' and 'Strongly disagree'. The statements were then rendered into Hindi. Pre-testing was done on 50 aged women living in Malviya Nagar (in South Delhi, very close to the study area). Following this, the responses to the statements were tabulated with a view to ascertaining the distribution. The statements having a concentration or near concentration on any of the five response categories were taken as having low discriminal power. As a result, forty-eight statements with low discriminal power were rejected. Next, the responses were assigned weight, '5' to 'strongly agree', '4' to 'agree', '3' to 'uncertain', '2' to 'disagree' and '1' to 'strongly disagree'. Unfavourable responses were given reverse weights. The weights of the items were summated across the 39 items. This was followed by statistical analysis using t-test. Again, 15 items having low t-test values were eliminated from the scale. Finally, 21 statements having the maximum discriminal power have been retained on the scale. At this stage, the reliability of the scale computes to 0.82, which is adequate for the present purposes. Subsequently, the 21 statements have been inserted in the interview schedule, which was administered on elderly women.

In order to calculate reliability-coefficient on a sample of 350, split-half method has been employed using odd-numbered statements as one-half and even numbered statements as the other. Its value is 0.79, which is indicative of a good internal consistency. Using Spearman-Brown formula, reliability value works out to be 0.88. This signifies that, hopefully, the scale is consistent and reliable.

The scale underlines a modicum of validity with high values of correlation between overall social adjustment (and its four components) and the respect the aged women get from their significant others, their involvement in family decision-making and activities they share with their family members, neighbours and friends. There is a strong positive association between feeling of economic security among the aged females and their social adjustment as seen by high values of product-moment correlation and rank correlation dealt in subsequent chapters. Similarly ability to adjust is also related positively to the physical health condition, well-being and life-satisfaction among the elderly females. The validity of the scale would become more apparent when test-retest is carried out in different cultural settings.

Attitudinal Adjustment

"No man is happy who does not think himself so", says Marcus Aurelius. In all likelihood, Aurelius is talking about attitudinal patterns. Indeed, attitudes determine the type of interaction that leads to satisfaction or dissatisfaction. Elderly, too, are no exception. What has been the impact of attitudes on the well-being of older people? Bhatia (1983) reports that many aged persons believe that it is their children's duty to consult them on important family matters. They feel that their children have deviated from traditional standards and norms of behaviour. They think that they are the best person to serve their children's interests. Jamuna (1989c) observes that some of the attitudes of devaluing self, adhering to stereotyped views of womanhood, and learned helplessness are detrimental to women's well-being. Dhillon (1992) brings out that the aged seem to have a stereotype view about the younger generation.

In Social Adjustment Scale, attitudinal adjustment has five statements out of which two are favourable and three unfavourable. In this component, attitudes of the respondents towards younger generation are scored. Following statements have been included in attitudinal adjustment.

1. Society has changed much, but youngers in the family generally agree with the opinion and advice of the elderly (favourable statement; t-value = +5.68).
2. These days, younger women are well-informed and educated and capable of managing household without the help and guidance from others (favourable statement; t-value = +5.95).
3. Younger people always want to have preference, even in taking bath (unfavourable statement; t-value = +5.44).
4. It is not good for the family and society to allow boys and girls to study and move around together (unfavourable statement; t-value = +5.43).
5. It does not make any difference whether or not you talk to others in the family about your unhappiness and frustration (unfavourable statement; t-value = +5.84).

Theoretical scores of the above statements range from 5 to 25; and observed scores are from 9 to 21. The mean score is 15.6. The data are quite homogeneous (standard deviation = 2.5) and somewhat negatively skewed (skewness = –0.44). In order to facilitate further analysis, the observed scores of attitudinal adjustment (9 to 21) have been divided into three, cutting points being 33rd and 67th percentile. The three groups are – low (9 to 14), medium (15 to 17) and high (18 to 21).

What is the impact of high or low attitudinal adjustment on the well-being and social acceptance of the respondents? Analysis shows that the attitudinal adjustment of the respondents does not significantly vary with their educational attainment (rank correlation = +0.17) and occupational status (rank correlation = +0.08). Data further bring out that 46.3 per cent respondents with low attitudinal adjustment have difficulty in sleeping. In contrast, all the respondents having high attitudinal adjustment report to having easy sleep. Perhaps they have a relaxed daily life-routine. Table 3.1 shows a strong positive association between attitudinal adjustment and feeling of loneliness among the respondents. It shows that among those

Table 3.1 : Association between attitudinal adjustment and feeling of loneliness among the respondents

Attitudinal Adjustment	*Loneliness*				
	Always	*Often*	*Sometimes*	*Rarely*	*Never*
Low	0.0	48.8	28.1	19.0	4.1
Medium	2.5	35.6	27.1	18.6	16.1
High	0.0	11.7	28.8	38.7	20.7

who often feel lonely, the proportion of respondents scoring low on attitudinal adjustment is almost four times higher than their counterparts having high attitudinal adjustment. Next, aged women scoring low on attitudinal adjustment more often consider their future as uncertain or hopeless (product-moment correlation = –0.47). Likewise, most (93.7 per cent) of the respondents with high attitudinal adjustment have a feeling that they have achieved everything or most of what they have aspired for, as compared to 32.2 per cent of their cohorts with low attitudinal adjustment. Perhaps, for understandable reasons those with high attitudinal adjustment have the satisfaction of achieving most in life.

Role in decision-making in family matters could be taken as one of the indicators of social integration of the aged. Results show that aged females with low attitudinal adjustment are, often, kept away from decision-making on matters like buying clothes for family members (see Diagram 3.1). The proportion

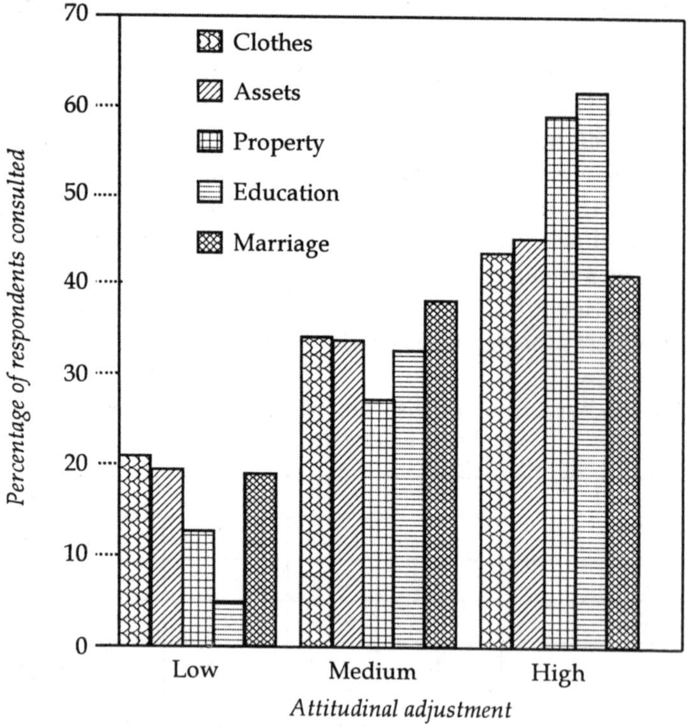

Diagram 3.1 : Attitudinal-Adjustment and Decision-Making

of respondents with high attitudinal adjustment (44.1 per cent) who are consulted on this matter is twice the proportion of those with low attitudinal adjustment (21.3 per cent). Likewise, the proportion of respondents with high attitudinal adjustment who have been consulted while buying household assets is more than two times higher than respondents with low attitudinal adjustment. Similar trends are observed in the case of consultation for gifts to be given to relatives and friends (rank correlation = +0.40) and matters related to property (rank correlation = +0.47). Also, the proportion of respondents with high attitudinal adjustment (67 per cent), who are satisfied and contented with their life, is more than six times higher than their age-mates having low attitudinal adjustment (10.4 per cent). Relevant statistics confirm the same (rank correlation = +0.54). Following is the case study of an aged female, Radha, rating low on attitudinal adjustment, exemplifies these findings:

Only sufferings are in my destiny

Radha recalls her past life with visible grief and sorrow. Being a middle class wife, she had faced financial crunch in bringing up her three children all along. She had pampered her middle-borne son giving him preference over two daughters. Before retirement of her husband, an Office Clerk, they could get her eldest daughter married. When her son attained marriage age, she looked for a girl from a very rich family. Ignoring her husband's wishes of not taking anything from their son's in-laws, Radha proudly demanded lots of dowry. Also, she expected her *bahu* to be docile, obedient and timid. Often, she tried to show her dominance over her son. Bitterness in the relationship of *saas-bahu* aggravated, when Radha tried to use the dowry of her *bahu* for her daughter's marriage. And when her son objected to this, she screemed, *"ye to kalyug hai, yahan apna hi beta jise doodh pila-pila ke bada karo voh hi das leta hai. Tu kyon apni bahan ke kaam aayega, tu to apni aurat ki hi gulami kar"* (this is kalyug, here your own child whom you nurtured on your milk, stings you. Why should you help your sister, you better be the slave of your wife).

After the death of her husband, Radha is forced to live in the *barsati,* leaving her own room. She is lonely. Two of her grandsons do not bother to talk to her even for weeks. Her son also hardly shows concern towards her. She is forced to do a lot of household chores including mopping, brooming, dusting, washing utensils and preparing foods. Her body also doesn't seem to co-operate with her. She is suffering from high blood pressure, arthritis, and stomach ulcer. She prays to God to take her life away and make her free from all bondages of grief and utter helplessness, while the God wishes otherwise.

The data show that aged women having high attitudinal adjustment generally get respect and love from their family. Respondents who score low on attitudinal adjustment more often are 'just wished' by their family members. Contrarily, aged women with high attitudinal adjustment, often get love and respect from their family members. The family shares their problems and emotions with them. To exemplify, the proportion of respondents with high attitudinal adjustment (50 per cent), whose sons/sons-in-law share their feelings and problems with them, is almost seven times higher than those who score low (7.3 per cent). Similarly, 43.2 per cent respondents with low attitudinal adjustment are 'just wished' by their grandchildren as compared to only 16.7 per cent respondents with high attitudinal adjustment. Likewise, the respondents with high attitudinal adjustment share friendly and cordial relations with their daughters-in-law. One mother-in-law expressing, *"Meri saas bahut rudiwadi thi, main koshish karti hun ki main aisi naa houn"* (my mother-in-law was strict orthodox, I try not to be like her), shares amiable relations with her *bahu*. Similarly, attitudinal adjustment is directly related to begetting respect from husband and also grandchildren.

Data have shown that attitudes influence the psychological well-being and social integration among the aged women. A respondent having an attitude that *"Budhapa to dukh takleef lata hi hai"* (old age does bring sorrow and pain), would, often, tend to focus on grief and sorrows in her life. Likewise, an aged woman expressing her mind set-as, *"Aaj-kal ki bahuyen ghar main kadam baad main rakhti hain pahle saas ko ghar se bahar nikalne main taiyari kar leti hain"* (now-a-days, the daughters-in-law do preparations to get their mother-in-law out even before stepping in the household), is more likely to share sneering relationship with her daughter-in-law. On asking about co-education system, one respondent articulates her attitude, *"Aajkal ki ladkiyan aise-aise kapde pehne hain ki pata na chal pawe ki ladka hai ki ladki. Aur upar se par kati aur ban janve, ye saath saath main jab ladka ladki padhe hain to bahut bura hove hain, ve katchi umar main bhag javen hain shadi kar leve hain"* (present day girls wear such clothes that it is difficult to recognise whether they are boys or girls. And on the above they cut short their hair and when boys and girls study together, it is very bad, they run away and get married at an early age). Such attitudes might pose hurdles for the aged women in establishing harmonious relationship with family members.

Conflict Adjustment

Relationships inevitably involve a combination of positive as well as negative interactions. All human beings have to deal with conflicting situations at one point of time or the other. Whether individuals fight or flee or compromise to a situation determines, to a large extent, the kind of response they are going to get from others. In a family where two or three generations are staying under a single roof, there may be many reasons of friction. Generation gap, with one member not being able to make the other understand his/her view points, differences in methods of cooking between daughter-in-law and mother-in-law and being at odds on possessiveness about son/husband are common issues of conflict in the family. Conflicting situations are unavoidable but a person can minimize such situations by compromising and adapting and, contrarily, can maximize clashes by exchanging hot arguments.

If elderly people continue with their earlier patterns of behaviour in exercising authority or control over children, they may face resistance. Their passionate concern about family matters may amount to interference to their youngers. Literature review gives some understanding of the effects of conflicting situations on the elderly. There are indications that negative dimensions of personal relationship are more psychologically potent than the positive ones (Rook, 1990). Evidence is recurrent that negative exchange can intensify the deleterious effects of life-crises (Dayton, Morgan and Antonucci, 1997). Such a negative exchange may be particularly problematic for ageing individuals, as many of their stressors are chronic ones

(Rook, 1990). Conversely, many researches show that positive exchange provides a buffer between stressful events and emotional distress (House, 1981; Stolar, MacEntee, and Hill, 1993). Though negative interactions are stressful for all, elderly people become much more susceptible to distress and pain in such negative life-events (Krause, 1993).

One respondent expresses the key for good conflict adjustment as, *"Bacchon ko apni jindgi jeene do aur khud apni jiyo to koi manmutaav nahin hota. Dikkat wahan aati hai jab hum aik dusre ko apni marzi se chalana chahte hain"* (if you let the children live their life according to their wishes and you live by your own wishes, there are no conflict. Problems arise when we try to impose our wishes on others). Another one also has similar views, *"Adjustment to hamen hi karna hoga. Young generation hamaare hisab se nahin badlegi. Agar hum adjust kar lete hain to sukhi rahenge, nahin to bacche hamen chhod kar alag rahna shuru kar denge"* (we only have to adjust. Young generation will not change according to our wishes. If you adjust then we will remain happy or else the children will start living away from us). On the other hand, one old lady communicates her clashes with her *bahu*, *"Aajkal ki bahuon ko sirf saas-sasur ko takleef dena aata hai aur kuch nahin aata, voh saas ko apni sabse badi dushman samajhti hain"* (these days daughters-in-law know only to give pains to their parents-in-law and nothing else, they consider their mothers-in-law as their biggest enemy). Such behaviour often aggravates negative interactions in the family.

In Social Adjustment Scale, Conflict Adjustment has four statements out of which one is favourable and three unfavourable. Following statements have been included in this component:

1. Some family members have the habit of being rude to the elders, no matter how many times they are forgiven (unfavourable statement; t-value = +6.58).
2. Whether you speak or remain silent, family members in day-to-day living manage to create issues and arguments (unfavourable statement; t-value = +6.85).
3. Self-centred as they are, younger people take long in the bathroom (unfavourable statement; t-value = +5.70).

4. If husband and wife in the household are having heated arguments, the elderly need not interfere unless asked to (favourable statement; t-value = +5.48).

During analysis, appropriate scores have been given to favourable and unfavourable statements. These scores have been summated to give the total score of conflict adjustment, ranging from 4 to 20 (theoretical as well as observed). Mean score is 13.1. The data are quite consistent (standard deviation = 3.7) and somewhat negatively skewed (skewness = –0.69). This range has been divided into three categories—low (4 to 12), medium (13 to 15) and high (16 to 20). As shown in the literature review, the data of the present study also bring to light that conflict adjustment plays a significant role in psychological well-being of the elderly females. Most respondents (84.0 per cent) scoring high on conflict adjustment do not have tension and anxiety as compared to 50.8 per cent of respondents with low conflict adjustment. Further, elderly females with low conflict adjustment are generally caught in loneliness than their age mates with high or moderate conflict adjustment. Relevant statistics confirm the same (product-moment correlation = –0.41; rank correlation = –0.42).

Positive interaction with significant others also helps in developing affirmative feeling about one's own health when physiological deterioration is on its way in old age. The data show that the respondents with high conflict adjustment often feel themselves healthy. On the other hand, aged women, with low conflict adjustment, generally, feel themselves sick and unhealthy (rank correlation = +0.51).

Similarly, conflict adjustment is also positively related to rating of past, present and future life. Table 3.2 depicts the association between conflict adjustment and self-rating of the respondents of their past, present and future life. It shows that aged females with low conflict adjustment often rate their life as unhappy or very unhappy. Among the respondents considering their past life as happy or very happy, the proportion of those scoring high on conflict adjustment is almost six times higher than their age mates ranking low on conflict adjustment. This trend is more peculiar while the respondents rate their future life. On the other hand, elderly women with high conflict adjustment generally rate their past, present and future life as happy or very happy.

Table 3.2 : Association between Conflict adjustment and self-rating of the respondents of their life

Rating of life		*Conflict Adjustment*		
		Low	*Medium*	*High*
Past	Very happy/happy	9.5	33.0	55.0
	Blend of happiness/unhappiness	77.2	56.0	42.0
	Unhappy/very unhappy	13.4	11.0	3.1
Present	Very happy/happy	5.5	31.9	59.6
	Blend of happiness/unhappiness	39.1	50.5	35.9
	Unhappy/very unhappy	55.5	17.6	4.6
Future*	Very happy/happy	5.5	33.8	64.2
	Blend of happiness/unhappiness	42.7	56.3	35.8
	Unhappy/very unhappy	52.1	10.0	0.0

*NA/DK/NR responses not included.

Further, data bring forth that conflict adjustment significantly influences the quality of relationship of the elderly female with her family members. Aged women with low conflict adjustment receive only nominal respect from her family, say, just a *namaste* by family members. Contrarily, aged women with high conflict adjustment generally enjoy greater respect from their family members. The family members consult them in household matters and share with them their feelings and problems. Among the respondents having low conflict adjustment, 58.0 per cent are just wished and only 4.2 per cent respondents are consulted on certain issues by their sons or sons-in-law. Conversely, among the aged females with high conflict adjustment, 9.2 per cent are just wished and 48.9 per cent consulted on personal and familial problems. Likewise, proportion of respondents with low conflict adjustment who are just wished by their daughters-in-law or daughters (69.2 per cent) is almost 10 times higher than their counterparts having high conflict adjustment (6.9 per cent). This trend is also sharply visible in the case of interactions of respondents with their husband (product-moment correlation = +0.37; rank correlation = +0.40) and grandchildren (product-moment correlation = +0.50; rank correlation = +0.51). So, conflict adjustment seems to be quite potent in influencing the respect and love the aged females get from their respective families.

Do personality dispositions like irritability and aggression have any link with the optimism-pessimism among the aged women? Study results show that optimism is positively related to conflict adjustment (product-moment correlation = +0.48). Also, among the respondents with low life-satisfaction, the proportion of those scoring low on conflict adjustment (30.5 per cent) is almost ten times the proportion of those with high conflict adjustment (3.1 per cent). Diagram 3.2 gives the association

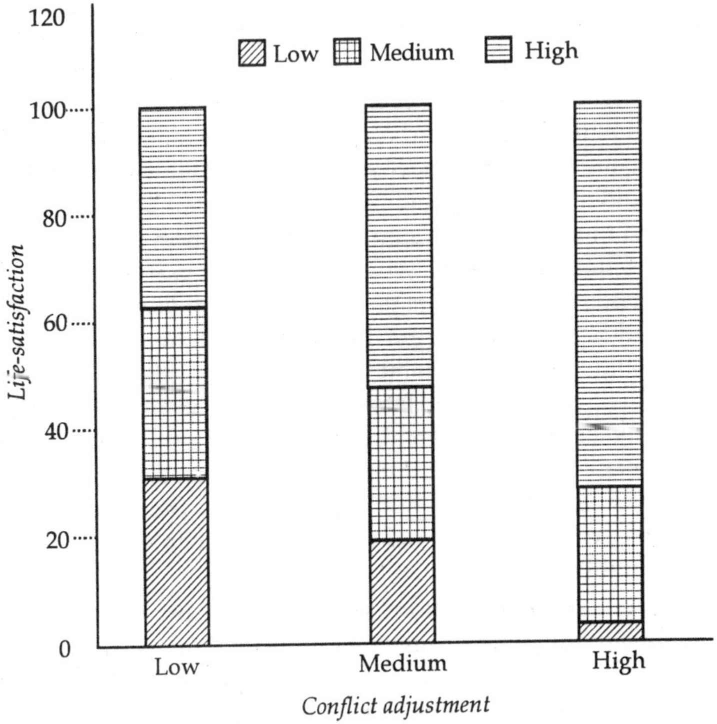

Diagram 3.2: Conflict Adjustment and Life-Satisfaction

between conflict adjustment and life-satisfaction among the respondents. It shows that 37.5 per cent respondents with low conflict adjustment have scored high on overall life-satisfaction as compared to 71.8 per cent of those with high conflict adjustment.

Apparently, conflict adjustment plays a crucial role in social integration of the elderly females. High conflict adjustment can reward an old female with harmonious relationships with significant others, satisfaction and contentment, low conflict adjustment can put her into despair and sorrow as in the case of Surender:

Power Politics in the Family

Surender Kaur (name is camouflaged), 60 years, is staying with her retired husband in Pushp Vihar in a four-member family. Her only son, an engineer, got married only eight months back. The proud mother-in-law expects her *bahu* to serve for all family members with devotion and obedience. She wishes that young daughter-in-law to cook new recipes everyday, make pickles, do embroidery, knitting and stitching. She often compares her *bahu* with others, in neighbourhood and relations. Contrarily, the *bahu* is not willing to be an all-rounder and wants to live her life in her own way. She feels that her parents-in-law are hurdles in her privacy. Moreover, the daughter-in-law wants to prove her full hold over her husband while Surender intends to show that he is still a son first and later a husband. This power politics is playing an important role in the family-dynamics and interactions. There is constant cold war between them and occasional exchange of hot arguments. Often, Surender expresses that her *bahu* knows nothing of kitchen work in front of her neighbours.

Surender's expectation is not fulfilled by her son and daughter-in-law, which frustrates her very much. She had an ideal image of *bahu* in which her daughter-in-law doesn't fit and as a result she curses her fate of making a wrong choice for her son's matrimony. She expresses her feelings with tearful eyes, "*Jab se yeh bahu mere ghar aayee hai ghar narak ban gaya hai.*

Aate hi pata nahin kaun saa jadoo fera hai ki beta usi ke gun gane laga hai. Barson maa-baap ne pala use bhool gaya hai" (with the approach of this daughter-in-law, my house has become a hell. With her arrival god knows what magic she has done that my son sings her praises. He has forgotten all the years of parent's nurturance).

Thus, respondents with high conflict adjustment are optimistic, free from tension and anxiety, healthy, satisfied with life and get respect and affection from family members more often than their age cohorts with low conflict adjustment.

Need Adjustment

Needs refer to some want or lack or deficit in an organism involving a physiological imbalance or a psychological tension. Stated differently, it is a motivational concept and is perceived as personal or social deficiencies of an individual or a group of individuals (Chowdhry, 1992). Maslow (1954) arranges the need hierarchy as—survival and security needs, need for love and belongingness, self-esteem and self-actualization. Chowdhry (1992) lists certain needs specifically for the senior citizens, other than basic human needs as—healthy and active life-style; financial security; development and maintenance of social support network and provision of opportunities for increased productive activity. Also, the elderly need meaningful interaction and intimate relationship, absence of which may lead to loneliness and unhappiness (Ramamurti, 1989). Similarly, Jamuna (1989a) assesses that majority of aged women have given priority to need for self-esteem, love and belongingness and security. When needs are unfulfilled, it might amount to abuse. Unfulfilled needs generally brings on several personal, social and other problems like feelings of frustration, emptiness, depression and feeling of inferiority among elderly (Sati, 1987). However, it may be important to keep in mind the other side of the coin. Fast pace of city-life and cut-throat competition force the youngers to work hard for the whole day. At the end of the day, they might not be left with energy to give time to their elderly relatives who might be waiting for them after the daylong loneliness. So, the elderly might feel neglected, if they fail to understand their youngers' constraints.

Need adjustment, here, means the ability of elderly females to recognize the limitations of younger generation in care giving. It involves emphasizing on incidence of care giving while ignoring the situation where the family members have failed to meet their needs appropriately. Those aged women who expect little from their family members in terms of giving time, importance and money, who can calmly wait for gratification of their needs, say, having food after earning members leave for their respective work place or getting their clothes mended when the female members are relatively free, are better adjusted.

In Social Adjustment Scale, the component need adjustment has six statements, three favourable and three unfavourable. In this component, the respondents are scored for their expectation about fulfilment of needs like food, medicare, clothing and care and support by their younger generation. Following statements have been included in this component:

1. As family members are busy with their own affairs they have no time for elderly suffering from ailments (unfavourable statement; t-value = +6.08).
2. When you need, say, some money, family members come at their own to help you (favourable statement; t-value = +5.27).
3. Younger generation is so preoccupied with themselves that they do not even worry whether elderly people have eaten food or not (unfavourable statement; t-value = +6.03).
4. If you are alone or silent, family members on their own come to you, sit and talk (favourable statement; t-value = +5.79).
5. When you, say, *sari* or *salwar kurta*, need mending, lady members in the family willingly do the work (favourable statement; t-value = +5.52).

6. Old people in the family have little to give and are a burden on the family (unfavourable statement; t-value = +6.00).

For analysis, appropriate scores have been assigned to favourable and unfavourable statements. Following this, these scores have been summated to give the total score of need adjustment. Theoretical range is 6 to 30; and the observed range is 6 to 28. Mean is 18.9 and the data are quite homogeneous (standard deviation = 5.3). Observed range has been divided into three categories – low (6 to 17), medium (18 to 22) and high (23 to 28).

It appears that need adjustment plays an important role in the quality of interaction of aged females with their family. One respondent, wishing deference, complains, "*Hum jo maan sammaan apne se badon ka apne buzurgon ka karte the voh aaj hamen nahin milta*" (what respect we used to pay to our elders we do not get that from our youngers). Data show that the respondents who score high on need adjustment gain more respect from their family than those ranking lower. Among the respondents, who are consulted during buying household assets, the proportion of those ranking high on need adjustment (95.0 per cent) is almost four times higher than those having low need adjustment (24.8 per cent). It is confirmed by relevant statistics (product-moment correlation = +0.63). Also, those mothers-in-law who score high on need adjustment mostly share cordial relation with their daughters-in-law (rank correlation = +0.69). Likewise, grandmothers with low need-adjustment are often just wished by their grandchildren. In contrast, grandchildren generally share their problems with their granny having high need adjustment (product-moment correlation = +0.60).

It appears that elderly with sound economic position are better able to meet their needs. However, since 92 per cent aged women, in the study, have remained non-workers or housewife, any generalization on their economic position and its association with need adjustment would not be feasible. Nonetheless, the correlation between need adjustment of the respondents and their feeling of economic security-insecurity can be looked into.

Table 3.3 demonstrates that those aged women who score low on need adjustment feel economically insecure, more often, than their age-mates who have high need adjustment. Among the respondents who feel economically unsecured, the proportion of respondents with low need adjustment is ten times higher than their counterparts with high need adjustment.

Table 3.3 : Association between need adjustment and feeling of security-insecurity among elderly women

Economic security-insecurity	*Need adjustment*		
	Low	*Medium*	*High*
Unsecured	65.0	22.8	14.2
Average	23.0	38.0	39.0
Secured	6.5	24.4	69.1

Analysis further shows that aged females scoring high on need adjustment also rank high on overall life-satisfaction (product-moment correlation = +0.67). Likewise, only 0.8 per cent respondents with low need adjustment consider a bright future ahead in comparison to 59.5 per cent respondents scoring high on need adjustment. Contrarily, among the aged females viewing their future as hopeless, the proportion of those having low need adjustment is 39.4 per cent compared to 0.8 per cent of those having high need adjustment (product-moment correlation = –0.58).

Similarly, a strong negative linkage (product-moment correlation = –0.66) indicates that respondents having low need adjustment mostly feel that only a few or none of their expectations from life are fulfilled. In juxtaposition, aged females with high rank on need adjustment feel that they have been fortunate enough to see most or all of their expectation from life fulfilled.

Apparently, aged women scoring higher on need adjustment are consulted on day-to-day matters in the family. Table 3.4 gives the association between need adjustment and aged females being consulted on various family issues. All the respondents having high need adjustment are consulted on buying gifts for relatives and friends. Similar trend is seen in the case of consultation in matters like sale or purchase of household assets, marriage of grandchildren. On the other hand, respondents ranking low on need adjustment are, many tines, not asked to give advice on certain family issues.

Table 3.4 : Association between need adjustment and consultation on family matters

Consultation on:	*Need adjustment*					
	Low		*Medium*		*High*	
	Yes	*No*	*Yes*	*No*	*Yes*	*No*
Gifts	54.0	46.0	95.3	4.7	100.0	0.0
Clothes	15.2	84.8	80.2	19.8	89.1	10.9
Household assets	18.9	81.1	76.7	23.3	98.8	1.2
Property	9.5	90.5	40.8	59.2	71.6	28.4
Education of grandchildren	1.1	98.9	8.5	91.5	19.7	80.3
Marriage of grandchildren	16.7	83.3	82.6	17.4	88.2	11.8

The foregoing discussion suggests that having realistic expectation is crucial for adjustment. Often, the gap between the expectation and reality is the cause of pain and frustration. *"Ab to apne hi bacchon se kutch ummeed karna hi fizool hai"*, one respondent expresses her anguish for unmet need of sharing time with children, *"Jin bacchon ke liye saari umar gavan di unke paas aaj itna bhi time nahin hai ki aakar pooch lain ki amma kutch khaya ki nahin"* (now it is futile to expect anything from our children. For them we spent our whole life and they don't have enough time to even ask 'mother! Have you eaten something or not'). Conversely, another aged lady in the study reveals her secret of harmonious relationship with the family, *"Budhape main aa kar sab chod dena chahiye tabhi mukti ho sakti hai aur insaan sukhi rahe sakta hai"* (in old age one must renounce all attachments only then one can be free and happy). So, fewer needs, realistic expectation and fewer attachments are key to happiness and better adjustment.

Role Adjustment

Old age, among others, brings changes in the roles of a person. As discussed earlier, roles determine status. Individuals derive satisfaction and status by fulfilling roles meaningful to them as well as to the society. As generally observed, in old age, such roles as home-management, child-care and economic employment shrink. This kind of change in roles often leads to lowering of status of the aged people. Such a condition is, at times, unsettling and threatening and increases the likelihood of psychological problems of low self-esteem, feeling of alienation and depression. Soodan (1975) observes that failure to remain an active member of the family may cause many mental disorders. In contrast, the aged who engage themselves in purposeful roles and activities have high self-esteem, better general health, lower depression and anxiety (see Bond and Feather, 1988). Adelmann (1994) observes that there is a strong positive association between multiple roles and psychological well-being among aged people. Multiple roles (like spouse, parent, homemaker, grandparent, caregiver, employee, volunteer, etc.) are associated with higher life-satisfaction and lower depressive symptoms. Jamuna (1994) brings out that, among others, satisfaction with role-activity is an important determinant of happiness in old age. Thus, the degree of adjustment appears to be dependent upon an elderly lady's activities and involvement in various roles appropriate to her age.

How conveniently an elderly female gives up her old key-roles and adopts new ones, determines her ability to adjust. *"Bacchon ki aazadi main khalal nahin daalna"*, one respondent expresses her role-change in the family, *"Main samajhti hun ki kabhi majhse ghar ke chote-chote kaamon ke baare main poocha jata tha. Main dhuri thi ghar ki, aaj yehe meri bahu hai. Mujhe uske adhikaar us se nanin cheenne hain"* (don't have to infringe the freedom of my children. I understand that there was a time when I was being asked for every little thing in the family. I used to be the pivot in the family, now my daughter-in-law is one. Well, I don't have to snatch her rights). It might not be easy for a female to hand over her authority and status to her daughter-in-law and accept a secondary position in the family. However, the aged who do so, happily adjust in their family. Contrarily, those aged females who are not able to accept this change, are overtaken by jealousy. *"Are, bahun aajkal khub saara make-up pot kar khin-khin karna jaanti hain"*, says one respondent, *"Rasoi ki zara si garmi bardash nahin hoti, hum to bees-bees jano ka khana banaya karti thi"* (oh! present day daughters-in-law know only overdoing make up and giggling. They cannot tolerate the heat of the kitchen. We used to cook food for twenty people).

Roles give a purpose, a sense of usefulness to the aged woman and add to her feelings of self-worth and belongingness. It follows that role adjustment would imply 'accepting' the change in roles and associated status. Adoption of new roles helps a great deal in accepting this change. It may be presumed that an aged woman who takes up new roles willingly, without having any grudges about the salient roles that she is no longer performing actively is having high ability for harmonious adjustment. In juxtaposition, the one who hesitates to hand over her roles, say, that of homemaker to the younger generation or shows her reluctance to adopt new roles in the family exhibits poor ability to adjust.

In the Social Adjustment Scale, the component—role adjustment has six statements. Among these, two are favourable and four unfavourable. In these statements, the respondents have been scored on their ability to willingly take up roles like grandmother, mediator and adviser in the family while allowing the youngers to enjoy key roles like parenting and home-manager. These statements are as follows:

1. Given free hand, elderly can bring up grandchildren in a better way than sometimes their own parents (unfavourable statement; t-value = +5.06).
2. Youngers in the family should first introduce visiting friends to the elderly before sitting down to talk to them (unfavourable statement; t-value = +5.11).

3. Even in casual discussions, youngers in the family often raise fresh and relevant points (favourable statement; t-value = +6.05).
4. These days, the younger generation tries to dominate the discussion, whatever the issue (unfavourable statement; t-value = +5.87).
5. Children and grandchildren ultimately resolve the matter of sharing of household assets like jewellery, radio, T.V., etc., without anybody's advice or interference (unfavourable statement; t-value = +5.47).
6. The role and importance of the elderly in the family remains the same although their physical strength declines (favourable statement; t-value = +5.84).

Theoretical scores are 6 to 30 while the observed scores are 8 to 27. The mean is 18.1 and the data are homogeneous (standard deviation = 3.9). In order to facilitate further analysis, the scores of role adjustment (8 to 27) have been divided into three—low (8 to 16), medium (17 to 20) and high (21 to 27).

Is role adjustment has any association with mental health of the elderly women? Sleep could be taken as an important criterion of mental health. Analysis shows a positive association between role adjustment and type of sleep. More than a half (54.9 per cent) of the aged women, having poor role adjustment, sleep with difficulty. On the other hand, 80.9 per cent respondents, scoring high on role adjustment, have easy sleep. Similarly, occurrence of tension and anxiety is almost three times more among respondents with low role adjustment (52.3 per cent) than their counterparts who are with high role adjustment (18.3 per cent). Also, role adjustment is strongly linked with feeling of loneliness among the respondents as shown by relevant statistics (product-moment correlation = +0.39).

Data further show that 82.1 per cent aged females, scoring low on role adjustment, consider their future hopeless compared to mere 3.6 per cent respondents ranking high. Likewise, the proportion of respondents having high role adjustment who consider bright future ahead is nine times higher than those scoring low. Relevant statistics show a strong correlation between optimism and role adjustment (product-moment correlation = +0.50). In the same connection, Table 3.5 shows the association between the role adjustment and fulfilment of life-expectations. Respondents with high role adjustment often feel that life has fulfilled all or most of their expectations while aged women with low role adjustment often crib that life has offered only little or nothing to them (product-moment correlation = +0.61).

Table 3.5 : Association between role adjustment and respondents' rating of their fulfilment of expectations from life

Role adjustment	*Fulfilment of expectations from life*				
	Everything	*Much of it*	*Some of it*	*Less of it*	*Nothing of it*
Low	2.5	26.2	46.7	18.0	6.6
Medium	14.4	55.1	26.3	4.2	0.0
High	50.0	44.5	4.5	0.9	0.0

Rest in NA/DK/NR category

There is a high correlation between life-satisfaction and role adjustment among the elderly females. Among those having low life-satisfaction, the proportion of respondents scoring low on role adjustment (67.8 per cent) is more than seven times those scoring high (9.1 per cent). Likewise, in the category of high life-satisfaction, aged females with high role adjustment have almost twenty-three times higher proportion (64.2 per cent) than those scoring low on role adjustment (2.8 per cent). Relevant statistics confirm the same (rank correlation = +0.59).

Analysis further shows that majority of the respondents (94.5 per cent) with high role adjustment willingly take up the household work. In contrast, 73.2 per cent respondents with low role adjustment unwillingly undertake the household activities as compared to only 8.9 per cent of those with high role adjustment (see Diagram 3.3). Further, the data bring out that the elderly women with high role adjustment receive affectionate treatment in the family (rank correlation = +0.38).

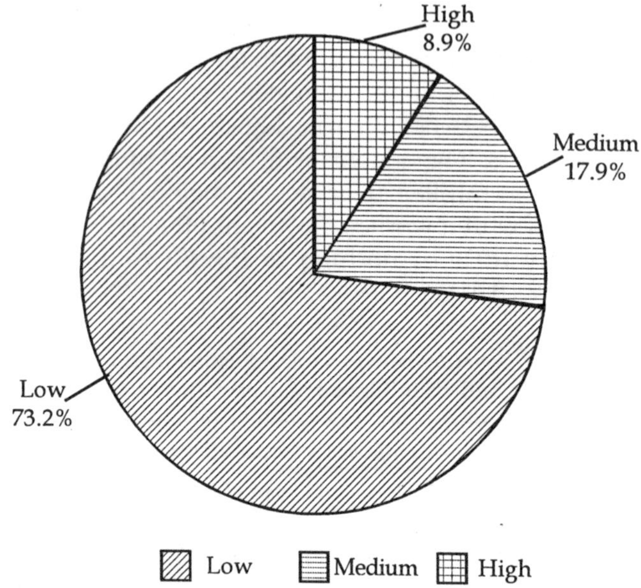

Diagram 3.3 : Role Adjustment and Unwillingness to do Household Chores

It appears that those elderly who are willing to take initiative for new social roles and responsibilities often get greater acceptance in the family and neighbourhood. Such activities as helping with family chores, providing care to grandchildren, baby-sitting, etc., would enable the elderly woman to make up for her lost key roles, say, that of home-maker as seen in the case of Nirmala (name is camouflaged).

Love Begets Love

Nirmala is a 76 years old married lady. She stays with her younger son, daughter-in-law, grandson and husband in Pushp Vihar. Her husband is a retired Government officer. Her son works in Ministry of Defence and daughter-in-law teaches in a private school. Her grandson is a class XII student. Her other children are well-settled. They visit her on regular intervals. Nirmala's daily activities starts at 4:30 a.m. by waking up her grandson to study for Boards and competitive exams. She prepares tea for both, takes bath, does prayer and prepares breakfast for the family. Her daughter-in-law helps a little bit only as she has to get ready and leave house at 6:30 a.m. for her school starting at 7:30 a.m. The old lady doesn't have traditional prejudices against working daughter-in-law. And the gratitude filled daughter-in-law praises her understanding mother-in-law everywhere for her contributions in home management and care to family members. Grandson also recognizes his grandmother's unconditional love and support she provides for his smooth study. In the day time, Nirmala gets the work done by maid. Her day is spent in chatting with her husband and watching T.V. In the late afternoon, daughter-in-law and grandson come back. All four members have their lunch together. In the evening Nirmala goes with her husband for an evening walk. After coming back she helps her *bahu* in preparing dinner. She watches TV with her family. They have their dinner, go for a walk again and she goes to bed at 11 p.m. The respondent has a cheerful calm disposition.

Thus, role adjustment plays a crucial role in psychological well-being and social integration of the aged females. Those elderly women who adapt to new roles, help the female members in the household work and accept secondary position in the household adjust better in the family. One aged female of Pushp Vihar, after handing over the key position of home-maker to her daughter in-law, expresses, "*Bahu ke raaj main main sukhi hun* (I am happy in my daughter's-in-law kingdom). On the other hand, aged women still attached to their previous roles, which have undergone change, often, feel the same as expressed by one respondent, "*Hum budhon ki koi zarurat nahin hai kisi ko. Bas bache-kuche din kaat rahen hain* (we oldies are no longer needed by anyone. We have to somehow manage to live rest of our life).

Overall Social Adjustment

Social adjustment is a process that involves a number of extrinsic and intrinsic factors interplaying to establish harmony and pleasure. McKinney observes, "Social adjustment is related to personality factors including motivation, values, goals, past experiences, conflicts, frustrations, ego-status, coping-patterns like compromise, withdrawal and attack, defence mechanisms, attitudes, which is goal directed or problem solving or self-centred" (1966). In the present study, an aged woman would be considered well-adjusted if she has the qualities like positive attitude, realistic expectations, takes up small but important roles without hitch or hesitation and generally avoids conflict-generating situations. Das (1994) reports that lack of rigidity and presence of flexibility are necessary for harmonious adjustment. Majumdar (1985) finds that, after retirement, many aged in New Delhi feel that everyone's attitude towards them has changed and they feel lonely and perceive a void in their life.

It may be restated that in the Social Adjustment Scale, scores of four variables—attitudinal adjustment, conflict adjustment, need adjustment and role adjustment have been added up to give the aggregate scores of overall social adjustment. Theoretical as well as observed range of scores is 4 to 12. In order to facilitate further analysis, the scores of overall social adjustment have been divided into three—low (4 to 6), medium (7 to 9) and high (10 to 12), cut off points being 33rd and 67th percentiles. Diagram 3.4 shows the frequency distribution of responses over all social adjustments.

Does age influence the ability to adjust? Richard, Livson and Petersen (1962) observe that overall adjustment to ageing was better among older retired respondents, as they tend to accept and internalize the norms for their age-group after the conflicts of transition are resolved. Dependency apparently becomes easier to accept in later life. However, the present study does not show the same results. Age, here, is not related to social adjustment of the elderly females (product-moment correlation = +0.08). In the same way, overall social adjustment has no statistically significant link with variables like religion, caste, educational and occupational status and income.

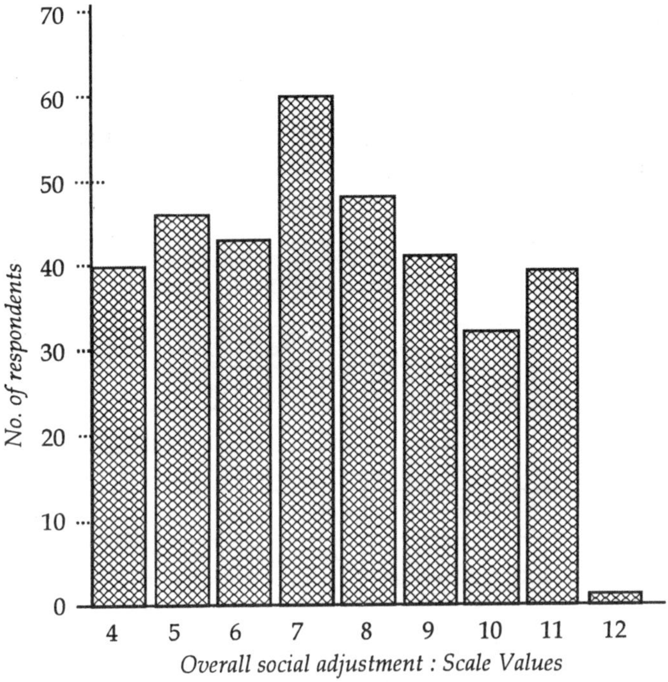

Diagram 3.4 : Frequency Distribution of Respondents over Social Adjustment

There is some association between type of sleep and overall social adjustment among the aged females. The proportion of respondents with high overall social adjustment (40.5 per cent) who reported to have easy sleep is almost two times more than those with low adjustment (22.5 per cent). Similarly, elderly females with high social adjustment rarely feel lonely but those with low scores on adjustment often feel so (product-moment correlation = –0.47).

Further, Table 3.6 gives the association between social adjustment and self-evaluation of health among the respondents. It shows that the proportion of respondents with high overall social adjustment (79.8 per cent) who consider their health as good or very good is almost seven times higher than those who score low (11.6 per cent). On the other hand, among the respondents regarding their health as poor or very poor, the proportion of those having low overall social adjustment is nearly eight times more than the aged women with high overall social adjustment. So, social adjustment is strongly related to the self-evaluation of health among the aged women.

Table 3.6 : Association between overall social adjustment and self-evaluation of health among the respondents

Overall social adjustment	*Self-evaluation of health by the respondents*				
	Very good	*Good*	*Uncertain*	*Poor*	*Very poor*
Low	0.0	11.6	45.5	38.8	4.1
Medium	4.2	45.0	37.5	11.7	1.7
High	6.4	73.4	14.7	4.6	0.9

As expected, overall social adjustment is strongly related to the respect the respondents get from their family. Relevant statistics (product-moment correlation = +0.60) show that sons/sons-in-law pay nominal respect just by saying *namaste* to their mother or mother-in-law who often show low social adjustment, while those with high social adjustment often share the problems and emotions of their sons/sons-in-law. Similar trends are observed in the case of daughter-in-law, grandchildren and husband.

It is, thus, observed that the overall social adjustment among the respondents goes a long way in getting respect and status in the family. It also has a significant relation with the maintenance of physical health condition and mental well-being among the aged females. Details of such associations would be dealt with a little later.

4

HEALTH, WELL-BEING AND SOCIAL ADJUSTMENT

Healthful longevity has always been a cherished dream. This is evident from a hymn of *Atharva veda "Jeewan Shardan Shatam, paysem shardan shatam"*, that is, life of one hundred years with functioning senses. It may be restated that health is not just absence of disease. It is a broad concept involving physical, social and emotional aspects. Health is man's normal condition, his birth-right. It is the result of living in accordance with the natural laws pertaining to body, mind and environment. These laws relate to air and sunlight, balanced diet, regular exercise, rest, relaxation and sleep, cleanliness, right attitudes of mind, healthy habits and good patterns of living (Park and Park, 1970). Thus, health means wholeness, physical fitness being only one of the dimensions. Shuval (1981) asserts that health is not a dichotomy of absolute health *vs.* absolute illness; it is rather health – ill-health continuum. There are various factors that influence an individual's position on this continuum – age being chief of them.

Ageing refers to the cumulative, progressive and degenerative changes that occur over a period of life course (Ramamurti, 1995). It suggests that the natural process of ageing is associated with a decline in specific functional abilities. Even though, in old age, body does become susceptible to a number of illnesses, yet this does not mean that ageing is synonymous to disease or illness. It implies that the criterion of 'being healthy' differs and should differ in different stages of human life-cycle including old-age. Attention may now be focused to certain factors influencing the health and well-being of the aged.

Physical Health

Ageing does make the body vulnerable to certain factors that lead to deterioration and eventual death. Kirkwood (1988) observes that bodies have 'in-built programme' to decay and die in order to make way for younger members of the species, preventing overcrowding, which is termed as 'programmed senescence'. In this process, tissues, such as the skin and muscles, become less elastic. Urinary system becomes slower and less efficient in excreting toxins and other waste-products, leading to a number of kidney-related problems. Gastrointestinal system reduces enzyme-secretion resulting in digestive upsets. There is decline in muscle-mass and strength, which may give rise to certain locomotor infirmities. Respiratory system takes in less oxygen leading to decrease in vigour (Hamilton, 1994). Aiken (1989) observes that an average 75 year-old person's cardiac-output, is approximately, 70 per cent of the average 50 year-old individuals. In old age, the cardiovascular system suffers a double blow—the heart decreases in strength and, simultaneously, arteries get hardened and shrunk making pumping of blood around the body more energy-consuming.

Psychological Well-being

In old age, there may be certain obvious changes in mental faculties, similar to ones at the physiological level. In brain, the cells become weaker as cerebral blood flow decreases, thereby less oxygen is available to the neurons. This somewhat reduces efficiency of the brain leading to delays in learning new things and creative thinking, poor recent memories but better remote memories, mental rigidity, tendency to reminiscing and forgetfulness (Hurlock, 1976). Eysenck (1987) notes that people become more introvert, as they grow older. Apart from physiological factors, that is, changing levels of neural excitement, it may also be due to societal indifference towards their needs. Similarly, Peck (1968) puts forth that, in old age, three conflicts need to be resolved. The first one is body-transcendence *vs.* body-preoccupation. The aged have to come to terms with their declining strength. Overemphasis on bodily well-being would bring disappointment. The second conflict is ego-differentiation *vs.* work-role preoccupation. To exemplify, in joint family system, an aged female is expected to handover her responsibilities of homemaker to her daughter-in-law and take a back seat. She needs to accept this change and take up new roles in order to maintain her self-esteem. The third of Peck's conflicts is ego-transcendence *vs.* ego-preoccupation. This essentially means that the aged start realizing that their end is round the corner.

Social Relationship

Does social adjustment of the aged can influence their physical health? Lynch (1977) observes that quality of social interaction actually affects our physical well-being and medical status. Relational difficulties are suspected to underlie problems like anorexia nervosa, cancer, heart-disease or even sudden death. Schmale (1958) reports that sense of failure in relationship may result in several types of physical symptoms among people. Shuval *et al.* (1973) point out that illness is also a mechanism for coping with failure or frustration. So, old women may pose sick in order to seek attention from their family members. It may be true that an urge to be sick, at unconscious level, can actually develop certain symptoms of illness in an individual. Cousins (1979), in his book *Anatomy of Illness,* cites many live examples claiming that positive thinking about one's health can even heal terminal illnesses. A clear impact of psycho-social factors on physiological functioning is shown by Mcintosh *et al.* (1993). They report that psychological adjustment and intimate relationship with kin elevates lymphocyte counts while tension and conflict with significant others lowers it. Further, Weiss (1972) asserts that bereaved people have disturbed sleep and appetite. These researches have indicated that health is a holistic concept and is significantly affected by our emotional investment and social relationship.

Life-style

"Most of us die of unhealthy life-style", asserts Rogers (1983). This is truly applicable in metropolitan cities like Delhi. Now-a-days, people are dying with life-style related diseases like asthama, ulcers, heart-attack, cancer, etc., and not due to previously considered killer diseases like cholera, plague, diarrhœa and malaria. The present life-style, characterized by imbalanced nutrition, lack of exercise, more or less constant stress, tension and no time for relaxation and enjoyment, is one of the major factors of non-communicable diseases. The World Health Organization, on World's Health Day, 1999, focusses on "active ageing makes the difference". It further says that aged people are prone to non-communicable diseases such as hypertension, heart diseases, stroke, diabetes, cancer, respiratory diseases, arthritis and mental problems. Presently, such non-communicable diseases account for about 56 per cent of all deaths worldwide and this proportion is expected to jump to 73 per cent by the year 2020. So, healthy body and healthy mind are crucial factors for well-proportioned life.

Gender

Covey (1992) observes that elderly females have higher rates of morbidity, though it has been observed that 'women are sicker but men die sooner'. Epidemiologically, apart from age-related ailments like diabetes, hypertension, deterioration in sensory capabilities, etc., females suffer from two broad health disorders, gynæcological and postmenopausal morbidities. Certain socio-cultural factors also add to the morbidity among females. All through the life-cycle, females are subject to various kinds of discrimination, oppression and exploitation. Parents' preference for male-child, right from birth to educational and health facilities, nutrition and other resource-allocation, early marriage, multiple pregnancies are some factors, accumulated effects of which, contribute to vulnerability of may gynæcological complications and nutritional deficiencies, fastening the ageing deterioration among females (Bagchi, 1997).

"Old age is multiple determined experiences", assert Butler and Lewis, "that depend on an intricate balance of physical, emotional and social forces, anyone of which can upset or involve others" (1977). Now, attention may be diverted to the health condition of elderly females in Pushp Vihar.

Health Condition of Elderly Females

With advancing years many age-related disabilities begin to appear. The capacity of the five senses also deteriorates. Hamilton (1994) observes that lens of the eye loses elasticity leading to *presbiopia* (long sightedness). Hearing impairment also begin to crop up and *presbycusis* (loudness recruitment) may develop. Ageing senses take longer time to give information to brain from the surrounding environment. O'Brien (1991) reports that usually old people lose full use of limbs and vital organs. Further, Desai (1991) finds gender-difference in health-condition, with elderly females suffering more from several degenerative diseases than their male counterparts.

In the present study, the health-status of the respondents, in terms of sensory conditions, bodily ailments, hospitalisation and their subjective health evaluation, has been assessed. Data on sensory capacities show that 65.7 per cent respondents complain of their vision going down and one-third face locomotion problems. Nineteen per cent of respondents have reported that there is deteriorative change in their hearing capacity and 9.7 per cent tremble. Deteriorating eye-sight is the most common problem faced by the respondents. These changes might be posing hurdles in their activities of daily-life and interaction with neighbours.

For further analysis, a composite variable, physical fitness-impairment, has been developed by combining the scores of the above four variables—vision, hearing, locomotion and trembling (see Q. 29 in Appendix A). Score '1' has been given if sensory capability has gone down, '2' for unchanged and '3' for improved. Theoretical range is 4 to 12 and observed is 4 to 8. Mean is 6.3 and the data are highly consistent (standard deviation = 1.1). The range 4-8 has been divided into two—low (4-6) and high (7-8), going by the 50th percentile.

In old age, due to certain anatomical and physiological processes the body becomes prone to various ailments like blood pressure, arthritis, diabetes, asthma, renal problems, etc. In Pushp Vihar, almost 60 per cent respondents are reported to have blood-pressure problem, 23 per cent are suffering from gynæcological ailments, 21 per cent are diabetic, 28.6 per cent have digestive up-sets and 13.7 per cent suffer from excessive coughing. Also, 13.7 per cent are having breathing problems. Almost 3 per cent respondents complain of lever or jaundice problems, 9 per cent have suffered from heart-attack in the past. Ten per cent have medical complaints like paralysis, cancer, bone-fracture, ulcers, skin-rashes and appendix pain. Having high or low blood-pressure is the most common problem cited by the respondents, followed by digestive up-sets, gynæcological ailments and diabetes. In the study, 37 per cent respondents have been admitted to hospital in the last two years.

What is the impact of these deteriorative changes on the psychological and social well-being of the elderly? *"Main bahut takleef main hun aur marna chahti hun"*, a 96 years old sick respondent tells, about the effect of deteriorating health in old age, *"Bhagwaan ne saare sukh diye lekin itni lambi umar aur us par itni rogi kaaya dedi – main aik bojh ban gayi"* (I am in great pain and want to die. God has given me all the joys but has given so long life and, above all, so many illnesses—I have become a dead weight). It shows the impact of physical ailments on the psyche and social relations of a person.

Gynæcological and post-menopausal problems often add up to the morbidity rate among the elderly females. Common gynæcological problems that dominate the health condition of aged females are urinary incontinence, bladder urgency, uterine cancer, ovarian cancer, breast cancer, etc. Ganesh (1997) reports that women are more vulnerable to osteoporosis, firstly, because of lighter bone structure and, secondly, oestrogen deficiency, after menopause, increases bone resorption indicating excessive osteoclastic activity. Analysis indicates that 41.3 per cent aged females between 60 to 62 years face gynæcological problems, another 45 per cent, in age category of 63 to 67 years, have such problems, and in 68 to 96 years age-group, 13.8 per cent respondents are suffering from gynæcological problems. Next, 27 per cent respondents, in the age-category of 60 to 62 years have digestive problems. In 63 to 67 years age-group, 25 per cent women suffer from digestive up-sets and, in 68 to 96 years of age, 48 per cent respondents are having such complaints. It seems, while gynæcological problems are more apparent in young-old age, stomach upsets are more frequent in old-old age-group.

All these changes have serious repercussions on the day-to-day activities of the elderly. This, in turn, may influence their interaction in the family and neighbourhood. So, deteriorating vision may hamper the aged female's creative utilization of her leisure time through, say, embroidery and, consequently, she may feel lonely and unattended. In another case, an elderly, with some locomotion problems, may not be able to initiate or maintain interaction in the neighbourhood. Though long life is cherished, deteriorating health-condition may gravely affect their quality of life, as seen in the case of a 92 years old respondent Imarti (name is camouflaged):

Is long life a blessing?

Imarti, 92 years old widow, stays with her son and his family in Pushp Vihar. Her son has retired a year back. Imarti is experiencing a decline in her body strength. Her eye-sight has decreased considerably and she has undergone cataract operation twice in both the eyes. She is suffering from high blood-pressure and heart-problem. Her hearing capacity has reduced markedly. She is suffering from acute pain in her left joint. Her health-problems aggravated with paralysis of right side of her body. After that, she has totally become dependent on others for her daily life-activities. Now, she is fully bed-ridden. The family also initially tried its best to provide her medi-care as well as full emotional support. However, when caring seems to become too taxing and unending, the family has, slowly and quietly, confined itself to providing food and medi-care to her. Her need to interact is overlooked. She often complains that she is not properly cared for by her family. The nagging and grumbling attitude of the old sick female has further driven her family members away from her. Their sympathy towards her deteriorating health-condition has gradually vanished. Now, she is left all alone in a small room with none to interact. Her daughter-in-law comes once a day to get her bathed and to give medicines. On regular intervals, her grandsons visit her. Helpless Imarti waits desperately for her death to come and free her from the pain and distress. *"Ab mujhe na theek se sunai de hai na dikhai de hai"*, in agony she murmurs, *"Shareer main bhi hazaar bimarian ho gayee hain phir bhi bhagwaan pata nahin kyon saans chalaye jaa raha hai"* (now, I am not able to hear and see properly. Thousands of ailments have occupied my body, still, don't know, why God is keeping me alive).

For analysis purposes, a composite variable, health—ill-health has been developed by combining the scores of ten variables on medical complaints (see Q. 30 in Appendix A). Score '2' has been given if the respondent reports to have the disease and '1' for not having it. Theoretical range is 9 to 18 and observed is 10 to 18. Mean is 16.1 and the data are highly homogeneous (standard deviation = 1.1). The observed range, 10-18 has been divided into two—low (10-16) and high (17-18), cut-off point being the 50th percentile.

Interviewer's Observation

During interviews, the researcher has observed and recorded the appearance of the respondents as younger, normal or older than their reported chronological age. Scores have been given as '1' for normal or older and '2' for younger. There are 85.4 per cent respondents who look normal or older and 14.6 per cent younger than their age. It is generally stated that elderly females who are hale and hearty tend to look younger than their contemporaries who have fragile health conditions.

Daily Life Activities

Personal autonomy is one of the indicators of quality of life in old age. It is, generally, achieved through good health-condition, proper exercise and adequate diet. Self-dependence, in activities of daily living, play crucial role in the life-style of an aged. More often than not, it determines type of roles and activities they can take up and their interactions in neighbourhood. It directly influences their self-concept. Roberts, Dunkle and Haug (1994) observe that, among elderly, greater independence in activities of daily life and greater perceived control of events significantly attenuated the adverse effects of strain on psychological well-being.

Data of the present study show that all the 350 respondents could eat at their own, without any help. Only 3 (0.9 per cent) respondents require help in bathing and dressing, 4 per cent need help in walking and 12.3 per cent could not get up and sit by their own. Almost 5 per cent aged females require help in the toilet. Another 12 per cent elderly women need help in handling money. Also, 84.6 per cent of the respondents are able to do small kitchen-work like preparing tea, coffee, heating rice, etc. Added to this, 69 per cent respondents are self-sufficient in taking medicines while 31 per cent need help. Further, 73.7 per cent aged females can do shopping at their own. Two-thirds of the respondents wash their clothes without help. Many among the respondents consciously try to maintain active life style with a view, *"Agar admi kaam na kare to haath pair jud jate hain, phir budhapa bahut takleef deta hai ki tum chote chote kaam ke liye dusron ke mohtaj ho jate ho"* (if one doesn't work, mobility decreases, then, old age gives pain as you become dependent on others even for little things).

It is often held that the aged become more dependent on others for their daily life activities with advancing age. Table 4.1 gives age-wise distribution of activities of daily-life among the elderly females. It shows that the proportion of respondents in the age-group of 68 to 96 years who need help in getting up and sitting (28.6 per cent) is almost five times higher than their younger counterparts (5.6 per cent). Similarly, the proportion of respondents in the age-group of 68 to 96 years is three times higher than those who are in the younger age-group (60 to 62 years). It appears that as we move from simpler to difficult activities of daily-life and from younger-old to older-old, there is a gradual but marked reduction in independence in performance of these activities. Relevant statistics confirm the same (rank correlation = +0.37).

Table 4.1 : Percentage distribution of the elderly females over the activities of daily-living in the three age-groups

Age	*60 to 62 years*		*63 to 67 years*		*68 to 96 years*	
Activities of daily life	*On my own*	*Require help*	*On my own*	*Require help*	*On my own*	*Require help*
Eating	100.0	0.0	100.0	0.0	100.0	0.0
Bathing	100.0	0.0	100.0	0.0	99.1	0.9
Dressing	100.0	0.0	100.0	0.0	99.1	0.9
Walking	100.0	0.0	100.0	0.0	96.0	4.0
Getting up and sitting	94.4	5.6	95.0	5.0	71.0	28.6
Toileting	99.2	0.8	98.3	1.7	86.7	13.3
Handling money	96.8	3.2	92.6	7.4	72.4	27.6
Kitchen work	95.2	4.8	90.1	9.9	65.7	34.3
Take medicine	80.6	19.4	81.8	18.2	40.0	60.0
Shopping	84.7	15.3	82.6	17.4	50.5	49.5
Washing clothes	79.8	20.2	73.6	26.4	41.9	58.1

In the study, widows are somewhat more dependent on their family for activities of daily living than their married counterparts (rank correlation = +0.22). Does it signify that distress makes the aged vulnerable to dependence on others for their daily-life activities? However, overall social adjustment is not significantly related to decline in body's capacity to handle daily activities independently (rank correlation = +0.12).

In order to facilitate further analysis, a 'dependence-independence in activities of daily-living scale' has been developed. For each of these eleven activities, respondents are given score 2 for performing independently and 1 for requiring help. Theoretical range for the scale is 11 to 22 while the observed range is 11 to 21. The mean is 12.4 and the data are highly homogeneous (standard deviation = 2.2). Data are positively skewed (skewness = +0.6), which means that distribution of frequencies is more towards the higher age group. The scores have been divided into two—low (1-11) and high (12-21), cut off point being the 50th percentile of the observed range. This composite variable would be added up with other variables to develop the variable, namely overall health condition.

Sleep

Sleep is one of the basic necessities of life. It relaxes body and mind while rejuvenating the cells and repairing tissues. It is also an indicator of mental well-being, as insomnia is a psychological disorder. Jarvik and Small (1995) observe that duration of sleep depends upon the social and psychological condition of the elderly. Thuesz (1990) reports that as many as half of the people, over the age of 65, suffer from insomnia in the United States.

Data of the present study show that 65 per cent of the respondents sleep easily while 35 per cent face difficulty in sleeping. In the same connection, attention is paid to the time the elderly females wake up in morning. Little less than a-half, (46.9 per cent) are early risers, that is, before 5 a.m. and 53.1 per cent have normal rising time, that is, after 5 a.m. Further, 11.1 per cent of the aged females are early bed goers, that is, before 9 p.m. Another 79.1 per cent of the respondents go to sleep at normal time, that is, from 9 p.m. to 11 p.m. and rest 9.7 per cent sleep late, that is, after 11 p.m. Apparently, sound sleep indicates physical as well as mental health condition.

Does overall health condition have any association with the quality of sleep among the elderly? Results show that 50 per cent of the respondents with poor health condition have difficulty in sleeping. Further, 80 per cent of the aged females, with medium health condition, enjoy easy sleep and all the respondents with good health status have easy sleep. Similarly, most (80 per cent) of the respondents with high conflict adjustment sleep with ease and only half of the respondents, with low conflict adjustment, enjoy easy sleep. Also, overall social adjustment has significant positive association with the type of sleep the respondents have. Among the respondents having easy sleep, the proportion of those who have high overall social adjustment (40.5 per cent) is almost twice the proportion of those having low social adjustment (22.5 per cent). It appears that aged women who are well adjusted often enjoy easy sleep.

Self-evaluation of Health

There is a definite deterioration in the health status in old age. Most often, these changes make the elderly susceptible to several ailments. It is important for the elderly to accept that they no longer will have that energy and vigour as in their youth and may have to live with certain health problems like high or low blood pressure, diabetes, sensory deterioration, etc. It is an important developmental task for the aged to come to terms with their waning body-strength and, therefore, consider minor ailments as 'normal' in old-age. Those elderly who are not able to do so become hypersensitive about their degenerating health-condition, which, may further affect their health negatively. It is a well-established fact that our beliefs influence our body functioning and, in turn, health and ailments (see Chopra, 1993; Cousins, 1979). So, self-evaluation of health is a crucial factor for the well-being of an individual.

In the study, 45.7 per cent respondents feel that their health is good or very good in comparison to their age-mates, 33 per cent are uncertain while 21.3 per cent consider their health poor or very poor. Do characteristics like age, marital status, have any association with the self-evaluation of health among aged females? Self-evaluation of health by the respondents has insignificant association with their marital status (rank correlation = +0.19). These results corroborate with the findings of Wolinsky and Johnson (1992). They report that becoming widowed has not altered previous reports of health-status and prior patterns of visiting physician or hospital-utilization.

Similarly, age of elderly females is not linked with evaluation of their own health (rank correlation = +0.07). However, there is a significant positive relation between the self-evaluation of health of the respondents and overall social adjustment (as seen in the previous chapter). It appears that satisfaction with familial relations often makes aged women less pre-occupied with the decreasing health condition, which in turn has positive impact on their health status.

Utilization of Leisure Time

In old age, people may have decreased energy but, most often, have plenty of time-resource, which needs to be utilized creatively. Such a 'free-time' is, commonly, termed as leisure time. Aristotle (1944) considers leisure as a state of being free from the necessity of being occupied (in work or any other form of obligation). A wide range of intrinsically rewarding creative activities that fell under the Greek school of leisure activities are music, writing, reciting poetry, dancing, singing, fine conversation with worthy companions and any form of mental cultivation that would be termed as 'serene contemplation'. Basu (1996) observes that the most preferred leisure activity is watching T.V., followed by listening radio, reading, gossiping and worshipping. Similarly, Chakravarty (1996) finds that T.V. assumes the role of a substitute for primary communication. Gupta (1993) reports that those elderly people who use their time more effectively and meaningfully score higher on emotional well-being, that is, show better psychological functioning.

In the present study, information on leisure activities has been extracted from daily-diary of the respondents (multiple choice). Most of the respondents (44.2 per cent) visit friends, neighbours and relatives when free, followed by 40.9 per cent respondents engaging themselves in household activities, say, making pickles, *chutney*, sweets, arranging-rearranging cupboards, and 38.9 per cent spend time with their grandchildren. Another 38.6 per cent respondents prefer having a nap and 31.4 per cent watch television in the afternoon free time. In winters, 23.4 per cent respondents bask in the sun in afternoons, do knitting and chat with neighbours. Further, 19.7 per cent respondents engage themselves in *bhajans, satsang* and the like. Another 10.5 per cent aged females pursue creative hobbies like embroidery, sewing, etc. in their leisure time. Also, 10 per cent aged women sit idle, 3.1 per cent read books and 1.4 per cent play cards with friends.

Do the type of activities adopted by the respondents in their leisure time have any association with their adjustment? Data show that the respondents who visit neighbours and friends and do household activities often show better adjustment than their counterparts who sit idle in their leisure time. For obvious reasons, aged females who initiate and maintain interaction within the family and neighbours and those who share the household work with family members show better adjustment.

Overall Health Condition

As discussed earlier, health is a holistic concept involving physical, psychological and social dimensions. Mechanic (1980) reports that psychological state can contribute to the occurrence of certain symptoms like headaches, insomnia, ulcers, etc. People are happy when relationships with significant others are harmonious, but develop side-effects when incongruent. Such side-effects can be as simple as stress or as complicated as physical or psychological conditions, which appear to be totally unrelated to the family problems. Lynch (1977) observes that divorce may accelerate loneliness and physical illness and can make a person prone to heart-failure. Paintal (1991) examines that poor health is related to poor adjustment among adults as well as elderly people. Unhappy and dissatisfied mental state seems to aggravate the ageing process while feeling of well-being, satisfaction and high morale appears to slow it down. In the same connection, Singh (1996) reports that general disability during old age and recurrent illness not only makes the aged vulnerable to neglect, destitution and dependency but also limits their role performance. This in view, attention may be paid to the health condition of the respondents.

In order to facilitate further analysis, a composite variable of overall health condition has been developed which is a sum of physical fitness-impairment, health-ill-health, dependence-independence in activities of daily living and appearance of respondent (interviewer's observation). Theoretical range is from 4 to 8 and observed one is from 4 to 7. Mean is 5.0 and the data are highly consistent and homogeneous (standard deviation = 0.8). The observed range is divided into three — low (4), medium (5) and high (6-7), cutting points being 33rd and 67th percentile.

What has been the impact of age on overall health condition of the respondents? Diagram 4.1 shows the association between the two variables. The proportion of respondents, in the age-group of 60 to 62 years, having high overall health condition is

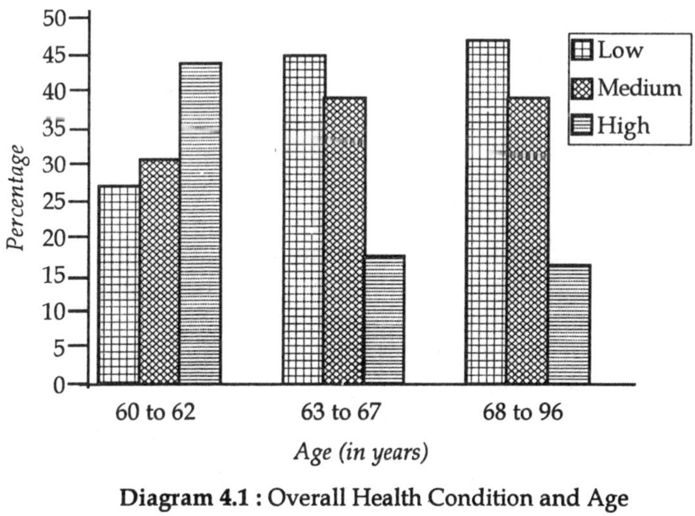

Diagram 4.1 : Overall Health Condition and Age

three times higher than their counterparts in the age-group of 68 to 96 years. Relevant statistics (rank correlation = +0.27) also shows that as age increases, there is decline in overall health condition.

Next, does widowhood increase the susceptibility to illness? Weiss (1972) observes that, those who have lost spouse, spend more days sick in bed, have more admissions to hospitals and have more emotional problems. Similar are the results of the present study. More often, widows have poor health condition than their married counterparts. The proportion of widowed respondents having poor health condition (66 per cent) is almost two times higher than their married counterparts (34 per cent). Table 4.2 gives the association between health condition of the respondents and their marital status.

Table 4.2 : Association between health conditions of the respondents and their marital status

Health condition	*Widowed*	*Married*
Low	66.0	34.0
Medium	42.0	58.0
High	15.4	84.6

Likewise, the proportion of married respondents having high overall health condition is, more than five times higher than the widowed respondents. Relevant statistics confirm the trend (rank correlation = –0.27). Widowhood seems to aggravate sorrow, tension and anxiety, which have negative repercussion on the health status of the elderly females.

Do elderly females sharing harmonious relationship with significant others also possess sturdy health condition? Table 4.3 shows the association between the overall health condition of the respondents and their social adjustment. Among the respondents possessing fragile health condition, the proportion of those having low social adjustment is more than four times than those with high social adjustment. This trend is further validated by relevant statistics (product-moment correlation = +0.31; rank correlation = +0.36). In the same way the components

Table 4.3 : Association between overall health condition and overall social adjustment among the respondents

Overall health condition	*Low adjustment*	*Medium adjustment*	*High adjustment*
Low	28.3	15.7	6.6
Medium	14.3	13.1	18.3
High	0.3	1.1	2.3

of overall social adjustment, i.e., attitudinal adjustment (rank correlation = +0.34), conflict adjustment (rank correlation = +0.32), need adjustment (rank correlation = +0.29) and role adjustment (rank correlation = +0.28) are also significantly related to overall health condition. It suggests that those elderly females who have harmonious interaction and relationship with significant others often enjoy good health.

Well-being of Elderly Females

Gerontologists assert that mental health problems among the aged are both organic and functional in nature. Catabolic process attacks on the nervous system and brain tissues increasing chances for mental health problems. Personality maladjustments coupled with stresses and strains give rise to functional disorders. Alzheimer's disease, also called 'primary degenerative dementia' and dementia, a marked decline in an individual's previously high level of intellectual performance are among the common mental disorders in old age. Added to this, Joseph (1991) brings out that in old-age, many people suffer from anxiety over finances, anxiety over health, feeling of being unwanted, isolated and lonely, feeling of guilt, irritation, and inability to adjust to changed condition and decreased social contacts and participation. Similarly, Gautam and Pant (1997) observe that depression often accompanies ageing. Hobman (1978) reports that, in Britain, just over half of adult-hospital beds and under half of psychiatric patients are over retirement-age. Let us look into those factors that are crucial for the well-being.

Loneliness

Loneliness is considered to be a major emotional problem experienced by aged people. As a subjective experience, loneliness is the discrepancy between one's desired and achieved levels of social relations (Perlman and Peplau, 1982). It is possible that a person may feel lonely in the crowd or, some other time, may feel perfectly happy on his own. Generally speaking, loneliness is a 'state', that is, a transient feeling—probably occurring in the aged on account of situational or environmental factors. On the other hand, 'trait loneliness' is a stable and persistent pattern of feeling. Trait lonely aged persons may have low opinion about themselves, dislike sharing their feelings and are low in intimate relations (Rubenstein and Shaver, 1980). Often, they may report high social anxiety, be prone to depression and feel that they are being judged or ridiculed by other persons (Perlman and Peplau 1982). Such elderly people lack effective coping strategies.

In the present study, respondents were asked to rate their feeling of loneliness as one of the five response categories—always, often, sometimes, rarely or never. Data show that 13.4 per cent of respondents never feel lonely while 1 per cent always feel so. Another 32.6 per cent respondents often have the feeling of loneliness, 28 per cent sometimes and 25 per cent rarely feel lonely. Does the feeling of loneliness increases with age? Analysis shows that, in the age-group of 60 to 62 years, 36.3 per cent of females always or often feel lonely while in the age-group of 68 to 96 years, 29.5 per cent respondents figure in this category. However, relevant statistics (rank correlation = –0.06) show insignificant relationship between age and loneliness. Data further show that generally respondents who willingly take up activities in the household such as cooking, dusting, cleaning (rank correlation = +0.34) and those who interact actively, say, go out for shopping, visit temple, play games with neighbours (rank correlation = +0.42) and friends (rank correlation = +0.38) rarely or never feel lonely. In contrast, aged women who are so to say introvert and less sociable often suffer from loneliness, as seen in the case of Sumitra:

None to Interact

Sumitra (name changed) is a 60 years old widow living with her only son. Her husband died 10 years ago. Her son, a police officer, often has long and odd duty hours. She is all alone in the house. She does all the household work but that too doesn't take much time. Sumitra doesn't socialize much with neighbours. Her relatives also live at far off places and hence rarely meet. On the top of it, arthritis has restricted her movements. She has no friends in the colony. Most of her leisure time is spent in past reminiscence. Everyday she has a lot of free time, which she does not know how and where to spend. Suffering from loneliness, she kills her time by watching T.V. Only her morning and evening time is spent in cooking foods for her son and herself. Her son also can't give much time to her mother. Loneliness has developed some psychological disorders like anxiety, fear and even hypochondriasis. Whenever her son gets late, she develops high blood pressure, perspires a lot and becomes too nervous. She often complains of palpitation, backache, stomach upset and many more. Sumitra is not very keen to get her son married as one astrologer has predicted that her *bahu* will be very dominating and dictatorial. She expresses her feeling of loneliness as, "*Akelapan bahut lagta hai, khali ghar katne ko dodhta hai*" (it is terribly lonesome staying all alone back at home).

Does loneliness affect the health condition of the elderly? Table 4.4 gives the association between overall health condition of the respondents and their feeling of loneliness. It shows that a little less than half (46.3 per cent) of the respondents with poor health condition always or often feel lonely while none of the respondent with high overall health condition figures in this category. On the other hand, most (92.3 per cent) elderly respondents with high overall health condition feel lonely only rarely or never. Relevant statistics (rank correlation = +0.43) confirm strong association between these two variables.

Table 4.4 : Association between overall health condition of the respondents and their feeling of loneliness

Overall health condition	*Loneliness*				
	Always	*Often*	*Sometimes*	*Rarely*	*Never*
Low	1.1	45.2	35.6	14.1	4.0
Medium	0.6	21.3	21.3	36.9	20.0
High	0.0	0.0	7.7	30.8	61.5

Anxiety and Tension

Anxiety and tension have become obvious characteristic of metropolitan life. One WHO sponsored study on "Global burden of disease and injury" (1996) covering eight geographical regions says that about 90 million people in India alone—more than the combined population of Delhi, Mumbai, Kolkata and Chennai, will suffer from major clinical depression at some stage in their life. However, this tension and stress have serious repercussion on the physical, mental and social well-being of a person.

In the present study, approximately every third respondent has been reported to be in tension and anxiety. Reasons for the tension and anxiety are many, ranging from husband's illness or death, financial problems, child ill, daughter's marital conflicts, ill-treatment by family, respondent's own illness to conflicts with daughter-in-law, etc. Data show that the respondents who take up household activities willingly often have fewer anxiety and tension (rank correlation = +0.43). Also, aged women who go out for walks with friends, sit and chat with them often remain away from anxiety and tension than their counterparts who try to remain within themselves (rank correlation = +0.44). Let us now, see the impact of anxiety and tension on health condition of respondents. Data show that 42 per cent respondents suffering from anxiety and tension have poor health condition and 92.3 per cent respondents having no anxiety and tension score high on overall health condition. It implies that anxiety and tension have a deleterious effect on the health of aged females.

Subjective Well-being

Well-being as perceived by people themselves, is one of the most important criteria for adjustment in old age. Rathore (1992) brings out that old people have significantly poor subjective well-being than their middle aged counterparts. Similarly, Raj and Prasad (1971) report that the most rural aged exhibit negative self-perception, particularly those belonging to better off classes. Soodan (1975) observes many aged people are reported to be distressed about the present-life. Also, older persons in non-institutionalized settings are better on psychological well-being and less depressed as compared to those in institutionalized settings (Chadha, 1989). These findings show that age, financial position, living arrangements and family atmosphere are important factors influencing subjective well-being. Let us see how elderly women feel in this regard.

Erickson (1982), in his psychosocial theory of development, asserts that old people review their past life and satisfaction that most goals of their life have been fulfilled, leads to ego-integration. Conversely, a feeling that not much has been achieved, brings a sense of despair because, with death approaching, it is too late to make amends. In the present study, respondents have been asked to rate the fulfilment of their expectations from life as—everything, much of it, some of it, less of it or nothing. Data show that 21.4 per cent respondents report that all their expectations from life are fulfilled. Further, 41.7 per cent respondents consider that they have got most of what they expected from life. Another 26.6 per cent have been able to fulfil only some of their desires. Eight per cent of the respondents feel that only very few of their expectations have been materialized. And 2.3 per cent respondents think that they have got nothing from life.

Respondents were asked to rate their past, present and future life as—very happy, happy, blend of happiness and unhappiness, unhappy or very unhappy. Table 4.5 gives the respondents' own rating of their past, present and future life. It depicts that majority of the respondents consider their life as blend of happiness and unhappiness. However, the number of

Table 4.5 : Respondents' rating of their past, present and future life

	Past		*Present*		*Future*	
	Number	*Per cent*	*Number*	*Per cent*	*Number*	*Per cent*
Very happy	8	2.3	8	2.3	14	4.7
Happy	106	30.3	106	30.3	95	36.5
Mixed	205	58.6	143	40.9	129	43.5
Unhappy	30	8.6	81	23.1	40	13.5
Very unhappy	1	0.3	12	3.4	18	6.0

respondents considering their past life (32.6 per cent) as happy or very happy, is more than three times higher than those having gloomy perception towards their past life (8.9 per cent). Like everyone, they have fond memories of their younger days. The rating by respondents of their present life is a little different. Happy and unhappy memories are differentiated but only marginally (ratio, 6 : 5). On the other hand, 44.2 per cent of the elderly women foresee very happy or happy future, 19.6 per cent give out gloomy prospects. On the whole, most of the aged women are more hopeful of their future, yet there are quite a few who are uncertain about it.

Interestingly, the interrelation between physical health and psychological well-being can be established by looking at the association between overall health condition of the respondents and their self-rating of past, present and future life (see Diagram 4.2). It shows that among the respondents considering their past life as happy the proportion of those having high overall health condition (76.9 per cent) is more than three times higher than their counterparts with low health condition (21.4 per cent). In the case of considering present life as happy this trend becomes more prominent as the proportion of respondents having high overall health condition (84.6 per cent) is almost six times higher than those who have low health condition (14.2 per cent). Similarly, among the respondents viewing happy future ahead, the proportion of those with high overall health condition (83.3 per cent) is almost five times higher than those with low health status (17.1 per cent). It suggests that

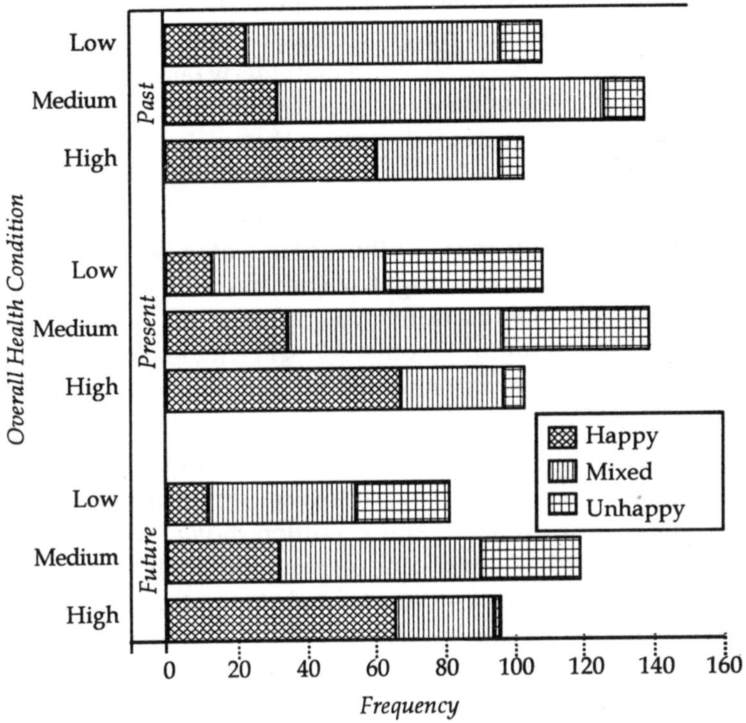

Diagram 4.2 : Overall Health Condition and Respondents' Rating of Life

the aged women with high overall health condition consider their past, present and future life as happy more often, than their age-cohorts who score low on overall health condition. Also, perception towards present and future life is much more potent in influencing the health status than the past one.

Optimism-Pessimism

Age is often considered as a state of mind. That is the reason we see 'young at heart' elderly even at the age of 75 years and, in contrast, we also come across young people who view the life with uncertainty and contempt. An optimistic person would tend to look at the brighter side of the situation and would be cheerful while pessimistic individual would be gloomy and melancholic. It is maintained that optimistic attitude goes a long way in maintaining good health—both physical and mental. Chadha *et al.* (1992) report that elderly females are rated high on hopelessness than old men. Does gender play crucial role in the well-being of elderly women? Let us view the situation in the present study.

In order to explore the dimension of personality trait, namely, optimism-pessimism, the respondents have been asked to rate their future as—bright, vague, no idea or hopeless. Approximately one-fourth (25.7 per cent) of the respondents perceive a bright future. Another 9.7 per cent view it as vague. Almost half (48 per cent) reported to have no idea about their future. Further, 16 per cent aged females are hopeless about their future and 2 (0.6 per cent) respondents did not reply.

Quite interestingly, relationship between optimism-pessimism and overall health condition indicates a positive association. Only 7.4 per cent respondents with low health condition consider their future as bright in contrast to 83.3 per cent of those with high overall health condition. Similarly, 11.9 per cent respondents with low overall health condition regard vague future ahead while none of the respondents with high overall health condition figures in this category. Relevant statistics confirm the same (product-moment correlation = +0.35; rank correlation = +0.41). These findings validate the trend of inter-linkage between physical and psychological dimensions of health. What has been the impact of this personality trait on the well-being of the aged women? *"Pahle zindgi main sukh aur dukh dono ạate rahte the"*, murmurs a respondent *"Ab sirf dukh hi hain"* (previously, life was a blend of happiness and sadness, now its only sorrows). Below is the case study of an elderly female, Gayatri, who knows how to seek happiness out of grief and has a positive outlook towards life.

Second Honeymoon

Gayatri, 62 years old lady knows how to convert challenges into opportunities in life. She happily stays with her husband—

a retired government officer. They have taken two rooms flat on sublet in Pushp Vihar. She is a mother of two daughters and two sons – all married and well-settled. Her eldest son is settled in abroad. Her younger daughter-in-law had refused to stay with her in-laws as it disturbs her privacy and free life-style. Gayatri, without grumbling, moved out of the house with her husband to celebrate her second honeymoon. Her husband's pension is more than enough for their subsistence. Here, the couple is living happily caring and sharing for each other. She gets up early in the morning and goes for a walk with her husband. Both prepare breakfast together. Then she gets the work done by maid. After that they both watch T.V. and have their lunch. In the evening they go out for a walk and buy vegetables and milk. Gayatri likes movies and they both enjoy standing in long queues and buying movie tickets. Many times, they go to visit some friends. "We were so busy in bringing up our children and could hardly share time with each other", says Gayarti, "Now our responsibility is over, my children are well-settled and we don't have any expectations from them. We are happy with ourselves. In our times, we didn't go out for honeymoon, now we are celebrating that".

Apparently, optimistic attitude is strongly related to adjustment among the aged females. Data show that among the respondents considering bright future ahead the proportion of those with high social adjustment is more than thirty times than those with low social adjustment (see Table 4.6). On the other hand, the proportion of respondents with low social adjustment considering their future as vague is more than eight times higher than their counterparts with high social adjustment. This trend becomes sharp when we look at the responses in the category of considering the future hopeless. The proportion of respondents with low social adjustment is more than twenty-two times higher than those with high adjustment. Relevant statistics also validate these findings (rank correlation = +0.53; product-moment correlation = +0.54).

Table 4.6 : Association between optimism-pessimism and overall social adjustment among aged females

	Bright	*Vague*	*No idea*	*Hopeless*
Low	0.6	5.2	15.5	13.5
Medium	6.9	4.0	21.6	2.0
High	18.4	0.6	11.2	0.6

It, thus, appears that optimism-pessimism and social adjustment go hand in hand. Let us take a look at other variables influencing the well-being of aged women.

Death-fear

Death can occur during any stage of the life of a person. However, advances in medicine have reduced instances of death during the earlier life stages of human beings and it has increasingly become a predictable function of old age (Kailash, 1976). So, one of the many difficult situations that the elderly have to face is the death of loved ones—spouse, close friends of long years and close relatives. Death is a biological event defined as "the transition from the state of being alive to a state of being dead (see Jeffers *et al.*, 1962). Rogers (1991) observes differential attitudes towards death and death-anxiety among the elderly and young persons. Those who are satisfied with their achievements, most often, accept the death while those couldn't achieve much, commonly, are fearful with death. Timing of death seems to be a significant factor in death-anxiety or acceptance. Young people are more afraid of death while old ones are found to be accepting with the concept of death. Fisherman (1991) brings out that religious older people are more prepared for death than those who do not practice any religious activity.

In the present study, 33.5 per cent respondents have reported to be not having death-fear while 39.7 per cent often feel so. Another 14 per cent aged females fear death sometimes, 9.4 per cent rarely have this fear and 3.4 per cent have refused to respond to these issues. While analysing death-fear in terms of age, findings show that in 60 to 62 years category, 34.4 per cent respondents often have death-fear. In the age-group of 63 to 67 years, 37.3 per cent often have fear of death and, in 68 to 96 years age-group, more than half (54.1 per cent) of the aged females often have fear of death. Thus, we see that with increasing age fear of death becomes more apparent among the aged women. *"Suna hai, yamraaj sota maar-maar ke le jata hai marne ke baad aur hazaaron bitchuon ke katne jaisa dard hota hai"*, comments one respondent, *"Main to bas yahi chahti hun ki bina dard ke chali jaun"* (I have heard that *yamraj* (God of death) takes you beating with rod after death and the pain is so excruciating as if thousands of scorpions have bitten you. I just wish to die without pain).

Do aged with sound health are less fearful of death? Does deteriorating health condition make the person more anxious about death? Data show that 60.4 per cent respondents, with low overall health condition, often feel death fear. With medium overall health condition, only 23.7 per cent aged females often have fear of death while no respondent with high overall health condition has reported to be having death fear. This signifies that health status of the aged does have an influence on their death-fear or else anxiety related to death tends to affect the health of the elderly. May be association of death with ill-health in old age makes a person with fragile health condition anxious about death. Next, overall life-satisfaction has quite low and inverse association with death-fear (product-moment correlation = –0.15).

It may be inferred from the foregoing discussion that the aged women with frail health condition often report to have anxiety and tension, feel lonely, are pessimistic and fearful of death. The respondents with high overall health condition have fewer anxieties, are more sociable and feel lonely rarely. They have positive outlook towards life and are less fearful of death. Whether sound heath condition contributes to well-being or positive attitude enhances health condition is a debatable matter. However, health condition and well-being are strongly related. To what an extent well-being is influenced by the adjustment of the aged in their family and neighbourhood?

Well Being and Social Adjustment

The deterioration of physical capabilities and mental faculties is considered inevitable in old age. However, how easily the elderly comes to terms with these age related changes, makes all the difference in their well-being. Richard *et al.* (1962) identify that the aged possessing constructive (adapting themselves easily to changing roles and status) and dependent (possessing mixed feelings of contentment and dissatisfaction about old-age) traits are better adjusted than those having defensive (carrying on high levels of activities so as to prove that they are independent), hostile (blaming others for personal shortcomings) and self-hatred (turning their hatred and resentment inwards) personality types. Certain factors like acceptance of changes that accompany advancing age, positive self-concept and social support are important for well-being in old age (Hobfoll and Walfisch, 1984; Ramamurti and Jamuna, 1987). Attention may now be focused on the factors ensuring or inhibiting well-being among the aged women of Pushp Vihar.

Data show that educational status, occupational patterns of the respondents and their husband, their income level as well as monthly family income do not show any statistically significant association with indicators of well-being like loneliness, anxiety and tension, optimism-pessimism, type of sleep and death-fear. This implies that well-being is an intrinsic factor and variables of socio-economic status does not have any influence on it.

Do socially well-adjusted people have fewer anxiety and tensions than those who show mal-adjustment? Is loneliness a salient problem for those who interact lesser? Data show that among the respondents who often feel lonely, the proportion of those with low social adjustment (60.9 per cent) is more than six times higher than their counterparts with high social adjustment (9.5 per cent). On the other hand, 33.3 per cent respondents with high social adjustment rarely feel lonely as compared to 13.3 per cent of those with low social adjustment. Relevant statistics show a strong association between the two variables (rank correlation = +0.49). For obvious reasons aged women who share harmonious relations with their family and neighbours often do not face the problems of loneliness. However, those elderly females who remain introvert or do not initiate or maintain interaction with significant others most often than not feel lonely. This signifies the importance of social interaction.

Data further show a strong association between anxiety and tension the respondents have and their social adjustment. Almost a-half (50.8 per cent) of the respondents having low social adjustment report to have no anxiety and tension as compared to 82.5 per cent aged females with high social adjustment. Among those respondents who have anxiety and tension, proportion of those having high social adjustment is only 17.5 per cent whereas those with low social adjustment are 49.2 per cent, almost three times higher than the former group. Anxiety and tension have deleterious impact on the psyche of a person. Support of significant others goes a long way in limiting the negative effect of anxiety and tensions. That may be the reason why respondents with high social adjustment tend to have fewer anxiety and tension. In consonance, Hobfoll and Walfisch (1984) find that positive self-concept and good social support have a combined effect in preventing a state of depression and of anxiety during an acute crisis. Following is the case study of an aged female, Ganga, suffering from schizophrenia, according to her medical papers. Her mental illness is not being understood by her family members and as a consequence she has become an object of humour and pity in the neighbourhood.

Nobody Understands Me

Ganga, 66 years old married woman is suffering from Schizophrenia. Her husband, two sons, daughters-in-law and four grandchildren have almost boycotted her, without understanding the nature and cause of her mental illness. She is being labelled as "mad woman" by her family as well as neighbours. This has further aggravated her problem. Nobody interacts with her. Her family avoids her and considers her a nuisance. She feels very lonely. She is miserable, as no body understands her. She couldn't recall what incidents have made her schizophrenic. The family also refuses to talk about her illness with anybody. She is not being treated properly and is malnourished. In utter helplessness she calls God to take away her life and free her from this agony. *"Sab mujhse dur bhagte hain"*, cries Ganga, *"Mera apna pati bhi. Jis parivar ke liye maine saari zindgi tabaah kar di voh hi parivar mujhe itni takleef deta hai, koi mujhse baat nahin karna chahta"* (everybody runs away from me, including my husband. The family for whom I have wasted my whole life, that very family gives me so much of pain, nobody likes to talk to me).

It may be restated that sleep is an indicator of well-being. Does social adjustment has anything to do with sleep? Data show that 47.1 per cent respondents with high social adjustment sleep easily while only one-fourth (25.1 per cent) of aged women with low social adjustment figure in this category. In the category of those respondents who report to have difficulty in sleeping, 57.8 per cent have low, 26.8 per cent have medium and 15.4 per cent have high social adjustment. Relevant statistics confirm a strong association between the two variables (rank correlation = +0.36). So, it appears that the nature of interactions aged females have, in the waking stage have an influence over their type of sleep.

Findings of the study show that 54 per cent respondents with low social adjustment report to often have death-fear. Another 23.7 per cent respondents with medium social adjustment and 22.3 per cent aged women with high social adjustment often have the fear of death. Among those respondents who rarely think about death, 36.4 per cent have low, 9.1 per cent medium and 54.5 per cent high social adjustment. Relevant statistics show an insignificant relationship between the two variables (product-moment correlation = –0.06). Death-fear seems to be somewhat independent of social relations the aged women have with significant others.

It seems obvious that the aged sharing harmonious

relationship with their family and neighbours tend to rate their life many shades better than those having incongruent relations. Table 4.7 shows the association between respondents' own rating of their past, present and future life and their overall social adjustment. It brings out that among the respondents considering their past life as happy, the proportion of those having high social adjustment is almost nine times higher than those with low social adjustment. Similarly, while rating present life, the proportion of those having high social adjustment is almost twenty-five times higher than those with low social adjustment. This trend become much sharper when we look at the rating of future life. Data further show that overall social adjustment is also highly associated with respondent's perception about their fulfilment of expectations. Relevant statistics confirm this strong link (product-moment correlation = +0.66; rank correlation = +0.69).

Table 4.7 : Association between overall social adjustment and respondents' rating of their past, present and future life

Rating of life		*Overall social adjustment*		
		Low	*Medium*	*High*
Past	Very happy/happy	2.3	10.1	20.4
	Blend of happiness/ unhappiness	27.8	21.8	8.9
	Unhappy/very unhappy	4.3	2.6	2.0
Present	Very happy/happy	0.9	9.5	22.3
	Blend of happiness/ unhappiness	12.9	21.1	6.9
	Unhappy/very unhappy	20.9	3.7	2.0
Future	Very happy/happy	0.3	10.4	26.0
	Blend of happiness/ unhappiness	12.5	24.3	6.8
	Unhappy/very unhappy	16.9	2.4	0.3

The foregoing discussion implies that social adjustment has a strong positive link with the well-being among the aged females. It signifies the holistic concept of health involving physical, psychological and social dimensions, affect on anyone has repercussions on the other dimensions.

Life-satisfaction and Social Adjustment

Old age is considered to be the last chapter of life. Though, a universal phenomenon, it is not a uniform experience for all senior citizens. Some elderly persons achieve a sense of fulfilment and satisfaction in later years, while others turn bitter and lament the decline of their physical abilities and social significance. Life-satisfaction is an important criterion of happy ageing. It denotes the quality of life. Ramamurti and Jamuna (1993) show that self-acceptance of ageing changes, self-perception of health, satisfaction with marital and familial relations are some of the factors that predict life-satisfaction among the elderly. Palmore and Luikart (1972) find a strong positive correlation between life-satisfaction and level of activity among the elderly. Ardelt (1997) asserts that wisdom (defined as a composite of cognitive, reflective and affective qualities) has a profoundly positive influence on life-satisfaction, particularly among aged women. Chadha (1991) observes that elderly females are less satisfied from life than their male counterparts. The reason for this gender difference could be seen from the findings of Prakash (1994), who asserts that restricting the females at home, leads to social isolation, alienation and hopelessness, which, in turn, may lead to a low life-satisfaction.

In the study, to measure life-satisfaction among the respondents, a scale developed by Neugarten, Havighurst and Tobin (1961), namely, 'life satisfaction index' has been used. The original scale has 20 items. The scale is based on the pattern of summated rating with three response categories—'agree', 'uncertain' and 'disagree'. The original scale has the reliability (split-half) as 0.82 ($p< 0.001$). These statements have been carefully edited to adapt to suit the study condition. The test was rendered into Hindi. Pre-testing was done on 30 aged women of Police-colony, Hauz-khas. Eleven statements were retained having high t-value. After making necessary changes, the scale was included into the main interview schedule. The scale has five favourable and six unfavourable statements.

During analysis, for favourable statements weight '3' has been given for the response 'agree', '2' for 'uncertain' and '1' for disagree. Reverse weightage has been given to unfavourable statements. Then, the scores of 11 statements have been summated to give the total score of composite variable 'overall life-satisfaction'. Theoretical as well as observed range of the scale is 11 to 33. Mean is 22.9. The data are homogeneous (standard deviation = 6.6) and slightly negatively skewed (skewness = –0.12). The range has been divided into 3 – low (11-19), medium (20-27) and high (28-33), cut off points being the 33rd and 67th percentiles.

"Bhagwaan ki kripa hum par saari jindgi bani rahi, badi acchhi jindgi gujri". (God's blessing have remained with me throughout life, I have lived my life contended) says an elderly female. What factors makes a person feel so? Kant and Sharma (1996) find that life-satisfaction is strongly associated with relational variables, say, marital happiness, rather than socio-economic factors like income-level and females more often score low on life-satisfaction. Can these findings be generalized? In the present study also, variables like religion, caste, age, past and present occupational patterns of the respondents and their husband are not related to overall life-satisfaction with any statistical significance. Educational status of the respondents does not appear to be related to life-satisfaction (rank correlation = +0.19).

Diagram 4.3 presents the association between life-satisfaction and marital status of the respondents. It brings out that the proportion of widowed or separated respondents scoring low on life-satisfaction (41.9 per cent) is almost twice higher than their married counterparts (22.6 per cent). Among those respondents who score high on life-satisfaction, 45.1 per cent are married and 21.0 per cent widowed. Relevant statistics show a positive relationship between the two variables (rank correlation = +0.27). So, apparently, presence of a life-partner in old age is crucial for the life-satisfaction.

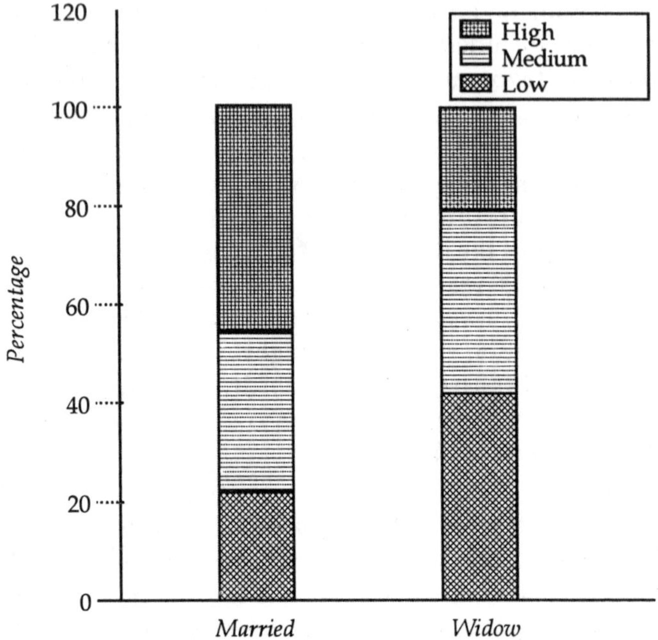

Diagram 4.3 : Life-Satisfaction and Marital Status

Does health status of the aged have any influence on their life-satisfaction? Findings of the study show that among the respondents having low life-satisfaction, almost a-half (49.3 per cent) have low health condition and only 6.8 per cent have high overall health condition. Similarly, among the respondents scoring high on life-satisfaction, the proportion of those having high health condition (69.9 per cent) is more than seven times higher than their age-cohorts having low overall health condition (9.3 per cent). Relevant statistics validate the findings (rank correlation = +0.49; product-moment correlation = +0.49). It implies that balanced diet, regular exercise and active life go a long way in achieving satisfaction in life in old-age.

Data bring out that life-satisfaction is strongly related to variables like loneliness (rank correlation = –0.67), anxiety and tension (rank correlation = –0.47), optimism-pessimism (rank correlation = +0.69) and type of sleep (rank correlation = +0.47). Death-fear shows somewhat weak association with life-satisfaction (rank correlation = +0.25). In the same way, respondents with high overall life-satisfaction often rate their health as very good or good than those having low life-satisfaction (rank correlation = +0.69). These results bring out that life-satisfaction has a very strong link with the well-being of the aged females. Does the same trend persist between overall life-satisfaction and overall social adjustment?

"Bhagwan yeh Budhapa aur mere jaisi takdeer kisi ko na de" (God should not give anybody old age coupled with the fate like that of mine) cries one respondent, scoring low on overall social adjustment. Analysis shows that among the respondents having low life-satisfaction, the proportion of those having low social adjustment (67.2 per cent) is more than eight times higher than those with high social adjustment (7.9 per cent). And among those respondents who score high on life-satisfaction, 2.7 per cent are having low, 18.6 per cent medium and 78.8 per cent high overall social adjustment. Relevant statistics reinforce the findings (rank correlation = +0.67; product-moment correlation = +0.67). It denotes that harmonious social interactions have profound influence over the feeling of life-satisfaction the aged women have.

To sum up, the elderly females should not just ensure their 'survival' rather they must sustain their productivity and enjoy a good quality of life conducive to satisfactory physical and emotional well-being. Considering the health in totality, WHO document, "Ageing: exploding the myths" (1999) recommends protection of income-security over the life course and involvement in family, community, a club or a religious organization along with regular exercise and balanced diet for active life in old-age.

5

SOCIAL ACCEPTANCE OF THE ELDERLY FEMALES

Everyone needs others for sharing, caring and support. Love and belongingness are among the basic needs of the human-being. These needs are fulfilled by social institutions like family, neighbourhood, religious institutions, work place, etc. Formal or informal acceptance of significant-others is crucial for the self-concept and well-being (see Cooley, 1930; Mead, 1937). The elderly are no exception to it. Interaction with family and significant-others, involvement in community affairs, respect from youngers bring a sense of acceptance and satisfaction among the aged (Stevens, 1992). Attention may be paid to the social acceptance of the elderly women in the family and neighbourhood.

The dynamics of interpersonal relationship rests on give and take protocol (Rosow, 1967). For harmonious interaction leading to social acceptance, the responsibility lies on both the relationship-partners. As a logical corollary, persons showing love and care to others often get the same in response. To exemplify, aged women who actively participate, say, in the household chores often get acceptance from the family members. On the other hand, elderly females taking up issues with the youngsters on every big and small matter tend to be avoided by them. So, the integration and, in turn, the well-being of the aged women in the family and community would be determined by the extent of their acceptance. Does the socio-cultural milieu have any influence on the social acceptance of the aged females?

In the agrarian society, the widely prevalent institution of joint-family had not only enabled the aged to be integrated in their family and community, but also provided them the privilege of being the head of the household, clan, village, tribe, and educational and religious institutions. They used to control the family-property. They would occupy the high status of decision-makers in family matters. It is, however, doubtful that aged women enjoyed same privilege as did elderly men. Nevertheless, they would enjoy authority over the younger females of the household. Their status would increase especially when their son brings home the '*bahu*'. They used to act as mediator, educator, doctor, and consultant in various day-to-day family matters. Also, they would play active role in performance of cultural practices, rituals and obligations. They were often consulted in matters related to childbirth and minor health care particularly of women and children not only by females of the family but also in the neighbourhood. They were often approached for matters related to kitchen work like pickle, *bari, chutney, papad* making, food preservation, etc. Elderly women would also play salient role in the socialization of their grandchildren. Story telling by grandmothers used to be not only a recreation for grandchildren but also an important instrument of inculcating manners and values among them. During marriage-fixation and performance and also functions associated with newborns like *annaprassana* (rice-eating ceremony), their advice and contributions were often considered pivotal. Their involvement in these activities helped them in social integration. All these salient roles played by the aged females contributed significantly to their acceptance in the family (Kakkar, 1982; Jamuna, 1995).

However, in modern times, social matrix has undergone changes due to factors, say, commercialization, industrialization and urbanization. Along with, modernization has profoundly influenced the values like inter-dependence, co-operation and self-sacrifice giving way to independence, personal mobility and personal achievement. All these factors have contributed to changes in the structure and functioning of the family system. In this regard, Chaney (1990) asserts that opportunities for empowerment at an older age tend to diminish with modernization. Truly, several salient roles of elderly females have been eroded due to these social changes having an influence over their social acceptance too. To exemplify, now-a-days, cheap plastic goods have replaced handicrafted traditional articles; doctors have replaced midwifery and curing arts of aged females. Similarly, television and computers have blunted indigenous lore, making story-telling by grandmothers an outdated task. And, once elderly females begin to be less productive and socially less useful, their position tend to become increasingly marginal. In view of these social, economic and technological changes, their contributions in the family has gone down, so is the case with their importance and acceptance in the family.

Apart from the family, community and state have also played an important role in ensuring the social acceptance, care and well-being of the elderly. Invariably, the *Panch* members used to be the elderly of the community. They would resolve the familial and property conflicts and would take decisions regarding the welfare of the village. This shows the high level of acceptance and status the elderly enjoyed. Viewing the scenario from the gender perspective, females would remain in the four walls of the household and, in general, would have restricted interaction with the community people. It seems that traditional Indian system puts the females at a disadvantageous position with regard to their acceptance in the community.

Further, in absence of family support, for any reasons, it would be the duty of the village-fellowmen to look after them. Also, community, in terms of *biradary,* has had exerted considerable pressure on families to care for their elderly relatives by making it a code of conduct for younger family members (Singh, 1995). These social institutions had been able to create the fear of social boycott and loss of prestige for the families, if the elderly are left uncared for. Further, religion as an instrument to social control, has played an important role in enforcing the support and care for the elderly. It preaches that, as it is the duty of parents to care for their offsprings, in old age, the children have to serve their parents. It places caring for parents as '*dharma*' or duty of children and goodwill of old parents will bring prosperity in the family. Thus, cultural, social and religious imperatives enjoin upon the younger members to look after their elderly relatives. But, do these institutions have been able to ensure the social acceptance of the aged?

This in view, Cattell (1993) asserts that, presently, the situations of old people in urban settings may vary markedly from those in rural settings, where kin and community relationships are likely to be more salient. In urban areas, the role of community has weakened noticeably. Metropolises, like Delhi, are characterized by impersonality where the neighbours do not even know names of each other. Though today also, the community often looks at the expressions of self-interest of younger generation amounting to abuse to their elderly relatives as somewhat shameful or selfish, but the power of the community to enforce its standards is by no means assured. Inability of the community to exert any pressure for safeguard of the elderly is one of the reasons of high rate of crime against elderly in the cities. Apparently, with the lack of active community-participation, the acceptance of the aged shows noticeable reduction in the urban set-up. Then, what is the situation of the aged women who have remained passive in interactions with the community people?

In India, role of the state in the care of elderly has, more or less, remained substitutive in nature. When the family and community fail to care for their aged, the state is expected to come into action. Constitution of India has made it mandatory for the state to ensure well-being of older persons (see Article 41 of Directive Principles of State Policy). The National Policy for Older Persons, aims to strengthen their legitimate place in society and help older persons to live their life with purpose, dignity and peace. The policy visualizes that the state shall extend support for financial security, health care, shelter, welfare and other needs of older persons, provide protection against abuse and exploitation, make available opportunities for development of the potential of older persons, seek their participation, and provide services so that they can improve the quality of their life. Special attention has been paid to older females so that they do not become victims of triple neglect and discrimination on account of gender, widowhood and age.

Also, for the aged who are not fortunate enough to have a family to care for them, there are around 155 old age homes run with the assistance of Ministry of Social Justice and Empowerment or some philanthropic organizations. Added to this, Criminal Procedure Code, section 125, has recognized the right of parents without any means, to be supported by their children having sufficient means. Does any forceful intervention or coercive approach ensure the acceptance of the aged in the family and community?

The foregoing discussion gives some insight into the social acceptance of the elderly in their family and community. Let us now have a look at the social acceptance of the aged females of Pushp Vihar.

Social Acceptance of Elderly Women

Acceptance of the aged females in the family and community is highly important for their well-being. It gives them a sense of self-worth. Assistance provided by social network helps the elderly deal more effectively with problems that confront them (Chadha, 1996; Krause, 1997). Sugisawa *et al.* (1994) observe that social participation, social support and loneliness have indirect but very strong influence on the mortality of the Japanese elderly. Similarly, Lin *et al.* (1979) bring out that social support is negatively related to the incidence of psychiatric symptoms, and absence of social support is a better predictor of disorders than occurrence of stressful events. Ramamurti (1978) emphasizes that activities that do not involve other people are likely to fail as sources of satisfaction and well-being. Social acceptance of the elderly women, in the present study, is assessed through the roles played in the family and neighbourhood, their involvement in decision-making and the respect shown to them by their family members. Let us look into the various roles played by the respondents in their respective families and neighbourhood.

Roles

Binstock and Shanas (1976) bring out that role-loss deprives people of their social identity. In old age, due to shrinkage of social roles, there is obvious deterioration in self-concept and social acceptance. The elderly are excluded from their prime roles like employment, home-management, parenting, which affect their well-being. However, those aged who replace their lost roles, take initiative in social participation often stay happy and contented. Kincade *et al.* (1996) examine that impressive number of older people in the United States provide assistance in different areas like personal care, child care, volunteer work and offering advice and support in numerous situations. Old people having close relationships, involvement and engagement in various activities exhibit fewer depressive symptoms (Jamuna, 1994; Lee *et al.* 1996). So, involvement in some kind of fruitful and satisfying activities is very important for the social acceptance of the aged. Attention may be paid to the acceptance the respondents get in their family and neighbourhood. What type of roles do they play? Do they mind household activities and looking after their grandchildren? What are the factors that enhance their acceptance?

Role as Wife

Marriage, or the status of 'being married' tends to be associated with decreased rate of mental disorders and a higher health status (Oberoi and Dey, 1991). Marital relationship is one of the closest and vulnerable ones. This relationship offers companionship, responsibilities, security and well-being. Asha and Subrahmanian (1990) report that married aged score higher on positive self-concept and life-satisfaction than their widow counterparts. Has marital status a bearing on the status and acceptance of elderly women?

In the study, married respondents (46.8 per cent) were asked about the most common activity they share with their husband. The range of activities has been arranged from most common ones to rare ones as follows—sitting and talking, going to doctor, evening and morning walks, going to bank, visiting family friends or relatives, going to church, temple, etc., shopping, participation in in-door games (chess, carom, cards, etc.), attending discourses/lectures/seminars and going to movies. Apart from the list of activities given above, some respondents report to watch T.V. with their husband and some prepare meals together. Most preferred activity as reported by the respondents is sitting and talking with their husband (32.4 per cent), followed by watching T.V. (16 per cent), going for morning and evening walks (13.8 per cent) and shopping (13.8 per cent). In old age, couples generally have ample time to share and support each other due to retirement and relative freedom from parental and household responsibilities.

Table 5.1 : Most commonly shared activities by elderly respondents with their husband

Activities	*Percentage*
Sit, talk, games, watching T.V.	57.2
Going to bank, shopping	14.5
Morning and evening walks	13.8
Other activities like going to friends, cooking	10.3
Going to temple, discourses	4.2

For the purposes of analysis, similar types of activities have been grouped as shown in Table 5.1. It brings out that most of the married respondents prefer in-door activities like sitting and talking, playing games and watching television with their husband (57.2 per cent). The proportion of respondents preferring to go out for morning and evening walks (14.5 per cent) is almost one-fourth of the previous category. In old age, certain ailments like cataract, arthritis and other locomotion problems of either partner often tend to hamper their outside-household activities. Another 13.8 per cent respondents go together for shopping and to banks. Such activities go a long way in maintaining healthy and active life-style. Further, 4.2 per cent respondents, considering spirituality a better way to cope with challenges of life, have reported to go to places of worship and for religious discourses with their husband as their most preferred activity. Lastly, 10.3 per cent respondents share other activities like cooking food, going to relatives and friends, etc., with their husband. So, we see, that aged women of Pushp Vihar share several activities with their husband within their limits. These activities ensure their acceptance not only by their husband but also by their family members.

Are the younger aged respondents better accepted than the older ones? Do the type of activities shared with husband has any association with the age of the respondents? Data bring out that in the age-group of 60 to 62 years most common activity the respondents share with their husband is morning and evening walks (40 per cent). In the age-group of 63 to 67 years, respondents attend discourses with their husband (48.3 per cent). Among the older age-group (68 to 96 years) most respondents sit and talk with their husband (58.9 per cent). It implies that when the respondents are in younger age-group, they often go out with their husband for walks, on getting older they often go to doctors together and when the body becomes weaker, they sit and talk with each other. However, relevant statistics show an insignificant relationship between the type of activity shared with husband and the age of respondents (rank correlation = +0.12). Does it signify that health status of the respondents rather than their chronological age influence their type of activities shared with husband?

Data show that among the respondents who go out for shopping with their husband, 20 per cent have low, 40 per cent medium and 40 per cent high health condition. Similarly, among the aged women who most commonly sit and talk with their husband, 28.4 per cent have low, 35 per cent medium and 36.6 per cent high health condition. Relevant statistics show somewhat significant relationship between the type of activity shared with husband and their health condition (rank correlation = +0.23). It suggests that health condition seems to influence the type of activities shared with husband. Healthier respondents tend to have greater acceptance than those with low health condition.

Apparently, type of family also seems to influence the type of activity the aged couple share with each other. Data of the present study show that in joint family system, the most preferred activity of the aged couple is sitting and talking, watching T.V., etc., (77.4 per cent). In nuclear family system, they often go out to bank and shop together (82 per cent). So, circumstances also play important role in the activities the aged respondents prefer to have with their husband. In joint family system, often, younger family members go out for shopping and the elderly sit and chat with each other, while, in families, where only husband wife stay together, they have to share all the responsibilities and activities among themselves. And it is good as far as the social acceptance of the elderly women is considered.

Does the ability to deal with conflicts influence the acceptance of the respondents by their husband? Stated differently, what is the association between the conflict adjustment and the type of activities respondents share with their husband? Among the respondents with low conflict adjustment, the most preferred activity is sit and talk (36.5 per cent). Respondents with medium (42.6 per cent) and high (49.2 per cent) conflict adjustment often go out for morning and evening walks. Relevant statistics also show a significant relationship between the type of activity shared with the husband and conflict adjustment (rank correlation = +0.31). Respondents with high conflict adjustment generally have greater acceptance by their husband. In the same way, overall social adjustment of the respondents also shows some association with the activities shared with husband (rank correlation = +0.27). Analysis shows that among the respondents who prefer to sit and talk with their husband, 41.9 per cent have low, 25.8 per cent medium and 32.3 per cent high overall social adjustment. Also, among the aged women going out to *satsang* with their husband, 20 per cent have low, 40 per cent medium and 40 per cent high overall social adjustment. It may be inferred that the respondents who prefer to just sit and talk often are ranked lower on social adjustment. Aged women having high social adjustment tend to prefer out-door activities. These respondents seem to have greater acceptance by their husband.

Does death of husband affect the acceptance of the aged women in the family and community? With the death of husband, the role of a female as a wife ends. Prakash (1994) observes that 'widowhood' weakens the kinship network from the husband's side. Loss of wife's role restricts certain social interactional patterns. Quite often, widows tend to be ignored, tolerated, rejected or viewed as liability. Doubtless, this adversely affects their sense of worth and self-esteem. Contrarily, study by Pellman, (1992) shows that widowhood, as a factor, doesn't influences the community integration among the elderly women. In the sample, in 58.6 per cent cases their spouses were not with them. Below is the case study of a widow respondent, Ramkali (name is changed) who has replaced her lost role as wife very effectively and has sought high acceptance in the family and neighbourhood.

Live Life Courageously

Ramkali is a 68 years old female living in Pushp Vihar with her two sons, daughters-in-law and three grandchildren. She is physically very active and mentally quite strong. She has a cheerful disposition. She is full of enthusiasm and courage. Ramkali's day starts at 4 a.m. She gets up and stores water as the area is facing water scarcity. She takes bath, does *puja* and prepares tea. Till that time, all other family members are fast asleep. She wakes them up with a cup of bed tea. She looks after her nine months old granddaughter to free her mother for daily chores. She helps her grandchildren in getting ready for school and then drops them to school bus. In her way back, she brings milk and vegetables. In neighbourhood also, she teaches women to make different types of pickles, *papad, chutney* and sweets.

Ramkali can't sit idle. She keeps herself engaged in some work. Her ability for adjustment is seen by the fact that she never insists anybody to do the work the way she likes. Her daughters-in-law praise her a lot and say that even if we are sitting and she is working, she never complains. Even at the time of her husband's death, almost a year ago, she was the one to help others normalize their daily-life. She is liked by her family members and neighbours very much.

It suggests that in old age there is a likelihood of change in roles and status. With the death of husband, long years of togetherness ends and it brings grief and frustration among the aged women. However, if the elderly women learn the skills of Ramkali to take initiative for new roles and responsibilities, it goes a long way in ensuring their social acceptance and well-being. Attention may now be focused to the other salient roles an aged female performs in the family and neighbourhood.

Role in Home Management

Aged women who continue to maintain their preferred active life-style by involving themselves in household chores generally have higher life-satisfaction (see Dhillon, 1992). Similarly, in a longitudinal study, Maddox (1963) explains that those old persons whose activity level has increased over a three-year period tend to have higher life-satisfaction than those whose activity level falls off. However, it may be restated that, due to factors like industrialization and modernization, a number of meaningful roles performed by the aged women, say, guidance to younger females of the family on issues like cooking, home management, child-care, health-care, etc., have shrunk. Does this mean that acceptance of the aged women has also reduced? Do the elderly women helping their daughters-in-law in various household activities are easily accepted by the family members?

In the present study, household activities performed by the respondents are also graded from most common ones to somewhat infrequent ones. They are as follows—preparing tea, coffee; cutting vegetables, salads; keeping things in place; dusting the furniture; mending clothes; preparing meals; cleaning utensils; cleaning/sweeping the floor; and washing clothes/laundering. Other most common activities the respondents perform are supervision of the household work, embroidery, knitting, pickle, *chutney* making and doing all the household work. Data bring out that cooking food is the most common activity the respondents perform (25.1 per cent), followed by dressing up of vegetables, salads (15.7 per cent), cleaning utensils (13.4 per cent) and dusting (12.6 per cent). For analysis purposes, these activities have been grouped into four categories as shown in Table 5.2.

Table 5.2 : Most common household activities performed by the respondents in their household

Activities	*Percentage*
Kitchen work	47.5
Sweeping, dusting, keeping things in place	41.9
Other activities like getting work done by maid, etc	7.6
Mending clothes, embroidery, knitting	2.9

It shows that kitchen work is the most common activity followed by sweeping and dusting the household. The proportion of respondents doing activities like mending clothes, embroidery is very low, may be because of lowering of eye-sight in old age. Many respondents also contribute in terms of getting the work done by maid and supervising the household. It may be inferred that unlike common belief that aged females' roles have shrunk in the modern times, respondents prove to be of significant help in urban families especially where the daughters-in-law are also the earning members. They not only help in small household activities like dusting, cleaning, mending clothes and the like but also in looking after the children and ensuring security of the house. So, household work enables the elderly women to get acceptance by their family members and also gives them a sense of self-worth.

Those elderly women who continue to engage themselves in some activities depending upon their body capacity often gets the benefits not only in terms of health but also in social acceptance. One respondent explains another benefit of involvement in household activity as, "*Main apna saara dhyan silai-kadhai main hi rakhti hun, naa galat sunti hun, naa galat kahti hun*" (I concentrate totally on my stitching and embroidery, neither I listen anything wrong nor do I say). Another one says, "*Ghar ka kaam nahin karen to din katna mushkil ho jayega*" (it would be difficult to kill time if I don't do household work). It implies that engagement in household work also helps them deal effectively with loneliness and sublimates their energy into creative work.

The above mentioned activities done by the respondents may lead to satisfaction if performed willingly. On the other hand, if the aged females are forced to work in the households, then, it may amount to abuse. Results of the present study show that almost three-fourths (75.7 per cent) of the respondents perform the household chores willingly. Another 8.3 per cent aged women feel some pressure in doing these activities and 16 per cent are compelled to do so. Do hale and hearty aged women readily take up household activities while those with fragile health condition often feel compulsion in doing so? Analysis shows that more than one-fourth (27.8 per cent) of the respondents having low overall health condition feel compulsion to do household work. On the other hand, 94.2 per cent respondents, in the category of high overall health condition, willingly do the work. Relevant statistics show a significant association between the health condition of the respondents and their willingness-unwillingness in doing the household activities (rank correlation = +0.31). It may be inferred that healthy respondents often willingly take up the household activities and get acceptance of the family easily than their counterparts with low health condition.

It is often believed that the aged women who actively participate in the household chores share harmonious relations with their family members and feel satisfied with life. What is the position of the respondents in the study? Among the respondents who willingly do the household activities, 17.4 per cent score low and 42.3 per cent rank high on life-satisfaction. Contrarily, 83.9 per cent respondents with low life-satisfaction feel compulsion to do the household activities while none of the respondents with high life-satisfaction figures in this category. Relevant statistics confirm a strong association between the two variables (rank correlation = +0.56). Further, respondents willingly doing the household chores often do not suffer from loneliness (rank correlation = –0.47) and generally have easy sleep (rank correlation = +0.39). Does social adjustment have any association with the willingness-unwillingness of the respondents to do household work?

The components of social adjustment, attitudinal adjustment, conflict adjustment, need adjustment and role adjustment and overall social adjustment are not related to the type of activities performed by the respondents with any statistical significance. However, all these variables are related to willingness or unwillingness of elderly females in doing the household activities. Among respondents with high conflict adjustment, 97 per cent do the household work willingly and those with low conflict adjustment, 45.9 per cent do it with their own choice (rank correlation = +0.49). In the same way, 31.3 per cent respondents with low attitudinal adjustment do the household work unwillingly while only 1 per cent aged females, with high attitudinal adjustment, do so with compulsion (rank correlation = +0.45). Similarly, respondents scoring high on role adjustment (rank correlation = +0.39) and need adjustment (rank correlation = +0.51) often do the household activities with their own choice than their counterparts ranking low on these variables.

Table 5.3 gives the association between the willingness-unwillingness among the respondents in doing the household activities and their social adjustment. It shows that the proportion of respondents doing the household chores out of compulsion is highest in the category of those having low social adjustment and lowest among aged women with high social adjustment. Among the respondents willingly doing the household activities, the proportion of those with high social adjustment is almost double the proportion of those with low social adjustment. Relevant statistics show a strong association between these two variables (rank correlation = +0.51). It suggests that respondents willingly participating in the household activities are often better adjusted and have high social acceptance.

Table 5.3 : Association between willingness-unwillingness among the respondents in doing household work and their adjustment

Overall social adjustment	*Willingness*	*Somewhat compulsion*	*Unwillingness*
Low	46.9	18.0	35.2
Medium	84.4	6.3	9.4
High	98.4	0.0	1.6

This in view, it may be inferred that it is not the type of activities performed by the aged females in the household but their willingness-unwillingness to undertake these activities makes all the difference in their physical, psychological and social well-being. The elderly women who work in the household as per their own wishes often have sound health condition, sleep easily, are satisfied with life, show better adjustment and greater social acceptance than their counterparts who feel compulsion in doing so.

Role as Grandmother

It is often said that in old age shrinkage of roles bring about a chain of deteriorative changes in the life-style of the people (see Sati, 1987). However grey years does bless people with a very significant and satisfying role of grandparent. In a study Roberto and Stroes (1992) find that grandchildren reported stronger relationships with grandmothers than grandfathers. Grandchildren perceived their grandparents, and grandmothers in particular, as influential in their value-development. Does fulfilling the role of grandmother make the path of social acceptance easier?

In this study, the respondents were asked to name the most common activity they have performed or are performing while caring for their infant grandchildren. Quite significant proportion of respondents (21.7 per cent) have never got the opportunity to perform the activities like bathing, dressing, feeding, their infant grandchildren. Table 5.4 shows commonly performed activities of respondents with their grandchildren.

The activities are arranged in the ascending order in terms of level of difficulty and quality of interaction. Helping the baby in sleeping is the easiest, followed by changing nappies, bathing and dressing, feeding and baby-sitting. Table 5.4 shows that the proportion of respondents helping the baby sleep and bathing and dressing are almost equal. The proportion of respondents doing baby sitting is the lowest.

Table 5.4 : Most commonly performed activities by grandmothers during care of their infant grandchildren

Activity	*Per cent*
Bath and dress	22.6
Help in sleeping	20.0
Feeding	16.9
Nappies change	11.1
Baby sitting	7.7
NA/DK/NR	21.7

Grandmother does several activities just after the little baby comes into the world. She helps the baby sleep, changes nappies, bathes and dresses the baby and gives the newborn full protection from harmful environmental conditions. Her long years of experiences in child rearing become handy for mothers in rearing up their child. She further helps the toddler learn sitting, standing, walking and speaking. Grandmother's stories not only have recreational elements but also inculcates in the child values and manners. In urban areas her role becomes all the more important when the young female is working. Though crèche facilities are available in cities but they can never be compared with the warmth of love and care provided by a grandmother to her grandchild. Granny acts as a friend, a guide, a counsellor, a teacher to the child.

In the study, one respondent, with her one-year old grandson in her lap, says, "*Mere pote ne mujhe jeena sikha diya, iske saath khelte hue main apne saare dhukh bhool gai*" (my grandson has taught me how to live, playing with him I forget all sorrows).

"Bhagwan ne mujhe yeh jiti jagti (her granddaughter) gudia dedi khelne ke liye", another aged female, playing with her little granddaughter, expresses, "*Ab araam se mere din kat jaayenge*" (God has given me this living doll to play with, now my days would be spent with ease). Grandchildren provide happiness and contentment to their grandparents, make them forget their loneliness, tension and anxiety and fulfil their life with several roles and activities, which obviously increase their acceptance in the family.

Is the age of the grandmother comes in the way of performing certain activities with grandchildren? Analysis shows that activities done during rearing of grandchildren is independent of age, marital status, educational level and occupational status of the respondents. Also, overall health condition of the respondents does not come in the way of performing activities in the care of infant grandchild.

Data show that 84.7 per cent respondents undertake the activities related to care of their grandchildren willingly. However, there is a substantial proportion of those respondents who do not do so. Among them, 9.1 per cent aged females report to feel some compulsion and 6.2 per cent have no choice to refuse.

Do the aged women who take interest in activities related to caring of grandchildren feel more satisfied with life and show greater acceptance? Does their keen engagement in such activities help them deal effectively with their loneliness, tension and anxiety? Data show that among the respondents who willingly do the child related activities 76.7 per cent do not have anxiety and tension. On the other hand, 88.2 per cent respondents who feel compulsion in doing these activities, often have anxiety and tension. Relevant statistics reinforce the strong association between the variables, having anxiety and tension and willingness-unwillingness in doing activities related to child-care (rank correlation = –0.34).

Likewise, among the respondents who often feel lonely, the proportion of those unwillingly doing the work related to their grandchildren (88.2 per cent) is almost four times (3.7) higher than their counterparts who work with interest (23.7 per cent). Relevant statistics confirm the same (rank correlation = -0.37). Similarly, respondents who willingly take up the activities related to child-care often score higher on life-satisfaction (rank correlation = +0.42). Data show that among the respondents who willingly do the activities related to their infant grandchildren, 18.5 per cent report to have low, 34.5 per cent have medium and 47 per cent have high life-satisfaction. On the other hand, all the respondents who do these activities unwillingly have scored low on life-satisfaction scale. It shows that unwillingness among the respondents to do such activities is more potent in influencing the life-satisfaction than their own choice. Apparently, respondents unwilling to perform activities related to infant-care tend to have lower acceptance of the family members.

Logically, aged females helping in the care of infants would have enjoyed greater social acceptance in their family. Data show that 96.1 per cent respondents with low attitudinal adjustment reluctantly undertake the activities related to infants while none of the respondents with high attitudinal adjustment figures in this category. It shows a significant relation between the two variables (rank correlation = +0.35). Similarly, respondents with low need adjustment often show unwillingness in undertaking child-care activities (rank correlation = +0.43). For obvious reasons, attitudinal adjustment and social acceptance go hand in hand so those respondents sharing high attitudinal adjustment often have greater acceptance in the family.

In the same way, no respondent with high conflict adjustment unwillingly do the activities related to their infant grandchildren in comparison to 96.1 per cent of those with low conflict adjustment. Relevant statistics confirm the same (rank correlation = +0.44). Most of the respondents (96.8 per cent) with high role adjustment keenly do the activities related to their infant grandchildren in comparison to 17.4 per cent of those with low role adjustment (rank correlation = +0.34). Apparently, the former group has greater acceptance by the family members.

The association between the willingness-unwillingness among the respondents in doing the activities related to their infant grandchildren and their social adjustment is shown in Table 5.5. It brings out that none of the respondents with medium or high social adjustment figures in the category of those undertaking the child-care activities unwillingly. This trend is confirmed by relevant statistics (rank correlation = +0.40).

Table 5.5 : Association between willingness-unwillingness among the respondents in doing household work and their adjustment

Overall social adjustment	*Willingness*	*Somewhat compulsion*	*Unwillingness*
Low	62.2	20.4	17.3
Medium	98.6	1.4	0.0
High	96.2	3.8	0.0

It, thus, implies that the aged women who participate in child rearing activities with their own choice often show high scores on life-satisfaction, overall social adjustment and acceptance by the family, they have fewer tension and anxiety and are generally away from loneliness. Does this trend persist when the grandchildren become somewhat older?

The respondents show active interactions with their somewhat grown up grandchildren. They have reported to perform several activities, say, story telling, looking after them after school hours, going to morning and evening walks, playing in-door games and sharing experiences and problems. Such activities go a long way in ensuring their acceptance not only by their grandchildren but also by other family members. Data show that 20 per cent respondents look after their grandchildren after school hours, 15.2 per cent go out with them for walks, 14 per cent talk casually with them. For analysis purposes, similar types of activities have been grouped.

In the sample, 29.8 per cent respondents have had no opportunity for interactions with their grandchildren. Table 5.6 shows the most common activities the respondents perform with somewhat older grandchildren. It brings out that casual talking and sharing experiences is the most frequent activity, followed by looking after the grandchildren after school hours, playing games and going out for morning, evening walks. Least common activity is problem-solving. Results depict high level of interaction between the grandmothers and grandchildren. What is the relation between social adjustment of the respondents and their activities with their somewhat older grandchildren?

Table 5.6 : Commonly performed activities by grandmothers with their grandchildren

Activity	*Per cent*
Story telling, sharing experiences, talking	22.8
Caring after school	20.0
Playing games, going for walks	16.3
Problem solving	11.1
NA/DK/NR	29.8

Analysis brings out some interesting findings about type of activities shared by the respondents with their grandchildren and their social adjustment. It shows that among respondents sharing problems with their grandchildren the proportion of those with high social adjustment is more than fifteen times higher than their counterparts with low social adjustment (see Diagram 5.1). Similarly, respondents with high social adjustment more frequently play games and go out for walks with their grandchildren than those with low social adjustment. However, among the respondents caring their grandchildren after school hours, the proportion of those with low social adjustment is more than double the proportion of those with high adjustment. Similar trends are seen in the case of casual talks and sharing experiences. It seems that caring after school hours and casual talks are the activities having some degree of compulsion while sharing problems, playing games and going out for walks are indicative of higher quality of relationship between grandmothers and grandchildren. That might be the reason for sharp difference seen in the last two activities between the respondents having low and high social adjustment. It may be noted that, in the study, 14 respondents having low scores on social adjustment, though live in the same household, do not have any interactions with their grandchildren for days together.

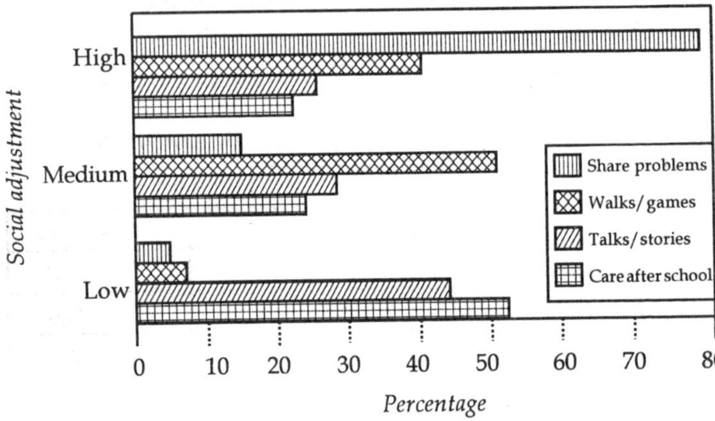

Diagram 5.1 : Social Adjustment and Activities Shared with Grandchildren

So, the aged women, as grandmothers, play a crucial role in the care and socialization of their grandchildren. The activities they share with their grandchildren, if with their own choice, often facilitate them in getting and ensuring acceptance of their grandchildren and also other family members. They do not feel lonely, tense and anxious. However, those elderly females who do not take keen interest in these activities often lose out on psychological well-being and social acceptance.

Role as Friend

Apart from the family groups, peers or friends play an important role in the life of the aged. Friendship is a source of pleasure to old people though less salient than family relationship. It may be noted that in Indian society, most often, women are confined to the four walls of the house. This is particularly true for those who are 60 and above years old today. Peers living in the close proximity of the household are likely to play the role of friend. Chances are these friends often tend to fulfil their relational and recreational needs, are antidote of their loneliness and neglect at the home front. Old females are likely to get sympathy, empathy and acceptance from friends. They tend to act as companion, counsellor and as a back up at the time of emergency. Let us look into the activities the respondents share with their friends.

Data show that 21 per cent of the respondents do not have any friends. Among the rest, 60.1 per cent respondents meet their friends daily, 29.7 per cent meet them once or twice in a week and 4.8 per cent meet their friends once in a month. Another 5.4 per cent respondents have no definite pattern of meeting with friends. Distance between place of stay of friends seems to affect the frequency of contact. Findings show that 70.3 per cent respondents have friends in the nearby place (less than one kilometre) and 29.7 per cent have friends living at far off places (one and more than one kilometres). It may be noted that since having friends is not mandatory, those respondents who have friends have greater acceptance in the community.

In Pushp Vihar, the researcher has observed the elderly females sitting in groups in parks and chatting. They also go to *satsang* with their friends in the nearby temple. Many go out to buy milk from Mother Dairy booth with friends as daily routine. In winters these old females sit and chat in the Sun for hours with friends and neighbours. For widows particularly, such engagements are quite helpful in combating loneliness and grief. Friends also act as a cushion for their catharsis, at some conflicting situations in the household, the aged females often ooze out their anger and frustration in front of their friends. One respondent humorously expresses the importance of friends as, "*Agar meri saheli na ho to main apni bahu ki burai kis se karungi*"? (If I have no friend, then in front of whom shall I backbite my daughter-in-law?)

Now, attention may be paid to the activities shared by the respondents with their friends. These activities, doubtlessly, ensure their acceptance by their friends. Data show that 37.4 per cent respondents sit and talk with their friends, 18 per cent attend religious discourses together, 13.7 per cent go to temple, 5.7 per cent go out for walks, 3.1 per cent do shopping together and rest 0.9 per cent play games and go to picnic with their friends. For analysis purposes, similar types of activities have been grouped. Diagram 5.2 presents the activities respondents share with their friends. It shows that most preferred types of activities have been of in-door in nature. Activities having religious connotation dominate the second position. Outdoor activities like going for morning and evening walks and shopping are in the third position.

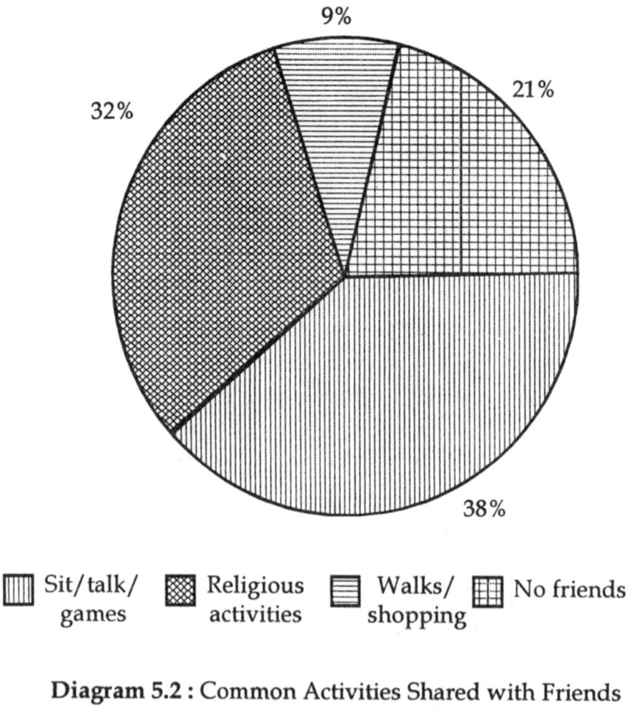

Diagram 5.2 : Common Activities Shared with Friends

Further, data show that religious affiliation, caste, marital status, educational level and occupational pattern are not statistically significantly related to the type of activities shared with friends. Analysis shows that type of activities shared with friends have no statistically significant association with loneliness (rank correlation = –0.10). However, having friends or not having them makes difference in their feeling of loneliness and tension and anxiety. Respondents who have friends with whom they can share their grief and happiness often do not suffer from loneliness (rank correlation = +0.25) and tend to have lesser tension and anxiety (rank correlation = +0.26).

As argued, social acceptance and social adjustment go hand in hand. It is, therefore, important to examine any association between having friends and social adjustment among the respondents? Data show that 30.8 per cent respondents with low social adjustment have friends as compared to 40 per cent of those with high social adjustment. It seems that having friends is not a strong indicator of high social adjustment or *vice versa* (rank correlation = +0.21). Interestingly, findings show that among the respondents who prefer to sit and talk, 42 per cent have low and 27.5 per cent have high social adjustment. On the other hand, among the respondents who go out for walks and do shopping with their friends, 14.1 per cent have low and 59.3 per cent have high social adjustment. Results show that there might not be a significant difference between the social adjustment of the respondents favouring in-door activities to share with their friends. However, the respondents preferring out-door activities often rank high on social adjustment and, thereby, they may have higher social acceptance at least in their peer group.

Thus, we see that though family is of prime importance for the elderly, friends do meet their interactional, recreational and acceptance needs and hence crucial for their well being. They help, to a certain extent, in combating loneliness and tension and anxiety. Also, health and adjustment, though play some role, are not quite significant for sharing activities by the respondents with their friends. In the same connection, attention may be paid to their interaction with neighbours.

Role as Neighbour

Neighbours provide security, assistance, companionship and guidance. Physical proximity makes the neighbours a source of immediate help in case of any need. Blau (1961) reports that older people suffering critical role losses are most likely to have neighbours as friends who have encountered similar losses. However, it is often claimed that cities, particularly metropolitan ones, lack the adequate role of neighbourhood and community in an individual's life. Fast pace of life does not leave any time for interactions with neighbours. In cosmopolitan cities like Delhi, often neighbours do not know even each other's name. This situation is disturbing for the elderly who need others to share their feelings and thoughts. With family members going out to their work place, elderly need friends and neighbours to interact with. What is the situation in Pushp Vihar?

Activity of the respondents with neighbours, to some extent, is an indicator of their social acceptance in the community. Findings of the study show that thirty respondents (8.6 per cent) do not prefer to interact with neighbours. Among the rest, most common activity of the respondents with their neighbours is sitting and talking (79.6 per cent), followed by going to places of worship (9.6 per cent), going for walks (4.0 per cent), attending discourses (2.8 per cent), shopping (2.5 per cent) and playing games (1.5 per cent).

During analysis, similar types of activities have been grouped as shown in Table 5.7. As seen in the case of activities shared with friends, here also, the most common activities shared with neighbours have been of in-door in nature, followed by activities related to going to places of worship and attending discourses. At the third position are the activities like going for walks and shopping.

Table 5.7 : Commonly performed activities by the respondents with their friends

Activity	*Per cent*
Sit, talk, play games	74.0
Go to religious places, attend discourses	11.4
Go for walks, shopping	6.0
NA/DK/NR	8.6

In the study, the researcher has observed somewhat uncommon trend of high level of interaction with neighbours. Often it is seen that the aged respondents have many age-mates in their neighbourhood who act as friends as well as neighbours also. Many respondents do interact actively with younger females in the neighbourhood. Market complexes and schools are within the vicinity of the colony. Aged women are often seen there doing shopping or dropping their grandchildren to school. Four-five places of worship have regular *satsangs* and *kirtans*. Elderly females routinely go there and offer prayers. The colony has several parks where aged women sit and chat with friends. Also walks in mornings and evenings by aged women with their grandchildren are quite beneficial for them. Thus, unlike nearby DDA flats in Saket where aged women have limited interactions with neighbours, this colony has been able to create a community living atmosphere. Still, personal initiatives for interactions are a must and nobody breaches privacy of others. In this backdrop we take a look into the interactions of aged females with their neighbours.

Analysis shows that type of activities shared with neighbours are not related significantly with variables like religious affiliation, caste, marital status, educational level and occupational pattern. Data bring out that health condition of the respondents does not come in way to their interactions with neighbours. Activities shared with neighbours do not show any significant association with loneliness and tension and anxiety (rank correlation = +0.11). Next, the variable social adjustment of the respondents also shows insignificant relationship with the activities shared with neighbours. It may be inferred that unlike family relations, interactions with neighbours are voluntary in nature. So, it is not the type of activity but just active interactions with neighbours that ensure their adjustment and acceptance in the community.

So, we see, that variables like health condition, life-satisfaction and social adjustment are significantly related to the roles of the respondents related to family, like, grandmother, home manager, wife but show not so significant relationship with their roles as friend and neighbour. This in view, it may be inferred that though friends and neighbours play valuable role for the well-being of aged women, acceptance in the family is of paramount importance. Let us pay attention to their involvement in decision-making on important family issues.

Decision-making

It may be restated that in agrarian societies, the aged would, more often than not, play the role of the head of the household. They would take decisions on important family matters, which would be obeyed by younger family members, without any questions. However, in the present day situation, the aged though have not the full authority to take the decisions but often they are consulted on important family matters. Luthra (1991) reports that though respect is shown to older people in rituals, but in everyday life their considerations are ignored. Role in decision-making in the family matters, among others, would signify social acceptance of the elderly females in their household. Let us see the situation in Pushp Vihar.

In the study, the respondents have been asked about various issues on which family consults them while taking decisions. These issues range from giving gifts to relatives and friends to marriage of grandchildren. Data show that 81.5 per cent respondents are consulted while giving gifts or presents to relatives and family friends. During buying clothes for family, 58.9 per cent respondents are consulted. Advice is sought from 62.7 per cent aged females while buying household assets like refrigerator, T.V., etc. Next, 39.6 per cent respondents are consulted in sale and purchase of property like house, car, and scooter. Only 8.9 per cent respondents are consulted during making decision about the education of grandchildren. The reason why only a few elderly females are consulted on this issue may be their low level of education and lack of adequate knowledge on this matter. Further, 69.2 per cent respondents are involved during taking decisions regarding marriage of their grandchildren. It shows that most common issue of seeking consultation of the aged women is giving gifts, followed by during marriage of their grandchildren.

One respondent, during interview, expresses, "*Hamari zarurat to bas shadi-byah main reet riwaz batane ki hi rah gayi hai*" (our importance is restricted only to guide in rituals during marriage ceremonies). Another one justifies the younger generation for not consulting them, "*Hamen kya pata hai? Aajkal zamana itni tezi se badal raha hai, nai-nai jankari jo nirnaya lete samaya honi chahiye woh hamare paas kahan hai, to bachhe hamse salaah kyon len?*" (what do we know, now-a-days world is changing so fast, we lack the recent information needed for taking decisions, so why should children consult us?) It seems that the involvement of the aged women in decision-making in the family is an important indicator of their acceptance.

Results show that age (rank correlation = +0.11) and marital status (rank correlation = +0.11) are not related to consultation on various family issues. It is often said that higher educational status empowers the female to have a say in certain family matters. Findings show that educational status (rank correlation = +0.06) and past occupational pattern (rank correlation = +0.08) have no statistically significant relation with involvement of aged females in decision-making on various family matters. Even the post-graduate respondents have not often been consulted for the education of their grandchildren. Apparently, either elderly females are marginalized or traditional mind-set predominates their educational status.

Data further bring out that the respondents who are consulted for, say, buying gifts for relatives or friends, often rate high on life-satisfaction (rank correlation = +0.46). Likewise, relevant statistics show a strong association between consultation on buying clothes and life-satisfaction of the respondents (rank correlation = +0.58). Among the respondents who have been consulted on this issue, nearly three-fourths (75.5 per cent) of them do not have tension and anxiety. Similarly, among the respondents who are consulted on the marriage of grandchild, 94.4 per cent respondents do not have tension and anxiety. The respondents who are consulted for the marriage of their grandchildren rarely feel lonely (rank correlation = –0.36). Findings show that 40.4 per cent of the respondents who are consulted on matters like buying gifts rate their present life as happy or very happy while none of the respondents who are not consulted figures in this category. Relevant statistics show a strong association between consultation and rating of present life by the respondents (rank correlation = +0.52). So, it may be inferred that consultation on family matters often helps the aged women in their social acceptance and in maintaining self-worth. It is strongly linked to their satisfaction with life and goes a long way in dealing effectively with loneliness and tension and anxiety. Is consultation by the family associated with the social adjustment of the respondents?

Table 5.8 presents the association between consultation by the family on important issues and the social adjustment of the respondents. It shows that, certainly, the respondents having high social adjustment are more frequently consulted while making decisions on certain issues, thereby indicating their greater acceptance in the family. As we move towards more

Table 5.8 : Association between consultation on family matters and social adjustment of the respondents

Issues of consultation	*Overall social adjustment*		
	Low	*Medium*	*High*
Gifts to relatives/friends	24.5	31.2	44.3
Clothes for family	11.9	31.2	56.9
Buying household assets	10.4	30.7	58.9
Sale/purchase of property	0.7	19.8	73.3
Education of grandchildren	0.0	9.5	90.5
Marriage of grandchildren	11.1	30.6	58.3

significant issues like buying household assets or sale or purchase of property or education of grandchild, the difference between respondents with high and low social adjustment becomes sharper. To exemplify, among the respondents consulted on buying household assets, the proportion of those having high social adjustment is more than five times the proportion of those with low social adjustment. Similarly, none of the respondents with low social adjustment has figured in the category of consultation on education of grandchild as compared to most of the respondents with high social adjustment.

The foregoing discussion suggests that it is not the age, marital status or educational status but the social adjustment of the respondents that contributes to consultation in important family matters. The aged women who are consulted, often, show lesser degree of anxiety, tension and loneliness and show high life-satisfaction. These respondents apparently have better social acceptance.

Respect in the Family

Giving unconditional respect to elderly has remained the norm in Indian society. However, as discussed earlier, forces of change has challenged the ascribed status of senior citizens. Nevertheless, many studies show that aged people are still getting love and respect in their families. Desai and Naik (1970) report that most of the old people (84 per cent) get respect from spouse and children as usual and a few (1.6 per cent) have reported that they are respected even more after retirement. So, most of the aged do not perceive that their status has come down with ageing. Kumar *et al.* (1996) discover that 85 per cent of the elderly, in their study, are loved and welcomed by family. Moreover, 60 per cent of elderly are still enjoying status as head of family. More than 98 per cent feel that they have the support of family and friends with them and a similar proportion report congenial home environment. What is the situation in Pushp Vihar?

Level of respect shown to the respondents by their family members appears to have a direct relation with their social acceptance. In the study, the respondents have been asked, "when the members of the family/household come from outside, do they do the following—come and wish you, sit and talk to you, consult you/share with you problems/feelings". Data show that among the respondents living with their sons or sons-in-law, 28.6 per cent are 'just wished' by them. Another

45.7 per cent sons or sons-in-law sit and talk to the respondents and almost one-fourth (24.8 per cent) consult them in personal or familial matters. Further, 0.9 per cent respondents do not share cordial relationship with their sons or sons-in-law, so there is no interaction between them. In the same way, among the respondents living with their daughters-in-law or daughters, 23.3 per cent are 'just wished' by them. In 38.3 per cent cases daughters-in-law or daughters sit and talk with them and 27.3 per cent consult them in the personal and familial matters. Eleven per cent respondents do not share mutually satisfying relationship with their female members of the household.

Further, there are 25.7 per cent respondents who either do not stay with their grandchildren or who do not have any grandchild. Among the rest, in 15.8 per cent cases grandchildren come and wish their grandmothers, 40.8 per cent sit and talk to them and 37.7 per cent consult them in their problems. Rest 5.7 per cent respondents do not have any interactions with their grandchildren. Next, 58.6 per cent respondents do not live with their husband. Among those who stay with them, 6.8 per cent are 'just wished' by them, 40.8 per cent sit and talk to them and 50.4 per cent consult them in their problems. Three (2 per cent) respondents reported to have limited interaction with spouse though they live in same household. It suggests that aged women who are consulted by their family members on certain personal and familial issues tend to have greater acceptance in the family than those who are 'just wished'.

Analysis shows that factors like religion, caste, age, marital status, educational level and occupational pattern are not related, with any statistical significance, to respect given to the elderly female by her family members. However, data show that those respondents who are consulted by their sons often do not face the problems of loneliness (rank correlation = –0.41) and tension and anxiety (rank correlation = –0.26).

Interestingly enough, respect shown by daughters-in-law or daughters does not appear to influence the state of loneliness (rank correlation = –0.10) and tension and anxiety (rank correlation = –0.01) among the respondents. Again, the respondents sharing problems and feelings with their grandchildren generally do not have problems of loneliness (rank correlation = –0.31). The trend becomes much more interesting when we look into the respect paid to the respondents by their husband. Relevant statistics show a significant association between the respect given by the husband and feeling of loneliness (rank correlation = –0.45) and tension and anxiety (rank correlation = –0.23) the respondents have.

It may be inferred that relations of the respondents with their daughters-in-law might be having the shades of traditional prejudices of *saas-bahu.* There are many factors that influence this relationship and, in turn, acceptance and well-being of aged females. The mother of the adult son, who has been habituated to receive affection and concern from her son all along, notices a shortfall in his emotional investment towards her, consequent on his marriage. Understandably, for the son, wife substitutes for most of the activities previously done by his mother. As a result, the degree of his dependence on his mother gets reduced noticeably. *Saas* holds her *bahu* responsible for this shift in attention of her son and starts feeling jealous of her. On the other hand, daughter-in-law no more gets the parental type of affection in the home of her husband, she was used to earlier in her home. She, thus, feels that her mother-in-law is an authoritarian and demanding female. These dynamics in the family colour perceptions between mother-in-law and daughter-in-law. It greatly affects the attention and quality of care that the elderly female receives in the family (see Jamuna, 1995).

Do aged women with high social adjustment get more acceptance and respect from their family members? Diagram 5.3 presents the association between overall social adjustment among the respondents and respect received from family members. Data show that among the respondents, whose sons or sons-in-law 'just wish' them, 69.1 per cent have low and 4.1 per cent have high social adjustment. On the other hand, among the respondents, whose sons or sons-in-law consult them on personal and familial issues, 10.7 per cent have low and 72.6 per cent have high social adjustment (see Diagram 5.3A). So, those aged women who score high on social adjustment, often get greater acceptance and respect from their sons or sons-in-law.

Likewise, among the respondents, whose daughters-in-law or daughters 'just wish' them, 55.3 per cent have low and 6.6 per cent have high social adjustment (see Diagram 5.3B). Contrarily, among the respondents, whose young females of the household share feelings and problems with them, 11.2 per cent have low and 74.2 per cent have high social adjustment. It suggests that the elderly females having high social adjustment generally get greater acceptance and respect from their daughters-in-law or daughters.

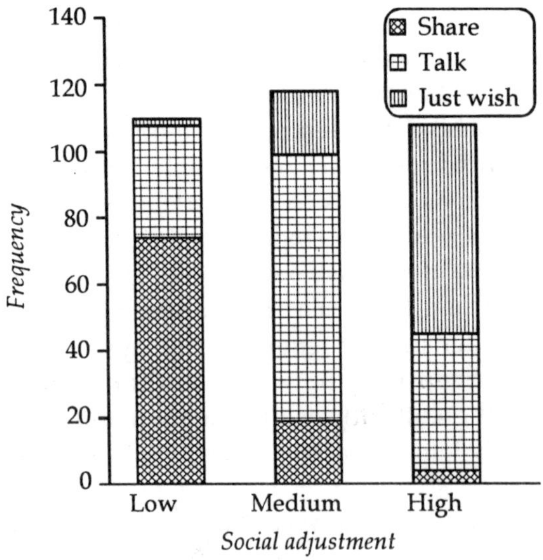

Diagram 5.3 : Social Adjustment and Acceptance by Family Members
A. Social Adjustment and Acceptance by Son/Son-in-law

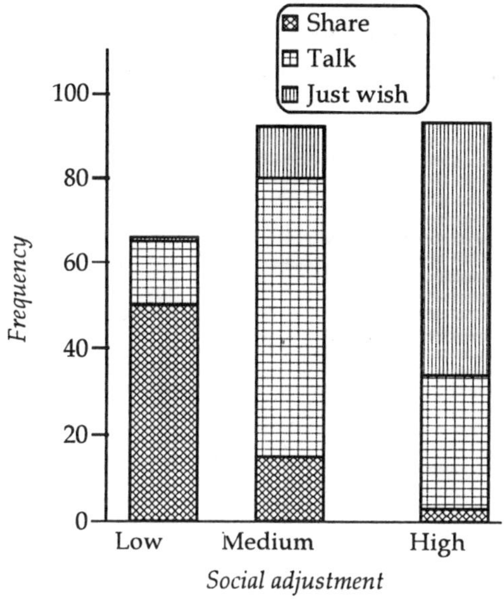

Diagram 5.3 (B) Social Adjustment and Acceptance by Daughter-in-law/Daughter

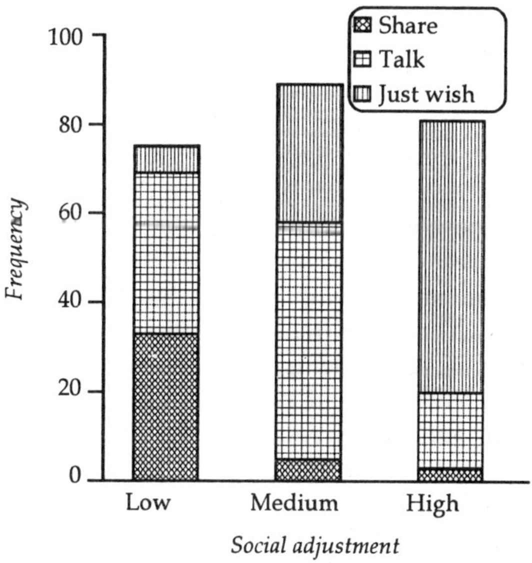

Diagram 5.3 (C) Social Adjustment and Acceptance by Grandchildren

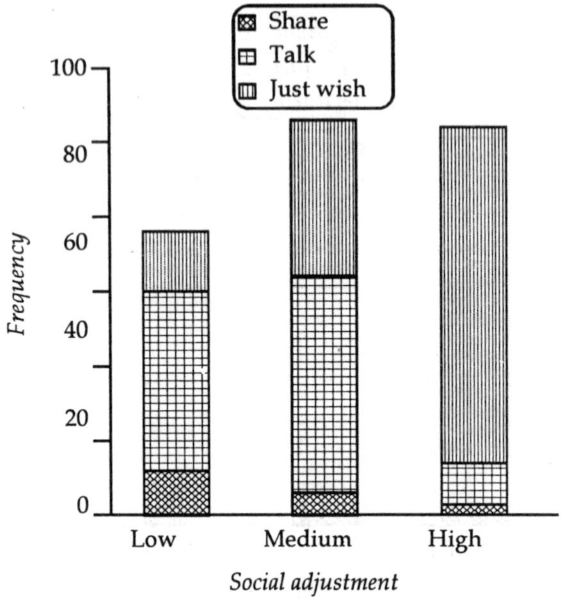

Diagram 5.3 (D) Social Adjustment and Acceptance by Husband

Does the trend of positive association between respect given to aged women and her social adjustment continue in the case of grandchildren and husband? Findings bring out that among the respondents, whose grandchildren 'just wish' them, 75.6 per cent have low and 9.8 per cent have high social adjustment (see Diagram 5.3C). Conversely, among the respondents, whose grandchildren share their problems and feelings with them, 8.2 per cent have low and 70.4 per cent have high social adjustment. Relevant statistics confirm the strong link between the two variables (rank correlation = +0.40). In the same way, among the respondents, whose husband 'just wish' them, 50 per cent have low and 10 per cent have high social adjustment. And, among the respondents, whose husband consult them on personal problems and familial issues, 10.8 per cent have low and 70.3 per cent have high acceptance and social adjustment (see Diagram 5.3D). It shows that the aged women with high social adjustment often get greater acceptance and respect from their husband. Relevant statistics confirm the same (rank correlation = +0.46).

It may, thus, be inferred that social acceptance of the aged women from their family and neighbourhood, to a large extent, depends up on their social adjustment. For better social integration of the aged, efforts should be made in the direction of helping the elderly and their family to develop and maintain harmonious relations with each other.

6

SENSE OF SECURITY AND ADJUSTMENT

In their prime of life, the elderly have contributed to the development of society. In old age, when their capacities wane, it is, therefore, obligatory for the society to stand by them and provide them support and security. The International Plan of Action on Ageing, 2002, also aims to ensure that persons everywhere are able to age with security and dignity and to continue to participate in their societies as citizens with full rights. Security in old age has many dimensions. It ranges from physical independence, psychological support, social integration to economic security. Sense of security is the confidence aspiring assurance for affection, attention, satisfying interaction, expectation to fulfil basic needs, like food, shelter, clothing, medi-care, and relational needs like visits to friends and relatives and symbolic gift-giving. Security is a broad concept with economic security being only one dimension of it.

Elderly and Security

What factors ensured security of the aged in the past? Agrarian economy encouraged joint family system. So, staying together of three to four generations under one roof was common. In the joint family system, property ownership would be in the hands of *karta,* the eldest male member in the family. He would control family's property, income and expenditure. Along with other factors, it ensured security and power to the aged. Often, the status and security of the aged women would be directly related to their husband's position in the family. However, the present-day condition is markedly different. Industrialization has, by and large, changed the earning patterns of the people. Modern technology, more or less, has made the know-how of the elderly somewhat outdated. Besides, specialization in occupational patterns has come up, giving rise to huge differences in earning capabilities of the household members. These factors, on the one hand, have contributed to the waning of joint family system and, on the other, have profoundly influenced traditional norms and values (Desai, 1998). As a consequence, the elderly, more or less, have become dependent on their offspring. The headship of the family changed from the oldest to the bread earner, usually the young. In urban areas the situation is much more grave as, more often than not, the authority and status is achieved on basis of financial position. Due to all these factors, the ascribed status of the aged is slowly becoming less evident. They are emerging as a vulnerable group. Then, what is the condition of aged females who often are considered economically dependent?

Gender Issue

More often than not, the elderly female, in Indian society, identifies herself with her husband. In fact, dependency, economic as well as social, on father, husband and subsequently on son, low level of education and health facilities and all other factors associated with it make an elderly female much more vulnerable than her male counterpart. "If men, who were once active in the labour force", asserts Prakash "and had made substantial tangible contribution, are considered as 'burden', then how will women, who always had been invisible contributors, be treated when they are no longer useful" (1996)? On the whole, Indian workforce is male-dominated with only 31 women working for every 100 men. However, when sectoral share is considered, the primary sector is dominated by women, with female-male ratio of 127.9 per cent. The secondary and tertiary sectors are predominantly male-dominated (Srinivasan and Shariff, 1997). In fact, mainly in the economic activities of primary sector, say, agriculture, where whole family is involved, it is the females who would do most of the work while males enjoy control and ownership. To exemplify, in the hill farming, two bullocks work for 1,064 hours, man for 1,212 hours and a woman for 2,485 hours, in a year, in one-hectare land. So, women work more than the bullocks and men together (Singh, 1987). Due to decreased activity in work place during old age, more and more elderly women have to stay back at home and engage themselves in domestic activities like cooking, house-keeping, child-caring and fetching water, etc., thereby making significant contribution to the family economy. Their economic value is invisible as it is neither remunerated nor acknowledged. Thus, their productive role in the domestic front is unnoticed, unaccounted and is not viewed as a resource in national development (Ramamurti, 1991). In spite of such a hard labour, women generally remain economically dependent on their family. Does it influence their security?

Offspring as Security

Leibenstein (1951) observes that one of the salient motives that determine the fertility behaviour is old age support motive. The third All India Family Planning Survey also reports that almost two-thirds of the couples considered children as their main source of old age support (ORG, 1990). In India, 'son-preference' appears to be synonymous with old age security motive. However, due to several reasons, the aged today cannot take for granted that their children would look after them. It is especially in view of longer life span requiring a longer period of dependency and higher costs to meet health and other needs. It is usually held that a person over 75 years uses eight times more health and social services than a normal adult (Getzen, 1992). These extra expenses start pinching in the family budget. Due to higher costs of bringing up and educating children and pressures for meeting their desires, old parents get lesser share of family income. The situation becomes much more precarious in the case of widows, majority of whom have no independent source of income, do not own assets and are totally dependent (Prakash, 1994). In metropolis like Delhi, many elderly couples live all alone, with relatives paying a few visits in the name of providing care and security. Sometimes children opting to make their career in abroad, leave their old parents behind. They may send enough money to compensate for their care and physical support. Such old persons often become soft targets for criminal elements. Also, it is not uncommon that old people become victims of deceptive dealings and of physical and emotional abuse within the household by family members to force them to part with their ownership rights (see Jamuna, 1995). It is important that security and protection is available to these old persons.

State and Security for Elderly

In Indian Constitution, Directive Principles of State Policy (Article 41) entrusts the state the responsibility of right to work, to education, to public assistance in case of unemployment, old-age, sickness and disablement and case of undeserved want. The Hindu Adoption and Maintenance Act, 1956, lays down obligations on a person to maintain his/her aged or infirm parents. Similarly, Criminal Procedure Code, section 125, has recognized the right of parents without any means, to be supported by their children having sufficient means. National Policy on Older Persons, 1999, sets one of its goals to provide financial security in old age on priority basis. It would also include sensitive taxation policies, special consideration to widows to ensure speedy settlement of benefits on demise of husband and extend the coverage of pension benefits, etc. At present, those who retire from government service, get pension and other retirement benefits, Death-cum-retirement-gratuity, and other benefits. Similarly those in private (organized) sector also get certain benefits from many social insurance schemes. In contrast, for those who are forced to leave work from unorganized sector, due to deteriorating health and old age, do not have any such benefits. In the name of social assistance, state governments do have a few schemes for the poor and destitute aged, main among them being 'Old Age Pension' scheme. However, benefits under this scheme are extremely small, not exceeding Rs.100 a month on an average, and that too is subject to several stringent conditions like age, domicile, absence of means of livelihood, absence of kinsmen (who could support them), etc. Consequently, many elderly persons facing deprivation and destitution, remain out the pail of Old Age Pension (see Khan and Kaushik, 1999).

The foregoing discussion gives a brief view of the social security system in India. What are the factors that lead to feeling of security or insecurity among the aged women? What is the impact of security or insecurity the elderly females have on their well-being? Let us now take a look at the economic condition of the respondents and their feeling of security-insecurity.

Economic Condition of Elderly Females

Certainly, economic condition of the people has a direct bearing on their quality of life. In this regard, although individual variations are significant, older people are considered to be at a disadvantageous position. This is, to a great extent, applicable to the aged women. Their low economic status is often indexed by their participation in comparatively low paying work. Demographic trends show that, as per 1991 census, 59.5 per cent elderly males and 11.2 per cent aged females were main workers. The category of non-workers included 39.4 per cent males and 83.8 per cent females. Several studies show the impact of economic condition of the elderly on their physical, psychological and social well-being. Bhogle and Reddy (1996) observe that the aged belonging to high socio-economic status often experience less depression. Dhillon and Chhabra (1989) highlight that the elderly belonging to lower income group most often tend to escape from the challenges in life. Similarly Monk (1979) reports that economic dependence of the older parents on children may make them suffer in various ways. In order to gain some insight into the economic condition of the aged women we need to take a look into their personal income, husband's income and total income of the household.

Income Distribution

A steady source of income is essential for meeting needs and maintaining the quality of life. It is often said that certain gender discriminating socialization practices like priority to males over education, employment opportunities, etc., have left the aged women with minimal skills to earn. They are, thus, more or less, dependent on their family for their maintenance. Apparently, families with ample resources, most often, do not feel the financial strain while caring for their aged relatives. On the other hand, when resources are scarce, most often than not, youngsters are given priority over the aged. In urban set up where children's education and high cost of living often create financial burden on the parents, care of the elderly especially for the middle and lower socio-economic class becomes a strain. So, the socio-economic background of the household becomes an important factor in meeting the economic needs of elderly females and ensuring their security. Let us first pay attention to the total monthly income of the household of the respondents.

Data show that the range of the monthly income of the household is from Rs.1000 to Rs.26,000. Mean is Rs.9968.2. The data are quite heterogeneous (standard deviation = 3986.76). Skewness (= +0.71) shows that concentration of frequencies is towards the higher income groups. To facilitate further analysis, total monthly income of the household has been divided into three – Rs.1000 to Rs.8000; Rs.8500 to Rs.11,500 and Rs.12,000 to Rs.26,000, cut off points being the 33rd and 67th percentiles.

Do religious affiliation and caste have any association with the monthly income of the family? Findings show that total monthly income of the household has no statistically significant link with religious affiliation as well as educational status of the respondents. However, caste shows some association with the monthly income of the household (rank correlation = +0.19), which is not a strong link. In the highest category of total monthly income (Rs.12,000 to Rs.26,000) the proportion of Brahmins (41.9 per cent) is more than four times higher than the respondents belonging to SC, ST or OBC (9.3 per cent). In lowest category of monthly income (Rs.1000 to Rs.8000), the proportion of SC, ST or OBC and Brahmin respondents is 32.7 per cent each, followed by Vaishya (22.8 per cent) and Kshatriya (11.9 per cent). It implies that the difference in the monthly income of the household between respondents belonging to higher and lower castes becomes acute with increasing income. The reason for this could be due to the differential educational and occupational opportunities available to the people belonging to different castes especially in the pre-independence era. Then, do aged women belonging to SC, ST or OBC more frequently feel unsecured than their counterparts of higher castes?

Husband's Income

It is often believed that married aged women, more often than not, first look at their husband to meet their economic needs than on their progeny. In this regard, past occupational pattern of the respondents' husband plays an important role. In unorganized sector where people earn their living by hard labour, old age may mean end of financial independence. Without any economic security, the aged become dependent on their relatives. If the family fails to care for them, they often become destitute. On the other hand, those elderly who work in organized sectors are covered by social insurance schemes such as pensions, gratuities, leave encashment and provident fund disbursement payable upon their retirement. They cover approximately 11 per cent of the aged population who are likely to be financially better off than their age mates in informal sector.

It may be restated that, in the present study, 48 per cent of the aged men (respondents' husband) were working in government or public sector undertaking. Rest of the 52 per cent elderly men remained out of the retirement benefit schemes. Findings on the past income of the respondents' husband show that 61.4 per cent respondents did not reply (were in the NA/DK/NR category). The range of past income earned by them is from Rs.1000 to Rs.10,000. Average monthly income is Rs.4466.6. The data are widely dispersed (standard deviation = 1725.8) and positively skewed (skewness = +0.47). So, in spite of living in the similar type of apartments, there is a significant difference in the earning patterns of the aged women's husband. Higher income of the husband appears to bring a feeling of security among the aged females.

A look into the old age security measures provided to 48 per cent of the aged men, those who worked in government or public sector undertaking, would be beneficial. They have received gratuity, provident fund and pension. After the demise of husband, the widow becomes eligible for family pension. Apparently, such measures are very valuable for old couple and provide them financial independence and a sense of security. Among the 48 per cent of the aged men, 39.3 per cent have received up to rupees one lakh by way of gratuity, provident fund, etc., 41.7 per cent have got upto rupees three lakhs and 19 per cent have received rupees five lakhs and above after retirement. Further, data on appropriation of the amount received at the time of retirement show that (multiple choice) 68.8 per cent of the aged men have spent it or plan to spend on marriage of their children, 22.6 per cent have kept it as savings, 8.3 per cent have spent it on their medical treatment, 12.4 per cent have utilized it for buying house or shop, 10.7 per cent have spent it on their children's career, 3.5 per cent have paid off their debts and 2.9 per cent have given it to their son for his appropriation. Next, 1.7 per cent of the aged females were not aware of its appropriation and in 1.1 per cent cases they have lost it by becoming the victim of some forgery deal. Does availing retirement benefits ensure security among the aged women?

Coming to the present income of the respondents' husband, the range is from Rs.1000 to Rs.30,000. The average income per month is Rs.3303.2, but with a wide dispersion (standard deviation = 2896.2). There are 64.4 per cent of the aged males in the missing category (NA/DK/NR). Among the rest, two categories have been formed cut-off point being the 50th percentile, first is Rs.1000 to Rs.3000 and second one is Rs.3500 to Rs.30,000. It implies that though quite a significant proportion of the respondents' husband are presently earning, their income distribution shows a wide gap. To what an extent husband's income influences the feeling of security-insecurity among the aged women? Do elderly females who have their personal source of income tend to feel more secured than their age-mates who are financially dependent on others?

Respondents' Income

It seems that elderly females can exercise considerable control over situations influencing them, if they have their own source of income. They can maintain respect, status and security if they are financially self-reliant. Income flows from property, past savings, pension and economically gainful work. Certain activities like household work are not measured in terms of economic gains. Traditional and cultural norms provided opportunities to males to be engaged in economically gainful activities while females were expected to remain financially dependent on the male members of the household. The impact of such norms is clearly visible through the demographic scenario of the economic independence of the elderly in India. There are only 8.78 per cent females in rural areas and 4.84 per cent in urban areas who are economically independent. The corresponding figures for males are 51.06 per cent and 45.71 per cent respectively (source: *Sarvekshana*, 1991). It suggests that, though, it is a fact that, unlike the present situation, most aged females of today had not got enough opportunity to become economically self-reliant. Most of them have remained invisible contributors in the family economy by doing household work. Do the findings of the present study confirm the same?

Data of the present study show that 93.4 per cent respondents had no income of their own in the past while only 8 per cent elderly females were involved in some kind of the economically gainful activities. The range of past income of the respondents is from Rs.200 to Rs.5000 a month. Average monthly income of the respondents is Rs.2069. Data are heterogeneous (standard deviation = 1478.7). Since the proportion of respondents who were engaged in some economically gainful work in the past is too small, no categories of the range of past income of the respondents have been made.

Among those who were involved in economically gainful activities, only 12 elderly women were working in government or public sector undertaking and have received retirement benefits. A look into the appropriation of amount received by the respondents during retirement would give some insight into their actual economic position. Those respondents getting these benefits have saved some part or whole of the amount.

Some of them have utilized certain part of this amount on the career of their children and others had to spend much of their amount on treatment of their illness. It suggests that though economic self-reliance might contribute to feeling of security, the proportion of respondents who were earning is too small. Majority of the respondents have to depend upon others for their needs. Let us look into the present income patterns of the respondents.

It would be recalled that, 84.6 per cent of the respondents, in the present study, are in the category of non-workers or housewife, 14 per cent are receiving pension and 1.4 per cent are doing economically gainful activities like running own shops or other self-employed activities like stitching, embroidery, etc. A large proportion of the respondents (83.1 per cent) have reported to have no income at present. Rest 16.9 per cent of the aged women earn Rs.1000 to Rs.6000 per month. Average present monthly income of the respondents is Rs.1822. Data are highly dispersed (standard deviation = 1169.0).

When asked about other sources of income, only 5 respondents (1.4 per cent) have replied in affirmation. These other sources include interest from bank accounts (4 respondents) and shop's rent (one respondent). Also, 12 per cent respondents (42) are getting money from their relatives like son from abroad (9), son from other city (24), brother (1), husband (6) and in-laws (2). Money sent by the relatives range from Rs.500 to Rs.2000 per month. Do aged females getting money from relatives feel secured?

Table 6.1 : Association between the past income patterns of the respondents and their religious affiliation

	Income of the respondents (Rupees per month)			
Religion	*Minimum*	*Maximum*	*Average income*	*Standard deviation*
Christian	1000.0	5000.0	2587.5	1310.8
Hindu	200.0	4000.0	1672.7	1360.2
Muslim	0.0	0.0	0.0	0.0
Sikh	500.0	5000.0	2125.0	2136.0

On expected lines, there is a strong association between the respondents' educational status and their past income. Relevant statistics confirm the same (contingency correlation = +0.52). Data show that, with a single exception, all the respondents, studied up to eighth standard, were earning between Rs.200 to Rs.2200 per month. On the other hand, respondents studied up to post-graduation were earning between Rs.700 to Rs.5000 per month. Data further illustrate that respondents belonging to Christianity were the highest paid among all working in the past. This is the group who has highest number of graduate and post-graduate respondents. No Muslim female was involved in economic activities outside home. Table 6.1 shows the association between the past income patterns of the respondents and their religious affiliation. It brings out that after Christians, Sikh respondents dominate the income distribution followed by Hindus. It suggests that along with educational qualification, religion also seems to play some role in influencing the past income pattern of the respondents. Religious affiliations, among others, enforce certain norms and practices related to the opportunities given to females for educational and career development.

Regular source of income is essential for elderly females for their subsistence, absence of which can create considerable tension and even misery as seen in the case of Janaki (name is changed).

Daughter's Marriage *vs.* Economic Compulsions

Janaki, a 65 years old widow, lives with her daughter in one bedroom flat. She is the mother of three daughters. Two years ago, her husband retired from CPWD. And, within two months he developed jaundice and was diagnosed as Hepatitis B positive. Money was spent like water on his treatment. There was no improvement. One day he died leaving behind the responsibility of two daughters on his wife, Janaki, eldest being married out during his life-time. After a few months, her eldest married daughter came with a marriage proposal for her younger sister with her brother's-in-law friend. Janaki was constrained to draw upon the money remaining from her husband's retirement benefits to get her second daughter married.

At present, her youngest daughter works in a beauty parlour and she happens to be the only bread earner in the family. With her meagre salary she can't think of anything else other than meeting the daily household expenses. She is crossing 29 years. The helpless mother doesn't have enough resources to marry her off. This is a major source of tension and frustration for the mother. No relatives, no friends come forward to help them. *"Yeh paise ki majboori meri beti ki zindagi tabah kar rahi hai"*, cries Janaki, *"Mujhe koi rasta nahin dikh raha. Mere saath kutch theek nahin hota dikh raha. Main aik besahara badnaseeb maa hun. Main kya karun?"* (This financial constraint is ruining my daughter's life. I can't see any way out. Nothing seems to go right with me. I am a helpless, unfortunate mother. What can I do?)

Aged females having such constraints tend to have feeling of economic-insecurity. Let us now pay attention to the linkage between ownership of property by the aged females and the sense of security-insecurity they have.

Economic Assets

Possession of economic assets symbolizes authority and power. It provides security and confidence to the possessor. In old age, ownership of valuables seems to influence care giving in the family. In the simplest terms, if property is owned and is at the disposal of the elderly, care may be provided primarily in hopes of inheritance. Dak and Sharma (1987) observe that aged women in Rattangarh (in Punjab) have to resort to somewhat coercive techniques to ensure their care and control which included keeping property under lock, secret purchasing of gold and silver ornaments and promising favours with valuables to those female members of the family who serve them best. Those elderly females who tend to distribute their property or other assets early to their children or daughters-in-law often run a risk of neglect in later life.

In the present study respondents were asked to tell whether they have any immovable property in their name such as house, shop, land, orchard, etc. Results show that 78 per cent of the respondents have no immovable property and 19.1 per cent have some property at their name. Rest of the 2.9 per cent respondents have remained quiet over this issue. Further, among those respondents having economic assets, only 10.6 per cent have some monthly income from their immovable property. Rest of the 89.4 per cent respondents do not gain any money regularly from their property or are unwilling to say anything about it. Does possession of economic assets bring a sense of security among the aged women? Do most of the respondents without any property in their name feel insecure? One respondent expresses the role of economic assets in ensuring security, "*Are beta! Aajkal apni aulad bhi tabhi tak apni hai jab tak aapke paas paisa hai*" (now-a-days, own offspring takes care only till the time you have money).

Ornaments are considered to be a female's weakness. In fact, in a society where the female commonly doesn't play active role in currency transactions, possession of jewellery seems to give her a sense of control and power. It is a traditional mean of economic security. In old age, when a female experiences change in her status and authority, ownership of silver, gold and diamond jewellery, to some extent, influences her 'bargaining power' in family in her favour. In the study, 53.4 per cent respondents have no jewellery with them. Next, 21.1 per cent aged females have jewellery up to Rs.10,000 and 25.5 per cent have jewellery up to Rs.20,000 and above. Among those respondents having some jewellery, 61.6 per cent keep it with themselves, 20.6 per cent with some relatives and 17.8 per cent in the bank locker.

As stated earlier, jewellery is an important source of economic security among the elderly females. It seems to have a direct link with the economic condition of the respondents. Analysis shows that possession of jewellery is not linked with the religious affiliation, educational and occupational status of the respondents. However, data show that among those respondents having jewellery worth Rs.20,000 and above, 36 per cent are Brahmins, 32.8 per cent Vaishya, 23 per cent Kshatriya and only 8.2 per cent are SC, ST or OBC. Among those having jewellery worth Rs.10,000, the proportion of Brahmin respondents is highest (33.9 per cent), followed by Vaishya (27.1 per cent), Kshatriya (20.3 per cent) and SC, ST or OBC (18.7 per cent). Among those respondents who do not have any jewellery, 40 per cent are Brahmins, 24.7 per cent SC, ST or OBC, 24.6 per cent Vaishya and 10.7 per cent Kshatriya respondents. It implies that caste seems to influence the purchasing capacity of the respondents and tends to have an effect on their economic status as well as feeling of security.

Having a substantial bank balance seems to provide economic security to the aged women. Results show that 43.7 per cent respondents have no bank account and rest 56.3 per cent have account in one or more than one banks. Looking at bank balance, 57.4 per cent respondents have refused to comment on it. Another 14.6 per cent aged females have amount of Rs. 5000 to Rs. 10,000 and 14 per cent respondents have Rs. 15,000 to Rs. 50,000 in their banks. Another 14 per cent have Rs. 60,000 to Rs. 8 lakhs. Analysis shows that bank balance of the respondents have no statistically significant association with their religious affiliation, caste, educational background and occupational status. What is the impact of bank balance on the feeling of economic security-insecurity among the aged women?

What property and assets mean to an elderly female? Does possession of assets give her power to control things around her? Does lack of it make her unsecured and miserable? Below are two contrasting cases. One demonstrates the power of money through her dictatorship, while the other has lost her mental balance when her property was taken away.

Money is Power

Sukhbir (name changed) is a 64-year old widow. She lives in Pushp Vihar with her two sons, daughters-in-law and five grandchildren. Six years back, after death of her husband, Sukhbir inherited his property, which includes two shops in prime locality and around fifteen lakh rupees. Though studied only up to eighth standard, she manages all money transactions. She has assumed the role of an authoritarian head of the household. Everyone has to ask her even on smallest matters in the family. She enjoys taking all decisions from menu for lunch or dinner to the export policy of their small business of garments. She decides which clothes to be worn by their sons, *bahu* and grandchildren on what occasion. She believes that as she has money she can buy anything from material goods to respect from others. She keeps on scolding her daughters-in-law on slightest opportunity even in front of guests. She insists her grandchildren to utter *"dadi ki jai"* by bribing them with chocolates. The grandchildren also imitate their grandmother when she rebukes their mother. Her sons also remain quiet under their mother's dictatorship, which has come due to power of money.

In sharp contrast we have the case of Mala.

I am a loser

Mala, a 68-year old female, lives with her husband in a two room flat in Pushp Vihar. The old couple does not socialize with anybody, nor do any relatives or friends visit them. They have taken the flat on sublet about five years ago. Mala, very painfully, recalls her golden old days. Her husband was making a lot of money through his business of semi-precious jewellery. She was living with her son and husband in a *kothi* in Greater Kailash. They had four cars and a bank balance of fifty lakhs.

Her husband would demand his unquestioned authority in office as well as at home. One day against their wishes, their son married a poor girl. The angry father asked their son to leave the home immediately. Grief stricken Mala called her orphan nephew to substitute her son's empty place in home. She treated him like her own son and got him married to a beautiful girl.

And one unfortunate day, they lost all their property. Her nephew deceived them by getting the property in his name in a disguised way. Their only one personal bank account, which was not a part of any business transactions was left with them. At present, they are meeting their daily needs through that bank interest only. In spite of best of their efforts, they couldn't get back their property. Mala consoles herself by putting all the blame on her destiny. Her old eyes are filled with tears whenever she remembers her past.

So possession of valuables seems to have an influence on the security the aged women have. No income can give a clear picture of people's economic position unless their expenditures are also taken into account. Let us see the expenditure pattern of the aged women.

Expenditure Pattern

In this study, total expenditure pattern of the family could not be taken into account, as during pre-testing, aged females were not able to tell (nor could it be expected) normal expenses incurred, say, on food, clothing, education, etc. However, expenditure on religious activities has been looked into. Performance of certain religious activities gives a feeling of contentment to the aged women having religious faith. Inability to carry out such activities, say, due to financial constraint seems to bring despair and anxiety among the elderly women. Data show that almost one-fourth (24.9 per cent) respondents spend up to Rs.1000 on religious activities in a year. Another, 29.7 per cent spend up to Rs.3000 and 20.8 per cent spend up to Rs.5000 and above per annum on these activities. Rest 24.6 per cent respondents did not reply.

Does religious affiliation play any role in the expenses incurred on religious activities? Table 6.2 gives the association between these two variables. It shows that among those spending up to Rs.1000 on religious activities, the proportion of Hindu respondents is 35 times higher than those belonging to Islam or Sikhism. Similarly, among the respondents spending Rs.5000 and above on religious activities, the proportion of Hindu aged women is more than three times higher than the second dominant group of Sikh aged women. It suggests that Hindu aged women have highest expenditure on religious activities while Muslim females spend the least on these activities. Analysis further shows that caste, age, educational status, occupational level and total monthly income of the family are not related to expenditure on religious activities. Similarly, overall social adjustment is also not related to this variable.

Table 6.2 : Association between expenses on religious activities and religious affiliation of the respondents

Religion	*Expenses on religious activities (per annum)*		
	Up to Rs.1000	*Up to Rs.3000*	*Up to Rs.5000 & above*
Christian	8.0	6.7	8.2
Hindu	81.6	72.1	64.4
Muslim	2.3	3.8	4.1
Sikhs	2.3	13.5	17.8
Other religions	5.7	3.8	5.5

Next, attention may be diverted to the money elderly women give for their maintenance in the family. Aged women contributing some amount in the family for their up keep are expected to have the feeling of security. On the other hand, aged women who do not or cannot pay anything may have a feeling of dependency on their progeny, which, in turn, seems to have negative impact on their feeling of security and well-being. There are 46 per cent respondents who do not pay anything for their up keep in the household. Another 30.6 per cent respondents pay up to Rs.1000 per month to their family for their up keep. Eighteen per cent aged females pay up to Rs.2000 or more in the family. Rest 5.4 per cent respondents did on reply on this issue.

Data present that religion, caste, occupational patterns and total monthly income of the family are not related to the payment to the family. Has payment for up keep any link with the marital status of the respondents? Relevant statistics show some association between the payment the aged women give to their family for their maintenance and their marital status (rank correlation = –0.26). Among those paying money up to Rs.2000, the proportion of married respondents is almost eight times more than their widow counterparts. In the same way, age of respondents is also related to the payment to family. Among the respondents who do not pay anything, the proportion of those in the age-group of 68 to 96 years (42.2 per cent) is almost one and a half times more than their younger counterparts (27.3 per cent). On the other hand, among those paying up to Rs.2000 and above, the proportion of respondents in the age group of 60 to 62 years (46 per cent) is almost six times higher than those in the age group of 68 to 96 years (7.9 per cent). Relevant statistics confirm the same (rank correlation = –0.24). Does payment to family ensure security among the aged women?

Many times, certain expenditures are held up for want of money. Such situations tend to have a deleterious effect on the well-being of the aged women. Let us see the situation in the study area. On asking whether any of their expenditures were held up for want of money, 4.3 per cent respondents have replied in affirmation. There are seven respondents who could not get their medical treatment due to financial stringency. Equal number (seven) of respondents wanted money for *puja* for survival of their husband and grandchild. One female was upset as because of economic hardship she is not able to get her daughter married off. Such conditions often lead to insecurity among the aged women.

Sense of Security

Security means safety, freedom from danger and anxiety. Does the sense of security only depend upon the financial position of the aged? Barge *et al.* (1994) observe that irrespective of economic development, progeny, particularly son, is considered some kind of a guarantee for old age security and support. D'Souza (1990) brings out those aged who are economically dependent upon their children often have tension and anxiety. Paintal (1991) reports that financial insecurity tends to increase with advancing age. Soodan (1975) highlights that in old age economic stringency brings insecurity and loss of social status. These studies show that age, children, financial position and economic dependence are associated with the feeling of economic security-insecurity.

In the present study, economic security is the feeling of assurance an aged woman has that, irrespective of her economic dependence-independence, her kith and kin would take care of her needs and wants. It is her confidence that she will get money whenever she needs. Her family will come forward for her help when required. In order to measure the feeling of economic security-insecurity, respondents were asked to tell whether they feel that they can get money as per their needs or wishes, say, for going to pilgrimage, for buying fruits, confectionaries, for their medical treatment, etc., (see Diagram 6.1). Data show that 86.3 per cent respondents feel that they can buy clothes for their

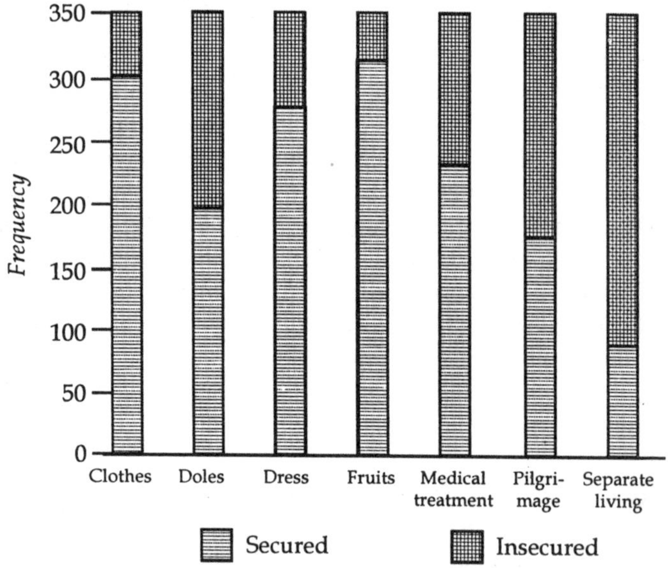

Diagram 6.1 : Respondents' Sense of Security to Buy/Arrange certain things

grandchildren whenever they want to do so. Similarly, 55.7 per cent respondents feel that they can spend money on giving doles, donations according to their own will. Further, 78.6 per cent respondents can buy dresses for themselves whenever they wish and 89.7 per cent feel that they can purchase fruits, confectionary, etc., when they feel like. On medical treatment, 65.4 per cent respondents feel that they can spend big amounts if the need arises and 49.1 per cent can go for pilgrimage or to their relatives, etc., whenever they want to. On issue of managing separate living, if need arises, one-fourth are comfortable and the rest have negated.

For further analysis, a composite variable, economic security-insecurity has been developed by combining the scores of the above seven variables (see Q.22 to Q.28 in Appendix). Score '1' has been given if the respondents have replied in the negative and score '2' in the affirmative. Theoretical as well as observed range of these scores is 7 to 14. Mean score is 11.5. The data are quite homogeneous and consistent (standard deviation = 2.1). For the purposes of analysis, the score has been divided into three—insecure (7 to 10), average (11 to 12) and secure (13 to 14), going by the 33rd and 67th percentile.

Having sons often gives a sense of security as expressed by one respondent, "*Budhape main paise ke liye hum apne bete ka munh nahin dekhenge to kiska dekhenge*?" (In old age, whom else we can depend on for money other than our son?) On the other hand, another elderly lady, feeling economically insecured, comments, "*Main sirf apni aulad par kharch kar sakti hun, khud par nahin*" (I can only spend on my child and not on myself). Economic security is an important factor for the well-being of the elderly women.

Do widows feel insecure more often than their married counterparts? Table 6.3 depicts the association between the feeling of security-insecurity among the respondents and their marital status. It shows that among the widow respondents, the

Table 6.3 : Association between feeling of security-insecurity among the elderly respondents and their marital status

Security-insecurity	*Married*	*Widow/separated/divorced*
Insecure	31.7	54.3
Average	39.0	28.5
Secure	29.3	17.2

proportion of those having feeling of insecurity is almost three times higher than those who feel secured. However, among the married respondents this difference is not so peculiar. Relevant statistics confirm the association between the two variables (coefficient of contingency = 0.22). It somewhat corroborates with the popular belief that a female is more or less dependent upon her husband to meet her needs and she faces financial stringency after the death of her life partner.

It is often held that sound financial position of the husband gives a sense of security to the aged females. However, analysis shows that feeling of economic security-insecurity is not related to husband's past or present occupation and the income raised by him. Further, economic security is also not ensured even by giving payment to family by aged females for their upkeep. Among the respondents who don't pay anything, 42.8 per cent feel insecured, 31.1 per cent average and 26.1 per cent feel secured. On the other hand, those aged respondents who pay up to Rs.1000 per month, 56.1 per cent still feel economically insecured and only 9.3 per cent have feeling of security. Among those aged females who are paying up to Rs.2000 or even more per month for their maintenance, only 39.7 per cent feel secured and 27 per cent respondents still feel insecured. Next, respondent's own income is also not the assurance for their feeling of security. Out of 23 respondents earning in the past, 13 feel secured, 7 average and 3 insecured. Very low number of respondents in the earning category makes the data unfit for any generalization. It suggests that feeling of economic security does not seem to be dependent on the financial position of the respondents.

Quite interestingly, possession of immovable property is not strongly related to the feeling of economic security-insecurity (rank correlation = +0.23). In the same way, there is not a sharp difference between the feeling of security-insecurity among the respondents who have some kind of regular income from their immovable property and those who do not have so (rank correlation = +0.19). In the same connection, data show that having valuable jewellery does not ensure feeling of security. Similarly, keeping jewellery with relatives or in bank locker has no association with the feeling of security or insecurity. It implies that possession of economic assets not necessarily bring the feeling of security among the aged females. Perhaps, traditional mind-set and values of dependence on others come in the way of feeling of ownership and security.

As would be expected, elderly females having bank accounts more often feel economically secured than their counterparts who do not have any bank balance. Table 6.4 shows the association between the feeling of security-insecurity and having one or more bank accounts. It shows that, among those respondents not having any bank account, the proportion of those feeling insecured is almost five times higher than those having feeling of security. However, this difference in the feeling of security or insecurity is not so significant when we look at those respondents having bank account(s). Relevant statistics confirm the same (rank correlation = +0.32). It suggests that not having a bank account is more potent in influencing the feeling of insecurity.

Table 6.4 : Association between the feeling of security-insecurity and having bank account among the respondents

Feeling of security-insecurity	*No bank account*	*Having bank account(s)*
Insecure	60.8	30.5
Average	27.5	38.1
Secure	11.8	31.5

Does dimension of security-insecurity has any relation with the bank balance of the respondents? Among the respondents having a low bank balance (Rs.5000 to 10,000), 47.1 per cent feel insecure and 19.6 per cent secure. On the other hand, among the respondents with a bank balance of Rs.60,000 and above, only 18.4 per cent feel insecure and 44.9 per cent secure. Relevant statistics (rank correlation = +0.27) reinforce the link between the feeling of security-insecurity and the bank balance of the respondents. Also, money sent by relatives does not contribute to sense of security among the elderly women. Next, there were only twelve respondents who have got retirement benefits and all have a feeling of security with two exceptions. Relevant statistics show a strong relation between the two variables (rank correlation = +0.53). On expected lines, all the 15 respondents (4.2 per cent) who complaint that their expenditure was held up for want of money are in the category of economically insecure. Among the rest 335 respondents, 41.2 per cent feel insecure, 34.9 per cent average and 23.9 per cent secure.

The foregoing discussion brings out some interesting trends. Feeling of security-insecurity, more or less, does not seem to be associated with ownership of immovable property, jewellery, and occupational and income patterns. However, it shows some association with the bank account and bank balance. It might be a chance factor or respondents having monetary liquidity have the feeling that money they have in the bank can be used immediately in case of any emergency. What is the impact of economic security-insecurity on the indicators of well-being like loneliness, tension and anxiety, optimism, etc.?

A strong link is observed between feeling of economic security-insecurity and type of sleep among the respondents. Among those who feel secure, 90 per cent have easy and 10 per cent have difficult sleep. Among those who are insecure, 58.8 per cent sleep with difficulty and 41.2 per cent have easy sleep. Relevant statistics reinforce the findings (rank correlation = +0.44). In the same way, tension and anxiety are related to economic security-insecurity (rank correlation = –0.39). Among the respondents feeling insecure, the difference, between the proportion of those having tension and anxiety (51.6 per cent) and those not having them (48.4 per cent), is not significant. However, among the respondents having a feeling of security, the proportion of those who are free from tension and anxiety (90 per cent) is nine times higher than their counterparts having tension and anxiety (10 per cent). Apparently, financial insecurity tends to bring tension and anxiety, which has a direct influence on the type of sleep. So, aged women having feeling of security seems to have easy sleep.

Table 6.5 gives the association between the feeling of security-insecurity and loneliness among the respondents. It shows that among the respondents who often feel lonely, the proportion of those having feeling of insecurity is more than 23 times the proportion of those with feeling of security. On the other hand, among the aged women rarely feeling lonely, the proportion of those with feeling of security is almost three times higher than their counterparts feeling insecure. Relevant statistics reinforce the trend (rank correlation = –0.59).

Table 6.5 : Association between the feeling of security-insecurity and loneliness among the respondents

Security-insecurity	*Feeling of loneliness*				
	Always	*Often*	*Sometimes*	*Rarely*	*Never*
Insecure	33.3	81.6	42.9	14.8	8.5
Average	66.7	14.9	41.8	44.3	38.3
Secure	0.0	3.5	15.3	40.9	53.2

Data further bring out that respondents who feel secured more often consider their health as good or very good. Contrarily, insecure elderly females often score low on subjective health evaluation. None of the respondents feeling insecure figures in the category of very good health condition. Among the respondents considering their health as poor, the proportion of respondents having a feeling of insecurity (77.3 per cent) is more than 25 times higher than those who feel secured. Similarly, none of the respondents, with average or secured feeling, figures in the category of rating their health as very poor. Relevant statistics confirm the same (rank correlation = –0.57). It implies that feeling of security and that of physical well-being go hand in hand.

In this connection, data show that the respondents who do not have feeling of security, more often, rate their past, present and future life as unhappy or very unhappy. On the other hand, aged females having feeling of security often rank their past, present and future life as happy or very happy. Relevant statistics show a strong association between the feeling of security-insecurity and self-rating by the respondents of their past (rank correlation = +0.41), present (rank correlation = +0.64) and future (rank correlation = +0.63) life. It may be noted that the association between economic security-insecurity and rating of present and future life is much stronger than rating past life. Similarly, respondents with feeling of security most often feel that all or most of their expectations from life are fulfiled (rank correlation = +0.60). In contrast, financial insecurity makes aged females often feel that they have not been able to achieve something or anything from life.

On expected lines, secured respondents tend to have bright outlook towards their future as compared to their counterparts with feeling of insecurity. Relevant statistics confirm the strong association between the two variables (rank correlation = +0.59). Diagram 6.2 shows the association between economic insecurity-security and optimism-pessimism. Among the respondents who consider their future bright, the proportion of those who are secured is more than 17 times higher than those with the feeling of insecurity. Similarly, among the respondents considering

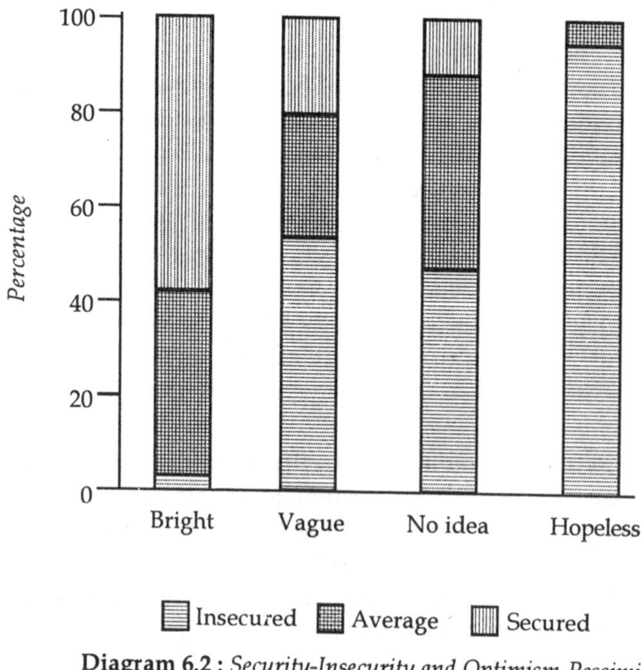

Diagram 6.2 : *Security-Insecurity and Optimism-Pessimism*

their future as hopeless, 94.6 per cent feel insecure and none of the respondents with feeling of security figures in this category. So, feeling of security and optimism show strong linkage.

Does the financial position of the respondents influence the treatment they get from their family? Analysis shows that past and present income of the respondents and their husband, possession of jewellery, immovable property and bank balance are not related to the treatment the respondents get from their family (respectful, indifferent, disdainful). It suggests that sound economic position of the aged women does not ensure their acceptance and respect in the family. In the same way, variables like past and present income of the respondents and their husband, ownership of jewellery, immovable property and bank balance do not have any statistically significant association with the type of dress the respondents wear (fresh, used, mended) and their living arrangement (exclusive room, shared room, *barsati*).

These findings do not confirm the common belief that possession of economic assets can guarantee respect and care from the family members. "*Aaj-kal bacche paise-jaaydad ke peeche thode` hi maa-baap ki izzat karte hain*", explains one respondent, "*Veh khud hi itna kama lete hain ki hamaara paisa unhen nahin chahiye, hum meetha bolenge aur pyar se rahenge to hi voh hamaare paas rahenge nahin to alag ho jayenge*" (now-a-days children don't respect their parents for the sake of money. They themselves earn so much that they do not need our money, if we speak nicely and show love, then only they will come to us otherwise they will live separately). It appears that if aged females have congruent relations with significant others, they have a sense of security and surety that their needs and wishes would be taken care of. On the other hand, incongruent relations often bring a sense of insecurity among elderly women.

Adjustment and Security

Do socially well-adjusted aged women more often have the feeling of security? Paintal (1991) observes that sense of economic insecurity, in old age, affects both, well adjusted and mal-adjusted aged males, equally. Can this finding be generalized? What is the situation in the present study? Diagram 6.3 shows the association between overall social adjustment and economic security-insecurity. It brings out that among the respondents scoring low on social adjustment, the proportion of those with feeling of insecurity is more than 18 times higher than those feeling secured. In the category of respondents with high social adjustment, the proportion of those feeling secured is almost three times higher than aged women having insecurity. Relevant statistics reinforce the trend (rank correlation = +0.50). Perhaps, harmonious interactions with significant others gives a feeling of security, that relatives are there to care for in case of any need.

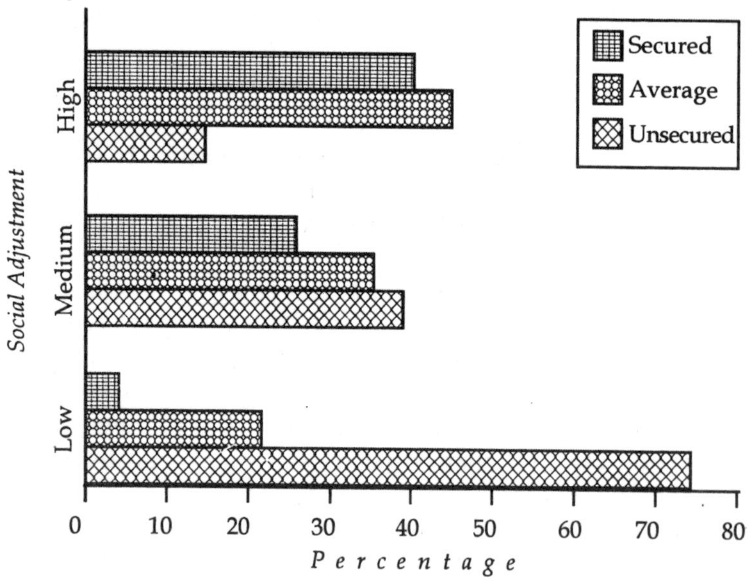

Diagram 6.3 : Sense of Security and Social Adjustment

Apparently, aged women who are accepted in the family often feel secured. Taking involvement of the respondents in decision-making as one of the indicators of acceptance, analysis shows a strong association between the feeling of security-insecurity and consultation of respondents on various issues. Table 6.6 depicts this linkage with relevant statistics. It implies that aged females who are engaged in the decision-making process in the family generally have a feeling of security as compared with those who are not consulted.

Table 6.6 : Association between economic security-insecurity among respondents and their consultation in family matters

Family matter	*Per cent*		*Rank correlation*
	Yes	*No*	
Consulted for gift	81.5	18.5	+0.41
Consulted for clothes	58.9	41.1	+0.44
Consulted for household assets	62.7	37.3	+0.49
Consulted for property	39.6	60.4	+0.53
Consulted for education	8.9	91.1	+0.29
Consulted for marriage of grandchild	69.2	30.8	+0.24

Data further show that respondents having feeling of security do the household work willingly more often than their age cohorts who are unsecured (rank correlation = +0.46). Same is the case with looking after grandchildren. Grandmothers with feeling of insecurity often consider the care of their grandchildren as a burden rather than an enjoyment. Relevant statistics confirm the same (rank correlation = +0.34). It implies that feeling of security influences the social relations.

Let us look into the linkage, if any, between feeling of security-insecurity and overall life-satisfaction. Table 6.7 shows the association between two variables. It brings out that among the respondents who score low on life-satisfaction, the proportion of those who are insecure is more than 46 times higher than their counterparts with feeling of security. Similarly, among the aged women who have high life-satisfaction, the proportion of those with feeling of security is more than 5 times higher than their age-mates with feeling of insecurity. Relevant statistics confirm a strong relation between the two variables (rank correlation = +0.59).

Table 6.7 : Association between security-insecurity and overall life-satisfaction among the aged respondents

Security-insecurity	*Overall life-satisfaction*		
	Low	*Medium*	*High*
Insecure	78.5	39.8	8.5
Average	19.8	36.6	45.3
Secured	1.7	23.6	46.2

Apparently, security often enhances the feeling of life-satisfaction. This confirms to the findings of Streib (1956) who reports that aged people, from higher and middle socio-economic strata, are more likely to show satisfaction with life.

Thus, security is one of the crucial needs of the aged females. As the feeling of security-insecurity is significantly related to the relational variables like social adjustment and acceptance, efforts should be directed towards harmonious relations along with interventions for economic self-reliance of the aged females.

7

CONCLUSION

The world is experiencing a 'grey-revolution' spearheaded by the senescence. Almost all the countries are found having slowly but steadily growing number of the elderly. From 200 million, in 1950, the number of elderly population has risen to 590 million in 2001. It is further expected to increase to 1,100 million by the year 2025. This inordinate increase is largely due to the advances in medical sciences, preventive medicines and improved diet. Furthermore, ageing is turning out to be a major social issue in developing countries. The highest proportion of the elderly population is found in China and India followed by Indonesia. The number of frail elderly population above the age of 85 years is also growing fast. In addition, ageing is being increasingly feminized, as the older population consists of more women than men. This trend is likely to further get accentuated almost worldwide.

For decades, India has been described as a 'young-nation'. However, with declining birth rates and longer life expectancies, elderly population is rapidly increasing. From only 12 million elderly people in 1901, the figure crossed 20 million in 1951 and 57 million in 1991. In 2001, it is estimated to have reached to 76 million. In the next 25 years, this figure may rise to 177 million. Further, 90 per cent of the elderly in India are from the unorganized sector and, hence, most often than not, remain uncovered by social security schemes. Added to this, 40 per cent older people are living below poverty line. Coming to educational background, in 1991, nearly 73 per cent elderly people were illiterate out of which 87 per cent were females. These demographic characteristics of the elderly and more so of elderly females pose a challenge for social planners.

At any rate, global attention is now being focused on elderly females due to several reasons. Firstly, they outnumber elderly males in most countries. Secondly, high rate of widowhood along with morbidity, social and economic dependency makes the aged female highly vulnerable. In 1991, 54 per cent elderly women were widows. Along with the problems of advancing age, aged women have to put up with the implications of prejudice and discrimination of a patriarchal social structure, which India mostly has. Illiteracy, malnutrition, poor health, multiple pregnancies, economic and social dependence on the family, often, aggravate their problems. These demographic changes have an impact at the macro- and also at micro-level.

Old age is an inevitable and universal phenomenon. However, certain socio-economic changes have made it a challenge for the individual as well as the family and community. Urbanization, industrialization, changes in the occupational and income patterns, etc., have noticeably altered the structure and functioning of the family and society, thereby profoundly affecting the situation of the elderly. At the macro-level, reducing dependency ratio is going to put the load of social security for the aged on the earning population. The economy of developing countries is as such burdened heavily to meet the basic needs of its citizens. Providing adequate social security cover to a large segment of elderly population is bound to be a daunting task for these nations.

At the familial level, senior citizens are, generally no longer enjoying the ascribed unconditional authority. The bread-earner, who is usually a young male, gets the headship. Compulsory retirement, vocational and familial engagements of children often shrink the roles of the elderly in the family and community. More so, shoddier is the situation of the elderly females. Earlier on, salient roles of elderly females used to be giving guidance to young females in the household, facilitating decision-making, providing child-care and often mediation. These roles are now seen as occupying a back-seat. Added to this, changing value-system, concepts of privacy and independence, competition and success also sharpen the generation-gap and increase the vulnerability of the aged.

Definitely, urban environment plays a crucial role in the well-being of the aged. While it provides opportunities for advanced educational, occupational, income, medical facilities and civic amenities, it has a darker side also. Characterized by the intense ruthless competition in all walks of life, lack of time for personal interaction, impersonality, growing crime-rate, the urban-life often remains unresponsive to the interactional and relational needs of the elderly. Also, changing roles and expectations of women, their career ambitions and employment outside the home implies considerably reduced time for care-giving to elderly relatives. Limited living space and financial stringency, in urban areas, contribute negatively to the well-being of senior citizens.

Therefore, with increasing number of elderly people in the population, almost every family would be dealing with issues like care-giving and adjustment of their elderly relatives. In this regard, while researchers have focused their attention on retirement and related issues of the elderly, aged females in urban areas have, by and large, remained neglected.

Keeping the foregoing discussion in view, the present work looks into the health, economic security, acceptance by the family and community and adjustment of the aged women living in an urban area. The study aims to find out the impact of the ability of an aged female to adjust, on matters relating to her health, well-being, economic security, life-satisfaction and acceptance by the family and neighbourhood. Towards this, attention has been focused on a large 'middle-income group' residential colony in Delhi, Pushp Vihar. In the light of the objectives of the study, information has been gathered from 350 elderly females in family setting. This has been supplemented by extensive official information, as also by observation.

In order to study the ability to adjust, a Social Adjustment Scale has been developed and administered along with the interview schedule. To gather a comprehensive insight into the situation of the elderly, attention has been paid both to qualitative as well as to quantitative aspects. While interview data have been subjected to extensive computer analysis, a few case records have also been developed which shed much light on the situation of the elderly, their relational and financial anxieties, their interactions with family members and neighbours, and provide a qualitative insight into their situation.

Overview

Chronological age is an important attribute. Not only does it signify role and status in the family and community but also gives some idea about the health condition and activity level of the people. In the study, the age of the elderly females ranges between 60 years to 96 years. Average age is 66 years, which means that most of the respondents are in the 'young-old' age-group. Elderly females in this age-group, in comparison to the 'old-old', are quite hale and hearty and independent in activities of daily-life. However, reduction in eye-sight and gynæcological problems are common. At the social level, aged women, in this age-group, often have to deal with change in role and status with the arrival of daughter-in-law in the family. Elderly females who accept role-change and age related changes without grudges, not only share cordial relations with their family members but also feel satisfied with their life. As would be expected, needs and problems of elderly women are different in different age-groups. Therefore, interventions should be age-group specific.

In patriarchal societies like India, females are culturally expected to be dependent on their father, husband and son at subsequent stages of life. This dependence further increases with widowhood, which is almost concomitant feature of old-age. This is what is shown by the present study. About a half of the respondents are widows. Widows have tension, anxiety and loneliness more often than their married counterparts. The proportion of widows having fear of death is almost three times higher than married aged women. Widows generally have pessimistic attitude. They often view their health as poor. Widowhood affects the well-being. Elderly widows merit special attention of social planners because of their specific needs.

Religion and caste form important components of a person's identity. In consonance with the national statistics, three-fourths of the elderly women, in the study, profess Hindu religion. Indeed, other faiths like Sikhism, Christianity and Islam (in order of frequency) are also represented in the sample. Among the Hindu elderly females, the predominance is of Brahmins, followed by Vaishya, Kshatriya and others. Religion and caste do have some linkage with educational and socio-economic status of the aged females, yet their psychological well-being (optimism, loneliness, type of sleep, social adjustment and acceptance) appear to be independent. Needs and problems, aspirations and adjustment of elderly women cut across the religious and caste differentiation.

In interpersonal relations and psycho-social integration, at all levels, mother tongue is extremely important. In the study, almost a half of the aged women have Hindi as mother tongue and a fifth Punjabi. It may be noted that the two lingual groups are able to interact albeit laconically. So is the case with those who have South Indian tongue. These aspects are likely to have a bearing on interpersonal relations or even on sharing of activities with neighbours.

Length of stay of the elderly women in Delhi influences their adjustment with metropolitan life-style. Majority of the respondents have come to Delhi when they were aged 50 years or more. They often find urban life-style difficult to adjust. Some urban features like fast pace of life, demanding jobs, indifferent neighbourhood may lead to alienation, loneliness, dissatisfaction and low self-worth among aged women until they come to terms with the metropolitan life routine and lower their expectation.

Joint family system used to ensure security and well-being of the aged. However, now-a-days nuclear family groups are becoming popular because of personal preferences and work demands. In the study, most of the respondents are staying in joint family groups, though quite a few adopted and nuclear family groups are also represented on the sample. In joint family system, though the chances of friction and conflicts increase, say, due to differences of opinion among family members, it ensures care and support to the elderly, particularly when, with advancing age, they become more and more dependent on others for daily-life activities. Interventions directed towards empowering the family to care for their elderly relatives and enhancing adjustment of aged women with their family would be a step forward towards realizing the WHO slogan, "Care for the elderly is home-bound".

It is commonly believed that size of the household denotes the opportunity the elderly get to interact and relate. In the study, on an average, six persons make up the household. Majority of the respondents are living with their one son, daughter-in-law and two grandchildren. Having large size of the household does not ease the problem of loneliness among aged females. Further, cordial relationship depends, it is seen, more upon the ability to adjust and not on exactly the number of members in the family.

Education is considered crucial for self-reliance, empowerment and adjustment. Aggregate data on aged females in India show that literacy rate among them is low. The question then arises: Do illiterate or less educated elderly females face adjustment problems? Three out of every ten respondents, in the study, are illiterate. Maximum number of illiterates are represented in the category of 68 to 96 years. Christian respondents are the most educated group particularly in terms of higher education. Similarly, SC, ST or OBC respondents more prominently figure in the category of illiterate respondents. Educational status of aged females' husbands is markedly superior. Psychological problems like difficulty in sleeping, loneliness, tension, anxiety, death-fear, pessimism and dissatisfaction with life affect the illiterate and educated elderly women in the same way. Quality of relationship is also independent of educational attainments of the aged women. So, illiterate, literate and highly educated aged females, more or less, share similar social and psychological challenges.

Most of the aged females have been deprived of skills for economic self-reliance in their youth. Since household chores are not accounted monetarily, being housewife is considered to be non-worker. Past occupational status of the aged women, in the study, gives a grim picture. Majority of the respondents have been housewife. For their economic needs, they have to, more or less, depend on their earning family members. Only a few aged women have been engaged in some economically gainful activities with meagre average monthly income. Present occupational status of the respondents is no better, with majority of the aged females being non-workers. Economic dependence and security of aged females is a prickly issue for gerontologists and social planners who aim to create a society for all ages.

Quite logically, well-educated aged women have had better occupational prospects. However, socio-economic variables like educational status and occupational patterns of the aged women are not linked with variables of psychological well-being like optimism, loneliness, death-fear, self-evaluation of health and life-satisfaction. Similarly, elderly women with high educational qualification and occupational achievement not necessarily show better adjustment in the family and neighbourhood. Qualities like empathy, liberal and understanding attitudes and optimism are independent of socio-economic status of aged females. Enhancing social skills of elderly females appear to be more potent in ensuring their well-being than improving their socio-economic status.

In the absence of their own earning capacity, the elderly females look at their husband for meeting their economic needs. Economic position of the husband has a direct bearing on the financial condition of the aged female. In the study, majority of the respondents' husband were in public sector undertaking or government service and, at present, getting pension. Representation of those in agriculture and private jobs is lesser. Pension, in terms of regular source of income, gives a sense of independence and security to aged women. However, majority of the elderly are not covered by such schemes. Initiatives to expand social security programmes would be beneficial for the security and well-being of aged women.

Family income of the respondents clearly shows the urban character—it is highly skewed and iniquitous. Range of monthly income of the household is from Rs.1000 to Rs.26,000, with an average of Rs.9968.2. Often sound financial position of the household enhances the capacity of the family to care and support their elderly relatives. In families with scarce economic condition generally preference is given to children's needs over the aged while allocating resources. Quite interestingly, feeling of economic security or insecurity among the aged females is not dependent on their family's economic position. Type of relationship the youngers share with their elderly relatives rather than the feeling of obligation towards aged parents seems to be gaining ground while spending money on the needs of elderly. This may explain the reason for no linkage between feeling of economic security the aged females have and the financial condition of their family.

Most of the elderly in the unorganized sector do not receive any social security except a few who are covered under old-age pension which is often too meagre to sustain livelihood. Aged working in organized sector generally receive the retirement benefits like gratuity, provident fund and pension. In the study, only 3.4 per cent respondents have received such retirement benefits. Almost a half of the respondents' husband have got gratuity, provident fund and pension on their retirement. Quite often, these retirement benefits were below five lakhs. This money generally has been utilized in or is kept for the marriage or career of their children. Irrespective of the appropriation of the amount of retirement benefits, aged women who have received some amount are more confident and secured than their counterparts who have remained only housewife. Efforts are needed in the direction of providing some gender specific social security schemes.

Possession of property gives confidence and power. It also influences caring behaviour of the family members in some cases. Majority of the respondents do not have any immovable property in their name such as house, shop, land, orchard, etc. Only about one-fifth of the aged women own some property. It shows the patriarchal character of our society where property is often in the name of males. Further, among those respondents having economic assets, only one in every ten report to have some monthly income from their immovable property. Jewellery is considered an important source of economic security. In the study, more than a half of the elderly females have no jewellery with them. Next, more than a half of the respondents have bank account(s) in one or more than one banks with an average of Rs.10,000. Elderly females having bank accounts, irrespective of the bank-balance generally feel economically secured. However, social adjustment is not related to the possession of immovable property or bank-balance. Property ownership does not ensure, it is observed, harmonious interaction of the aged women with their significant others.

Performance of religious activities gives some kind of psychological satisfaction to the aged. In the study, majority of the respondents spend up to Rs.3000 on religious activities in a year. A significant proportion of them spend up to Rs.1000 and for many this expenditure goes up to Rs.5000 and above per annum. On religious expenditure, Hindus followed by Christians top the list while Muslim females spend the least. Caste, age, educational status, occupational level and total monthly income of the family are not related to expenditure incurred on religious activities by the respondents. Similarly, expenditure on these activities is not related to the adjustment of the aged women in their family.

Many aged females pay some amount to their family for their up-keep. This somewhat reduces their dependence on their offspring and gives them feeling of self-reliance and confidence. In the study, majority of the respondents do not pay anything for their maintenance. Married women more often pay for their up-keep than their widow counterparts. However, even payment to family does not ensure feeling of security among the aged women.

Sometimes certain expenditures are held up for want of money affecting the well-being of aged women. In the study, a few respondents report to have faced their expenditures holding up. Such expenditures have been medical treatment, *puja* for survival of their husband and grandchild and marriage of daughter. In such situations, for obvious reasons, elderly females feel economically insecure. They tend to have low life-satisfaction. To ensure well-being of the aged females, their economic self-reliance is an important aspect.

There are deteriorative changes in the health condition in old age. Sensory capacities reduce and several ailments raise their head. In the study, most aged females complain of their vision going down and one-third face locomotion problems. About 19 per cent of respondents report deteriorative change in their hearing capacity and a few aged women also report of trembling. Majority of the elderly females have blood-pressure problem, followed by gynæcological ailments, diabetes, digestive up-sets and prolonged coughing. Some respondents complain of lever or jaundice problems and a few have had heart-attack in the past. A little over one-third of the respondents have been admitted to hospital in the last two years. Degeneration of health status in old age affects the aged women in their daily-life activities and role performance. Still, decline in health condition can be reduced with adequate nutrition, moderate activity level and positive outlook.

With increasing age, the aged become dependent on others for their day-to-day activities. Almost all the respondents could eat, bathe, dress and walk at their own. A few need help in getting up and sitting and toilet. About one-tenth of the elderly women need help in handling money. Majority of the respondents are able to do small kitchen-work like preparing tea, coffee, heating rice, etc. Added to this, 69 per cent respondents are self-sufficient in taking medicines. About three-fourths of the aged females can do shopping at their own. Two-thirds of the respondents wash their clothes without help. With increasing age, the independence in activities of daily-life decreases. In old-old age group, many elderly women become frail and dependent on others, which significantly affects their well-being and social relations. Caring of frail elderly may be quite taxing for urban families. Short-term care and day-care centres can share the responsibility of such aged people.

Well-being among aged females can be assessed through variables like optimism-pessimism, loneliness, death-fear, tension and anxiety, type of sleep, etc. Generally any psychological discomfort affects natural sleep. Sleep is, thus, an important indicator of well-being. In the study, majority of the aged women sleep easily while some face difficulty in sleeping. Often incongruent relationships affect sleep. Aged women having ability to adjust harmoniously with others often enjoy easy sleep. Further, almost one-third of the respondents have reported to be in tension and anxiety. About one-fourth of the elderly women consider bright future ahead and some feel hopeless. Data trends show that generally respondents who have fewer tension and anxiety have good health condition. Apparently, an attempt to live a tension-free life with 'let-go' attitude goes a long way in maintaining health in old age.

Loneliness and death-fear are often taken as frequently reported problems in old age. Enough free time is considered to be the cause of loneliness. However, it is the discrepancy between the expected and actual size of social interaction and relation. 'Trait-lonely' people feel loneliness even when in crowd. About one-third of the elderly females often feel lonely, 28 per cent sometimes and one-fourth rarely have this feeling. Further, advances in public health have made 'death' a more predictable phenomenon in old age. Almost one-third of the respondents do not feel death-fear and four aged females out of every ten often have this fear. Some of the aged women have fear of death sometimes and a few rarely have this fear. With increasing age fear of death becomes more persistent among the aged women. Poor health condition often aggravates the feeling of loneliness as well as death-fear among the aged respondents. Mal-adjustment generally adds up to loneliness. However, fear of death is independent of social adjustment among the aged women. Counselling and psycho-therapy are important measures to tackle 'trait-loneliness' among the aged women.

Interlinkage between physical health and psychological well-being has been proved beyond doubt. Healthy body gives a feeling of contentment and happiness. Hale and hearty respondents consider their past, present and future life as happy more often than their age cohorts who are frail. Health condition and optimistic attitude go hand in hand. Health status also has significant influence on the roles and relations of the aged women. Poor health condition limits interactions and activity performance. Data show that respondents suffering from poor health condition, more often than not, unwillingly do the household work. Aged women who are healthy take initiative in doing household activities. Interestingly, tension and conflict in relationship with significant others also contributes to rating of own health condition as poor or very poor by the respondents. Congruent relation leads to the feeling of being healthy. Those elderly females who take initiatives for harmonious interactions often enjoy good health. Contrarily, respondents who exhibit poor social adjustment generally suffer from poor health. It, further, emphasizes the importance of enhancing social skills of elderly females for cordial relations.

Mutually satisfying social interactions are crucial for the well-being of aged women. They help in curbing the feeling of loneliness and alienation. Data bring out that those elderly women who are rigid in behaviour and conservative in attitudes often remain in tension and stress. Respondents sharing cordial relations with others consider that all or most of their expectations from life have been fulfilled. On the other hand, aged women frequently engaging in conflicts and tensions with others feel that life has offered only little or nothing to them. It reinforces the linkage between psychological well-being and social adjustment.

Old age often brings ample leisure time as many salient roles shrink. Creative utilization of leisure time brings satisfaction and contentment. Failure to do so may lead to loneliness and alienation. Majority of the respondents, in their leisure time, visit friends, neighbours and relatives, engage themselves in household activities like making pickles, *chutney*, sweets and look after their grandchildren. Many respondents prefer having a nap and about a-third watch television in the afternoon free time. In winters, they bask in the sun do knitting and chat with neighbours. About one-fifth of the respondents do *bhajans, satsang* and the like. A few of them also pursue creative hobbies like embroidery, sewing, etc., in their leisure time. Poorly adjusted elderly females, most often than not, sit idle while those who adjust well, often, utilize their leisure time creatively. Hobby clubs, day-care centres, *satsangs*, can help elderly females to creatively utilize their leisure time as well as adjust well within their family and neighbourhood.

Acceptance by significant others gives a feeling of self-worth. Acceptance and approval depends upon the ability of the aged women to interact and relate harmoniously with others. It is assessed through the roles aged women play, say, that of wife, grandmother, home manager, neighbour and friend, the respect she gets from others and her involvement in decision-making in the family. In the study, majority of the married respondents sit and talk, play games and watch television with their husband. Some prefer outdoor activities, say, morning and evening walks, shopping and going to banks with their husband. So is the case with a small proportion of aged women who go to places of worship and for religious discourses. Perhaps their life mostly hovers around their husband. It is, therefore, hardly surprising to find that these activities have little or no bearing on their level of adjustment with others.

Engagement in household activities provides the elderly female opportunity to win acceptance and respect of the family members. However, a few aged women feel abused when they are made to do household chores. In the study, respondents perform a number of activities like preparing tea, coffee; cutting vegetables, salads; keeping things in place; dusting the furniture; mending clothes; preparing meals; cleaning utensils; cleaning or sweeping the floor; and washing clothes/laundering. Almost three-fourths of the respondents perform the household chores at their own will and others feel compulsion. Poor health condition often makes the aged women unwilling to take up household activities. Also, aged females having incongruent relationships with family members often undertake household chores unwillingly. Enhancing the adjustment ability of aged females and encouraging them to take up small household activities would ensure their greater acceptance in the family.

Old age often blesses people with the role of grandparents. Elderly females, as grandmothers, play crucial role in the care and nurture of infants when young mothers have to devote time to their work-place. In the study, respondents help their infant grandchildren in sleeping, change their nappies, bathe and dress them and help them in feeding. A few aged females take full care of their grandchildren. Elderly women willingly taking up activities for care of their grandchildren often get greater love and respect from their family members.

Grandmothers perform several useful activities while caring for their somewhat grown up grandchildren. Sharing time and activities with each other helps building up bond of affection and respect between grandmothers and grandchildren. Respondents take care for their grandchildren after they come from school, tell stories, share experiences and have casual talks. Some aged women go out for walks and play games and share problems with their grandchildren. Grandmothers having greater ability to adjust often share those activities that involve high quality of interaction and relationship. Aged women having calm disposition and qualities like adaptation and liberal attitudes often share cordial relations and more frequently discuss problems and feelings with their grandchildren. On the other hand, aged women with poor adjustment abilities often crib that they have to do work of caring for their grandchildren at the cost of their own free time. They often face problems in getting love, affection and respect from their family members.

Friendship offers opportunity for companionship, recreation, catharsis, acceptance and support. In the study, almost one-fifth of the respondents do not have any friends. Among the rest, about three-fourths of the aged females have friends in the nearby place (less than one kilometre) and rest of them have friends living at far off places (one and more than one kilometres). Distance between places of stay of friends affects the frequency of contact. A large number of respondents sit, talk and play games together with friends. It is followed by the proportion of respondents going to places of worship and attending religious discourses, going for walks and doing shopping with their friends. Age is not related to the type of activities shared among the friends. Adjustment of the aged women is also not associated with the activities they share with friends. Interaction with peers and friends brings psychological satisfaction to aged women. Elderly club for senior ladies can be an important institution for their recreation and well-being.

Role of neighbourhood is often underlined in metropolitan cities like Delhi, due to characteristics like impersonality, fast pace of life and lack of community feeling. However, in Pushp Vihar, neighbours play an important role for their aged female residents. Almost three-fourths of the elderly women sit and chat, play games, go out for picnic with their neighbours. Some respondents quite frequently go to temples and attend discourses with their neighbours. A few of them go out for walks and do shopping with them. Peers and neighbours, though not a substitute for family, play crucial role for aged females. Participation of elderly women in community work would not only contribute to their greater acceptance but would also increase their self-worth and confidence.

Involvement of aged women in decision-making in family matters indicates their acceptance and integration. Majority of the elderly females are consulted in decisions regarding giving gifts to relatives and friends. It is followed by their involvement in decisions regarding marriage of their grandchildren, buying household assets like refrigerator, T.V., etc., buying clothes for family, sale and purchase of property like house, car, scooter. Only a few grannies are consulted during decision making about the education of grandchildren, may be due to lack of enough information regarding present educational scenario. Consultation of the aged women in household matters gives a sense of worth and acceptance. It also gives a feeling of security among the elderly women. Socially well-adjusted aged women are often involved in decision-making in family matters. Undoubtedly, qualities like adaptation, amiable and loving nature of the aged women go a long way in getting respect and status in the family.

Love begets love and respect begets respect. An aged female who takes initiative for harmonious interaction generally gets respect and affection from her family members. On the other hand, an elderly female with authoritarian and rigid behaviour often receives avoidance and disdainful treatment from the family. Data trends show that respondents with poor adjustment are 'just-wished' by their family members. In juxtaposition, with aged women, having friendly and affectionate behaviour, family members discuss problems and share feelings. Efforts for enhancing adjustment ability among aged females would significantly help in ensuring their acceptance and integration in their family.

Sense of security is a crucial factor for the well-being of the elderly. It is the assurance the aged female has that, irrespective of her economic condition, her significant others would not only fulfil her basic needs, like food, shelter, clothing, medicare, but also provide affection and attention. In the study, majority of the respondents feel that they can purchase fruits, confectionary, etc., and buy clothes for their grandchildren whenever they want to do so. Similarly, more than a half of the aged females are confident of spending money on giving doles, donations as per their will. A little over three-fourths of the aged women feel that they can buy dress for themselves as they wish. On medical treatment, about two-thirds of the respondents feel that they can spend big amounts if the need arises and almost a half of the aged women can go for pilgrimage or to their relatives whenever they feel like. One-fourth of the respondents are confident of managing separate living, if need arises. In the study, most respondents are economically dependent on their family and still majority of them are confident of getting money whenever they need or wish. Sense of security is crucial for the well-being of aged women.

Sense of security is a multi-dimensional concept. Economic security is only one of its dimensions. Data trends show that feeling of security-insecurity, more or less, is not associated with the ownership of immovable property and jewellery the aged females have. It is also not related to the occupational and income patterns of the respondents as well as their husband. Rather, it is significantly related to the relational variables like social adjustment and acceptance. Strained relationships not only psychologically disturb the aged women but also enhance their feeling of insecurity. Aged females having poor ability to adjust often crib over financial insecurity. On the other hand, elderly women scoring high on social adjustment generally feel secure and confident that their kith and kin would stand by them at times of need. In order to enhance the sense of security, efforts should be directed towards harmonious relations along with interventions for economic self-reliance of the aged females.

Sense of security denotes quality of life. Certain factors of psychological well-being are significantly related to the feeling of economic security-insecurity. Sense of security is inversely proportional to the feeling of loneliness. In the same way, feeling of security considerably reduces tension and anxiety. Sense of security lowers fear of death to some extent. Also, secured aged women, most often, consider themselves hale and hearty. Contrarily, insecure elderly females often score low on subjective health evaluation. In the same connection, insecure aged women generally rate their past, present and future life as unhappy or very unhappy. Sense of security and optimism go hand in hand. Feeling of insecurity often makes aged females feel that they have not been able to achieve something or anything from life. Security is positively associated with life-satisfaction. Congruent relationships with significant others is the base of this sense of security. National Policy for Older Persons, 1999, and International Plan of Action on Ageing, 2002, highlight special measures to provide security to elderly women.

Harmonious interaction and relation with others, to a large extent, depends upon the aged females themselves. Elderly women having abilities like good communication skills, tolerance, empathy, acceptance of ageing changes and flexibility adjust better and readily develop congruent relations. They get acceptance, love and respect from significant others. They have a sense of security and feel satisfied with life. They have fewer psychological discomforts like disturbed sleep, loneliness, tension and anxiety, etc. Also, they feel physically fit and healthy. On the other hand, elderly females who are rigid, irritable, authoritarian and punitive fail to get love and acceptance from the family and community, more frequently fall sick and have more psychological disturbances. It highlights the need for helping the aged females enhance their ability for harmonious relations.

Intervention Strategies

In the present study, a typical aged female is 'young-old' in the urban setting. She is a widow and lives with her son, daughter-in-law and two grandchildren. She has not been to school and has been a housewife (non-worker) in her prime time. Nonetheless, the fulfilment of basic needs, generally, is not a problem with her. But, what bothers her is the shrinkage of her erstwhile roles, mainly on account of the presence of her daughter-in-law and, hence, she is required to re-adjust her perceptions and behaviours with the changing situation. Health-wise, her vision has somewhat gone down and she has some ailments like diabetes and gynæcological problems. She is quite capable of maintaining her activities of daily-life independently. As her world revolves around her family, she very much needs acceptance and companionship of her significant others. Given congruent relations with family members and neighbours, she feels secured, contented, happy and free from loneliness, tension and anxiety. Should she have qualities like good communication skills, adaptation, realistic expectation, empathy, optimism, acceptance of ageing and social changes, tolerance, sharing and caring, she is able to forge a bond of harmonious relationship with the family and neighbourhood.

International and national environment are responsive, at least theoretically, to the needs of elderly, particularly elderly females. International Plan of Action on Ageing, 2002, urges up on the nations to create an environment where persons, as they age, enjoy a life of fulfilment, health, security and active participation in the economic, social, cultural and political life of their societies. It further directs to enhance the recognition of the dignity of older persons and to eliminate all forms of neglect, abuse and violence. At the national level, National Policy for Older Persons, 1999, aims to ensure the well-being of older persons by extending support for economic security, health, shelter, and other needs and protection against abuse and exploitation. Older females merit special attention by way of safeguard against becoming vulnerable to discrimination and exploitation on account of gender, widowhood and age. The main issue, however, is how to add satisfaction and happiness to the life of older females—at the ground level.

In the light of the present study certain intervention strategies that emerge are as follows:

1. Health is considered to be the most precious wealth. Among older females, deterioration in strength, impairment and certain ailments are common. Besides, these accompany reduced autonomy in activities of daily-life. Some of them are hypersensitive about their health condition and often feel disappointed. Many aged women have specific nutritional needs and there is a wide scope to create awareness on this. A mechanism needs to be created among them to ensure awareness about nutrition and balanced diet, disease prevention, active ageing life-style, light physical exercise and Yoga and meditation.
2. The aged females who are frail, particularly those in 'old-old' age-group, need constant care and attention which urban households are rarely in a position to provide. Given this scenario, there is a need for short-term hospice (and ambulatory facility) where they would stay for a small period of time and return to their household.
3. Health care needs of older people are given high priority in the National Policy for Older Persons. In order to realize the goal of 'Health for all', there is a need for specialized geriatric services, exclusive geriatric wards and OPDs in hospitals. Geriatric care needs to be a part of the medical curriculum and also a component in the training of paramedics and nurses.
4. Mental health problems like anxiety, depression and dementia afflict quite a few older women. On the other hand, our socio-cultural milieu is not sensitive enough to deal with such problems. Social work professionals and psychologists need to come forward to fill in this gap. There is a wide scope for counselling services for the aged and their family groups on mental health issues. Social workers could also initiate measures to form self-help groups of older females at the neighbourhood level, which would go a long way in alleviating many of the psycho-social problems.

5. Many older females are found facing adjustment problems. Much of it owes to certain personality dispositions like rigidity, conservative attitudes, poor communication skills, aggression, etc. Non-governmental organizations (NGOs) need to take up sensitization programmes to enable the aged females to enhance their social skills for better adjustment.
6. In old age, there is a shift in the role of aged women from a 'provider' to a 'dependent'. This change often brings dissatisfaction. Aged women need to realize that they are capable of leading an active and pro-active life, may be on a restricted scale. Social workers need to closely interact and encourage older women to involve themselves in child-care activities like baby-sitting, dropping and receiving grandchildren at the school bus, giving food after grandchildren come from school, sharing their experiences and problems, accompanying them to playground, story-telling, helping them to go to sleep, etc. Similarly, in household management aged women may be encouraged to oversee the activities of domestic help, facilitate tasks like getting electricity and telephone bills paid (if agencies located within convenient distance). Such an initiative in taking up new roles may greatly help the aged women in better adjustment.
7. The impression gathered during data collection brings out that many school going boys and girls are less than mindful about elderly women in the household. Youngsters need to alter their perspective on ageing and the aged. School social work programmes and socially useful and productive work need to include a focus on elderly and initiate such programmes as 'adopt a granny'. Efforts should be made to inculcate respect and a sense of responsibility towards the elderly.
8. Many aged females are weighed down by certain urban characteristics like impersonality and a lot of free time. They sometimes feel lonely, alienated and neglected.

Towards this, 'day-care centre', a scheme of Government of India, offers them services as reading room, indoor-games, medical check-up, outings, lectures and vocational activities. However, there is a pressing need for the services of day-care centres to expand, both in number and quality. The scheme should have the support of state governments and union territories as a social welfare programme at the neighbourhood or *moholla* level.

9. A large proportion of aged females do not have acute or visible economic problems. On the contrary, many elderly women have jewellery and bank balance. More often than not, they fritter them away. There is a scope to make them aware of the proper management of whatever assets they have. NGOs are in a better position to take up this task. Also, for health related emergencies, options like subsidized health insurance could be worked out.
10. During field-work, the impression was clear that many elderly women suffer from feeling of insecurity, as in the neighbourhood itself, one or two elderly couples were robbed during day-light (in one case, they were even put to death). Elderly persons especially elderly women living alone need to be closely interacted with and advised by social workers and even police men on ways and means to avoid criminal victimization. Further, verification of domestic help, wide publicity of telephone helplines would go a long way in this direction.
11. In the emerging social scenario, older women face a plethora of problems without having a corresponding change in the perspective and attitude of the upcoming generation. In this, media of mass communication have a major role to play. Both print and electronic media need to focalize ungainly intergenerational conflicts and highlight ways and means which younger persons and the aged need to adopt to resolve them.

12. During data collection, the researcher had a close contact with five Resident Welfare Associations (RWAs). Most of the Delhi neighbourhoods have these RWAs. These have a major role to maximize the psycho-social satisfaction of the elderly particularly elderly women. These institutions could assign elderly women specific roles and responsibilities, paying due attention to their age and physical strength, for looking after the upkeep of the neighbourhood or for organizing recreational and cultural activities for children, adolescents and others.
13. Detailed data-base on the elderly is required, having information about their economic condition, type of family, health status in order to make reasonable policies and programmes. Also, social work research has a wide scope in this relatively under-researched area.

Ageing and the elderly is not a new phenomenon. However, due to certain socio-economic changes the aged and especially aged females in urban areas are face to face with several psycho-social problems. Insightful and adequate policy initiatives for the well-being of aged women based on the information regarding their needs and problems gained through research would bring, hopefully, a better, happier and more satisfying 'tomorrow'.

APPENDIX

DEPARTMENT OF SOCIAL WORK
JAMIA MILLIA ISLAMIA,
NEW DELHI-110025

Interview Schedule for the Elderly Women in Delhi

Namaste! I am a research scholar from Jamia Millia Islamia University, New Delhi. I am studying elderly people and their life-style. Towards this, I am meeting and ascertaining the opinion of those who have fund of rich and varied experiences. In this connection, I have a few questions to ask. This may take about 30 minutes. Whatever information I shall gather will be treated as confidential and used only for research purposes. I thank you for all the help and cooperation.

(A) Identifying Information

1. Name:
2. Religion:
3. Caste:
4. Marital status:
5. Mother Tongue:
6. Were you born and brought up in Delhi? If no, when did you come to Delhi (in completed years)?
7. For how long have you been living in this *moholla?*
8. For how long have you been living in this Household?

(B) Family Background

9. Please tell us about your natural family:

S. No.	*Relationship*	*Age*	*Educational level*	*Occupation*		*Monthly Income*	
				Past	*Present*	*Past*	*Present*
1.	Self						
2.	Spouse						

10. Now, please tell us about the household in which you are living at present:

S. No.	*Relationship*	*Age*	*Educational level*	*Occupation*		*Monthly Income*	
				Past	*Present*	*Past*	*Present*
1.	Self						
2.	Spouse						

11. Please tell us, if you don't mind, why you preferred to stay with this household instead of your family?

Economic Condition

12. Do you have any immovable property such as house, shop, land, orchard, etc.? If yes, do you have any idea how much is it worth of? How much income does it give to you?
13. Do you have personal jewellery? If yes, what would be its approximate value? If its value is Rs. 30,000/- or more, where do you keep it?
14. Do you have a bank account? If you have a bank account(s), would you mind telling me what would be the balance as at present?

15. Do you have a son, brother or relative, etc., who gives/ sends you money for your general expenses? If yes, please give details.
16. If your husband was in Government service or any organized sector, did he get any gratuity, P.F., etc.? If yes, how much was it? Could you give me some details of its appropriation?
17. If you were in Government service or any organized sector, did you get any gratuity, P.F., etc.? If yes, how much was it? Could you give me some details of its appropriation? Do you have any other source of income? If yes, please specify.
18. Do you make any payment to the family/household for your upkeep/maintenance? If yes, how much was it?
19. How much is your expenditure on religious festivals like *Holi, Diwali, Shivratri*, etc., during the year?
20. Are there any items of expenditure, which are held up for want of money? If yes, please give details.

Economic Security

21. Can you easily spend money for buying clothes or toys for your grandchildren?
22. Should you feel like can you make large '*daan*' or donations to temple/church or other religious institutions?
23. Are you in a position to buy new sari or dress for yourself whenever you feel like?
24. Off and on, can you buy fruits, biscuits, confectionaries, sweets, etc., whenever you feel like?
25. If ever you need some expensive medical treatment for yourself, do you think you can arrange it?
26. If you wish to visit some of your relatives or to go on pilgrimage can you arrange travelling and other expenses?

27. If ever the need arise, do you think you can make separate living arrangements (house, foods, etc.) for yourself?

Health and Well-being

28. Let us talk about your physical condition. During last five years, what has been the position of the following:

    a. Vision b. Bones/joints
    c. Hearing d. Psychomotor (Trembling)

29. During last two years, have you had any of the following medical complaints:

    a. Blood Pressure (high/low)
    b. Heart problem c. Gynæcological problems
    d. Sugar/Diabetes e. Digestive upsets
    f. Prolonged coughing g. Lungs/breathing troubles
    h. Liver/Jaundice i. Any other, specify

30. During the last two years, have you ever been admitted to a hospital/nursing home?
31. We would like to have some information about your daily life activities. Can you do the following at your own or require some help:

    a. Eating
    b. Bathing
    c. Dressing
    d. Walking
    e. Getting up and sitting
    f. Toilet
    g. Handling money
    h. Simple kitchen work (preparing tea, coffee, heating/preparing rice, etc.)

i. Taking medicines/pills
j. Shopping (nearby market)
k. Washing/Laundering

32. Generally at what time do you sleep?
33. At what time do you rise from your bed?
34. There are people who go to sleep easily and there are those who do so with difficulty. How about you?
35. Sometimes people become much concerned with personal/familial problems, and worry about them day and night. During last one year has it ever happened with you? If yes, please give details.
36. Sometimes people feel lonely, do you feel so?

a. Always
b. Often
c. Sometimes
d. Rarely
e. Never

37. Do thoughts of death ever come in your mind? If yes, how often?
38. How do you rate your health, when you compare it with your age mates?
39. How do you rate your life: Five years ago/ At present/ Five years from now?

a. Very happy life
b. Happy life
c. Blend of happiness and unhappiness
d. Unhappy life
e. Very unhappy life.

40. Often people think of life in the days to come. What is your position? How do you see the future?

a. Bright
b. Vague and uncertain
c. No idea/can't say
d. Hopeless

41. Do you think that whatever you expected from your life you have been able to get it?

    a. Everything of it b. Much of it
    c. Something of it d. Less of it
    e. Nothing of it

Social Acceptance

42. Now please tell us, what are the most common activities, which you share with your husband: Sitting and talking/Going to doctor/Evening/morning walks/Going to bank/Visiting family friends/relatives/Going to temple/church, etc./Shopping/Participating in the in-door games (Chess, carom, etc.)/Attending discourses/lectures/seminars/Going to movies/Any other, specify.
43. When the members of the family/household come from outside, do they do the following: 1. Come and wish you 2. Sit and talk to you 3. Share problems with you 4. None.

    a. Son/son-in-law b. Daughter/daughter-in-law
    c. Grandchildren d. Spouse
    e. Any other

44. What are the most common activities, which you perform in the household:
    Preparing tea, coffee/Cutting vegetables, salads/Keeping things in place/Dusting the furniture/Mending clothes/Preparing meals/Cleaning utensils/Cleaning/sweeping the floor/Washing clothes/laundering/Any other, specify.

    a. Handling of the above chores is your own choice or you have to do it?

    <u>Only to be asked from those having grandchildren in the house</u>

45. At present or earlier on did you do something in looking after your grandchildren? If yes, among the following, which chores did you handle most often: Helping the baby to go to sleep on bed or swing/ Changing the nappies/Bathing and dressing the baby/ Baby feeding/ Any other, specify.

    a. Handling of the above chores is/was your own choice or you have to do it?

46. Your grandchildren are so smart and close to you. We would like to know about your most common activities with them. If yes, among the following, which chores did you handle most often: Story telling/Looking after them after school hours/Going for morning/evening walks/Playing in-door games/Sharing your experiences/Sharing their problems/Any other, specify.
47. You must be having many friends. We would like to know where does your closest friend stay?

    Distance.........................km.

    How often do you phone her/visit her?

    What are your most common shared activities: Sitting and talking/Morning/evening walks/Going to temple/church, etc./Attending discourses/lectures/ Shopping/Outings/picnics/Participation in in-door games (chess, carom, cards)/any other, specify.
48. Now please tell us what are the activities that you most often share with your neighbours: Sitting and talking/Morning/evening walks/Going to temple/ church, etc./Attending discourses/lectures/ Shopping/Outings/picnics/Participation in in-door games (chess, carom, cards)/ Any other, specify.
49. Now, in the last two years, had your family consulted you in the following matters: Gifts/presents for relatives/family friends; Clothes for the family; Buying of household assets like refrigerator/T.V., etc.; Sale/

purchase of property like house/car/scooter; Education of grandchildren; Marriage of grandchildren; Any other, specify.

Life Satisfaction

51. Now would you mind sharing us, how do you rate your life satisfaction (Agree/uncertain/disagree)?

    a. Compared to others of your age, you make good appearance.
    b. As you grow older, things seem to be better than before.
    c. Old age is the most pleasant time of your life.
    d. You are just as happy as when you were younger.
    e. Most of the things you do are boring and monotonous.
    f. You expect some pleasant and interesting things to happen to you in coming years.
    g. The things you do are as interesting to you as they were 30-40 years ago.
    h. You feel old and somewhat tired.
    i. As you look back on your life, you feel satisfied and happy.
    j. You have made plans for things you will be doing in a month or year.
    k. Compared to other people, you get disappointments too often.
    l. In spite of what some people say, the lot of the average man is getting worse, not better.

Social Adjustment Scale

52. Society has changed much but youngers in the family agree with the opinion and advice of the elderly.
53. Given free hand, elderly can bring up grandchildren in a better way than sometimes their own parents.

54. These days, younger women are well-informed and educated and capable of managing household without the help and guidance from others.
55. As family members are busy with their own affairs they have no time for elderly suffering from ailments.
56. Some family members have the habit of being rude to the elders, no matter how many times they are forgiven.
57. When you need, say, some money, family members come at their own to help you.
58. Younger generation is so preoccupied with themselves that they do not even worry whether elderly people have eaten food or not.
59. Younger people have always want to have preference even in taking bath.
60. If you are alone or silent, family members at their own come to you, sit and talk.
61. It is not good for the family and society to allow boys and girls to study and move around together.
62. Even in casual discussions, youngers in the family often raise fresh and relevant points.
63. Whether you speak or remain silent, family members in day-to-day living manage to create issues and arguments.
64. When your, say, *sari* or *salwar-kurta*, needs mending, lady members in the family willingly do the work.
65. Self-centred as they are, younger people take long in the bathroom.
66. Youngers in the family should first introduce visiting friends to the elderly before sitting down to talk to them.
67. If husband and wife in the household are having heated arguments, the elderly need not interfere unless asked to.
68. These days the younger generation tries to dominate the discussion, whatever the issue.
69. Old people in the family have little to give and are a burden on the family.

70. Children and grandchildren ultimately resolve the matter of sharing of household assets like jewellery, radio, T.V., etc., without anybody's advice or interference.
71. The role and importance of the elderly in the family remains the same although their physical strength declines.
72. It does not make any difference whether or not you talk to others in the family about your unhappiness and frustration.
73. Now please tell us what did you do yesterday from morning till night?

Thank you very much

Researcher's Observations

74. Appearance of R: Younger/Normal/Older/NA/DK/NR
75. Dress of R: Fresh/Used/Mended/NA/DK/NR
76. Living Arrangement: Exclusive/Shared/Barsati/NA/DK/NR
77. Posture towards R: Affectionate/Indifferent/Disdainful/NA/DK/NR

REFERENCES

Abrams, Robert C. (1991): The Aging Personality, *International Journal of Geriatric Psychiatry*, Vol.1 (Jan.), pp. 1-3.

Adam, H.E. (1972): *Psychology of Adjustment*, New York: The Reinhold Press.

Adelmann, Pamela K. (1994): Multiple Roles and Physical Health among Older Adults: Gender and Ethnic Comparisons, *Research on Aging*, Vol. 16 (2), pp. 142-166.

Aiken, L.R. (1989): *Later life*, Hillsdale. New Jersey: Lawrence Erbium Associates.

Anastasi, Anne (1990): *Psychological Testing* (6th ed.), New York: Macmillan Publishing Company.

Anderson, Lars (1992): Loneliness and Perceived Responsibility and Control in Elderly Community Residents, *Journal of Social Behaviour and Personality*, Vol.7, No.3, pp. 431-443.

Anklesaria, Firdosh (2001): Stay Fit, Stay Longer, *Indian Express*, October 30, Tuesday, A Fortnightly Express Report.

Aoki, R., Ohno, Y., Tamakoshi, A. and Kawakain, N. (1996): Life-style Determinants for Social Activity Levels among the Japanese Elderly, *Archives of Gerontology and Geriatrics*, Vol. 22(3), pp. 271-286.

Ardelt, Monika (1997): Wisdom and Life-satisfaction in Old Age, *Journal of Gerontology -Psychological Sciences*, Vol. 52B, No.1, pp. 15-27.

Aristotle (1944): Leisure and Lives: Personal Expressivity across the Life Span. In Binstock, R.H. and Shanas, E. (Eds.): *Handbook of Aging and the Social Sciences*, Van Nostrand Reinhold Company.

Asha, C.B. and Subrahmanian, K.A. (1990): Problems of Elderly Women, *Indian Journal of Community Guidance Service*, Vol. 7, No. 3, pp. 61-67.

Bagchi, Kalyan (1997): The Plight of Elderly Females in India. In Bagchi, Kalyan (Ed.): *Elderly Females in India: Their Status and Suffering*, New Delhi: Society for Gerontological Research and Helpage India, pp. 11-22.

Bali, Arun P. (1995): Role of the Family in Elderly Care, *Research and Development Journal*, Vol. 2, No.1, pp. 30-40.

Bali, Arun P. (1995): Status of Gerontology and Geriatric Research in India: An overview and Guidance for further Research, *Research and Development Journal*, Vol. 1, No. 2, pp. 17-29.

Barer, Barbara M. (1995): Men and Women Aging Differently, *International Journal of Aging and Human Development*, Vol. 40, No. 3, pp. 187-207.

Barge, S., Patel, B.C. and Khan, M.E. (1994): Old Age Security in a Changing Employment Environment, *Social Change*, Vol. 24, No. 3-4, pp. 166-179.

Basu, Sanjay (1996): A Study on the Leisure Patterns among Aged Individuals in an Urban Metropolis in India through an Anthropological Perspective. In Kumar, Vinod (Ed.): *Aging: Indian Perspective and Global Scenario*, New Delhi: All India Institute of Medical Sciences, pp. 242-248.

Bhatia, H.S. (1983): *Aging and Society: A Sociological Study of the Retired Public Servants*, Udaipur: The Arya Book Centre Publishers.

Bhogle, S. and Reddy, R. (1996): Depression and Family Jointedness among Aged. In Kumar,Vinod (Ed.): *Aging: Indian Perspective and Global Scenario*. New Delhi: All India Institute of Medical Sciences, pp. 178-181.

Binstock, R.H. and Shanas, E. (1976): *Handbook of Aging and Social Sciences*, New York: Van Nostrand Reinhold Company.

Birren, J.E. and Renner, V.J. (1977): Research on the Psychology of Aging. In Birren, J.E. and Schale, K.W. (Eds.): *Handbook of Psychology of Aging*, New York: Van Nostrand Reinhold.

Birren, J.E., Butler, R.N., Greenhouse, S.W., Sokoloff, L. and Yarrow, M.R. (1963): Human Aging, *Public Health Service*, Publication number 989, Washington.

Birren, J.E., Woods, A.M. and Williams, M.V. (1980): Behaviour Showing with Age: Causes, Organization and Consequences. In Poon, L.W. (Ed.): *Aging in the 1980's: Psychological Issues*, Washington, D.C.: American Psychological Association.

Birren, James E. (1959): Principal of Research on Aging. In Birren J.E. (Ed.): *Handbook of Aging and the Individual: Psychological and Biological Aspects*, Chicago: The University of Chicago Press.

Birren, James E. (1960): *Handbook of Aging and the Individual: Psychological and Biological Aspects*, Chicago: University of Chicago Press.

Biswas, S.K. (1994): Implications of Population Ageing in India. In Ramchandran, C.R. and Shah, Bela (Eds.): *Public Health Implications of Aging in India*, New Delhi: Indian Council of Medical Research, pp. 22-35.

Blau, Zena Smith (1961): Structural Constraints on Friendships in Old Age, *American Sociological Review*, Vol. 26, No. 2, pp. 429-439.

Blazer, D. and Palmore, E. (1971): Religion and Aging in Longitudinal Panel, *The Gerontologist*, 16, Vol. 1, pp. 82-85.

Bond, M.J. and Feather, N.T. (1988): Some Correlates of Structure and Purpose in the Use of Time, *Journal of Personality and Social Psychology*, 25(1), 321-329.

Bose, A.B. and Gangrede, K.D. (Eds.), (1988): *The Aging in India: Problems and Potentialities*, New Delhi: Abhinav publications.

Bose, Ashish (1996): *India's Basic Demographic Statistics*, Delhi: B.R. Publishing Corporations.

Bose, Ashish (1998): *Demographic Diversity of India, 1991 census, State and district level data supplement*, New Delhi: Ministry of Human Resources Development.

Bose, Ashish, (2000): Demographic Transition, *Seminar*, 488, April 2000, pp. 35-39.

Bosworth, Hayden, B. and Schaie, K. Warner (1997): The Relationship of Social Environment, Social Networks, and Health Outcomes in the Seattle Longitudinal Study: Two

Analytical Approaches, *Journal of Gerontology- Psychological Sciences*, Vol. 52B, No. 5, pp. P197-P205.

Bromley, D.B. (1974): *The Psychology of Human Aging*, (2nd Ed.), Baltimore: Penguin Books.

Burgess, R.L. (1981): Relationships in Marriage and the Family. In Duck, S.W. and Gilmour, R. (Eds.): *Personal Relationships*, London and New York: Academic Press.

Butler, R.N. and Lewis, M.I. (1977): *Aging and Mental Health*. C.V. Mosby, St. Louis. MO.

Cannon, W.B. (1963): *The Wisdom of the Body*, New York: W.W. Norton and Company.

Cappella, J.N. (1988): Personal Relationships, Social Relationships and Patterns of Interaction in Social Work. In Duck, S.W., Hay, D.F., Hobfoll, H.E., Ickes, W.J. and Montgomery, B.M. (Eds.): *Handbook of Personal Relationships*, Chichester Wiley, pp. 325-342.

Cattell, Maria G. (1993): Caring for the Elderly in Sub Saharan Africa, *Aging International*, Vol. 20 (2), pp. 13-19.

Chadha, N.K. (1989): *Impact of Institutionalization on the Psychological Well-being and Depression among the Aged*, MS, National Symposium on Stress, Anxiety and Depression in Modern life, (Nov., 3-4, Patiala), Panjab University.

Chadha, N.K. (1991): Self-concept and Life-satisfaction among Aged, *Indian Journal of Gerontology*, Vol. 5, No.1-2, pp. 47-54.

Chadha, N.K., Willigen, John Van and Kedia, Satish (1996): Late Life Changes in Social Networks and Disengagement: Perspectives from a Delhi Neighborhood, *Research and Development Journal*, Vol. 2, No. 3, pp. 7-15.

Chadha, N.K., Aggarwal, Vandana and Mangla A.P. (1992): Hopelessness, Alienation and Life-satisfaction among Aged, *Indian Journal of Gerontology*, Vol. 6., Nos.3-4, pp. 82-92.

Chakravarty, Indrani (1996): Television and the Elderly: Indian Scenario. In Kumar, Vinod (ed): *Aging: Indian Perspective and Global Scenario*. New Delhi: All India Institute of Medical Sciences, pp. 235-236.

Chaney, E.M. (1990): Empowering Older Women: Evidence from Historical and Contemporary Sources. In Chaney, E.M. (Ed.): *Empowering Older Women*, Washington DC: AARP, pp. 5-11.

Chopra, Deepak (1993): *Ageless Body, Timeless Mind: The Quantum Alternative to Growing Old*, New York: Harmony Books.

Chowdhry, D.P. (1992): *Aging and the Aged* (A Source Book), New Delhi: Inter India Publications.

Cochran, C.D. and Hale, W.D. (1983): Sex Differences in Patterns of Sex Reported Psychopathology in the Married Elderly *Journal of Clinical Psychology*, Vol. 39 (5), pp. 647-650.

Coleman, Peter and McCulloch, Andrew (1990): Societal Change, Values and Social Support: Exploratory Studies into Adjustment in Late Life, *Journal of Aging Studies* Vol. 4, No. 4, pp. 321-332.

Cooley, C.H. (1930): *Sociological Theory and Social Research*, New York: H. Holt and Co.

Courtenay, Bradley C., Poon, Leonard W., Martin, P., Clayton, Gloria, M. (1992): Religiosity and Adaptation in Oldest-old, *International Journal of Aging and Human Development*, Vol. 34 (1), pp. 47-56.

Cousinsm Norman (1979): *Anatomy of an Illness as Perceived by the Patient*, New York: W.W. Norton and Co., Inc.

Covey, Herbert C. (1992): The Definition of the Beginning of Old Age in History, *International Journal of Ageing and Human Development*, Vol. 34(4), pp. 325-337.

Cumming, E. and Henry, W.E. (1961): *Growing Old*, New York: Basic Books.

D'Souza, Alfred (1982): *The Social Organization of Aging among the Urban Poor*, New Delhi: Indian Social Institute.

D'Souza, Victor S. (1990): The Simmering Problem of Aging in India: Some Emerging Issues, *BOLD Journal of the International Institute on Aging*, Vol. 4, No. 1, pp. 17-21.

Dak, T.M. and Sharma, M.L. (1987): Changing Status of the Aged in North Indian Villages. In Dak, T.M. and Sharma, M.L. (Eds.): *Aging in India*, New Delhi: Ajanta Publications.

Dandekar, Kumudini (1996): *The Elderly in India*, New Delhi: Sage Publications.

Daniel, Robert (1995): *The Influence of Involvement Retirement and Cognitive Age on the Age-related Learning Deficit*, Montgomery, DBA, Mississippi State University, pp. 228.

Das, Nimai Charam (1994): Psychology of Aging, *Journal of Community Guidance Research*, Vol. 11 (3), September, pp. 201-203.

Dayton, B.I., Morgan, D. and Antonucci, T. (1997): The Effects of Positive and Negative Social Exchanges on Aging Adults, *Journal of Gerontology-Social Sciences*, Vol. 52B, No. 4, S190-S199.

De Alvarez, Julia Tavares (1991): Special Problems Facing Elderly Women in Developing Countries, *BOLD Journal of the International Institute on Aging*, Vol. 2, No. 1, pp. 2-4.

Desai, H.M. (1991): *Disabled Senior Citizens*, MS, WAB Workshop for the Blind, Bombay.

Desai, K.G. (1983): *Aging in India*, Bombay: Tata Institute of Social Sciences.

Desai, K.G. and Naik, R.D. (1970): *Problems of the Retired People in Greater Bombay*, Bombay: Tata Institute of Social Sciences.

Desai, Murli (1998): *Marginalization of Older Persons*, MS, Paper Presented at the National Conference on 21st Century: A New Environment for the Elderly, New Delhi, March 13-17, 1998.

Dhillon, Paramjeet Kaur (1992): *Psychosocial Aspects of Aging in India*, Concept Publication Company, New Delhi.

Dhillon, Paramjeet Kaur and Chhabra (1989): *The Coping Strategies of the Aged*, MS, Delhi University, Delhi.

Dhillon, Paramjeet Kaur and D'Sousa, Sheila (1992): The Effect of Age and Sex on Needs, Social Adjustment and Reactions to Frustration. In Dhillon, Paramjeet Kaur (Ed.): *Psychosocial Aspects of Aging in India*, New Delhi, Concept Publication Company.

Dowd, J.J. (1975): Aging as Exchange: A Preface to Theory, *Journal of Gerontology – Social Sciences*, Vol. 30B, No. 2, pp. S84-S94.

Duck, Steve (1986): *Human Relationships: An Introduction to Social Psychology*, New Delhi: Sage Publications.

Edwards, Allen L. (1969): *Techniques of Attitude Scale Construction*. Bombay: Vakils, Feffer and Simons Pvt. Ltd.

Erikson, E.H. (1982): *The Life Cycle Completed: A Review*. New York: Norton.

Everson, T.C. and Cole, H. (1966): *Spontaneous Regression of Cancer*, Philadelphia: W.B. Saunders.

Ewart, C.K., Taylor, C.B., Kraemer, H.C. and Agras, W.S. (1991): High Blood Pressure and Marital Discord: Not Being Nasty Matters More than Being Nice, *Health Psychology*, Vol. 10(1), pp. 155-163.

Eysenck, H.J. (1987): Personality and Aging: An Exploratory Analysis, *Journal of Social Behaviour and Personality*, Vol. 3 (1), pp. 11-21.

Fairchild, Henry Pratt (1966): *Dictionary of Sociology* (Ed.), New Jersey: Littlefield, Adams and Co.

Feinson, M.C. (1987): Mental Health and Aging: Are there Gender Differences? *The Gerontologist*, Vol. 27(1), pp. 303-311.

Fisherman, Sarah (1991): Relationships among an Older Adult's Life-review, Ego-integrity and Death Anxiety, International Psycho-geriatrics, Vol. 4, Supplement 2, pp. 267-277.

Ganesh, Kamala (1997): Common Gynaecological Morbidity Pattern in Elderly Females. In Bagchi, Kalyan (Ed.): *Elderly Females in India*, New Delhi: Society for Gerontological Research and Helpage India, pp. 65-78.

Gangrede, K.D. (1989): Emerging Concept of Ageing in India: A Socio-cultural Perspective, *Eastern Anthropologist*, Vol. 42, No. 2, pp. 151- 169.

Gautam, Shiv and Pant, Anshuman (1997): Depressive Disorders in the Elderly, *Indian Journal of Gerontology*, Vol.11, Nos. 3-4, pp. 52-67.

Getzen, Thomas E. (1992): Population Aging and the Growth of Health Expenditures, *Journal of Gerontology: Social Sciences*, Vol. 47, No. 3, S98-S104.

Government of India (1995): *The Country Paper For Beijing Conference*. Department of Women and Child Development, Ministry of Social Justice and Empowerment.

Government of India (1999): *National Policy on Older Persons*, Ministry of Social Justice and Empowerment, Shastri Bhawan, New Delhi.

Government of India (2002): *India 2002: A Reference*, New Delhi: Annual Publication Division, Ministry of Information and Broadcasting.

Grewal, Hirdaipal (1991): Lively and Cheerful, Though Retired, *Social Welfare*, Vol. XXXVII, No. 11-12, Feb.-March.

Gupta, P. and Vohra, A.K. (1987): Pattern of Psychiatric Morbidity in the Aged. In Dak, T.M. and Sharma, M.L. (Eds.): *Aging in India*, New Delhi: Ajanta Publications.

Gupta, S.P. (1993): Perspectives on the Sociology of Leisure : Reexamined, *Man in India*, Vol. 73, No. 3, pp. 315-320.

Hall, G. Stanley (1922): *Senescence: The Last Half of Life*, New York: Academic Press.

Hamilton, Ian Sturat, (1994): *The Psychology of Aging: An Introduction*, 2nd Edition, London: Jessica Kingsley Publishers.

Havighurst, R. J. (1973): History of Developmental Psychology: Socialization and Personality Development through the Life-span. In Baltes, P.B. and Schaie, K.W. (Eds.): *Life-span Developmental Psychology: Personality and Socialization*, New York: Academic Press.

Havighurst, R.J. (1961): Successful Aging, *The Gerontologist*, Vol. 1(2), pp. 8-13.

Havighurst, R.J. (1963): Successful Aging. In Williams, R.H., Tibbitts, C. and Donahue, W. (Eds.): *Processes of Aging* (Vol. 1), New York: Atherton.

Herzog, A.R., Rodgers, W.L. and Woodsworth, J. (1982): *Subjective Well-being among Different Age Groups*, Ann Arbor: Institute for Social Research, University of Michigan.

Heyns, Roger W. (1957): *The Psychology of Personal Adjustment*, Ann Arbor: University of Michigan.

Hobfoll, S.E. and Welfisch, S. (1984): Coping with a Threat to Life: A Longitudinal Study of Self-concept, Social Support and Psychological Distress, *American Journal of Community Psychology*, Vol.12(1), pp. 87-100.

Hobman, David (1978): *The Social Challenge of Aging*, London: Croom Helm Ltd.

House, J.S. (1981): *Work Stress and Social Support*. Reading, M.A.: Addison-Wesley.

Hurlock, Elizabeth B. (1976): *Developmental Psychology* (4th Ed.), New Delhi: Tata McGraw-Hill Publishing Company Ltd.

Idler, Ellen L. and Kasl, Stanislav V. (1995): Self Rating of Health: Do They also Predict Change in Functional Ability? *Journal of Gerontology – Social Sciences*, Vol. 50B, No. 6, pp. S344-S353.

Jamuna, D. (1989a): Self-acceptance among Aged Women Belonging to Forward Class and Backward Class Groups, *Journal of Personality and Group Behaviour*, Vol. 9(1), pp. 13-18.

Jamuna, D. (1989c): Psychological Problems and Perspectives of Aged Women. In Pati, R.N. and Jena, B. (Eds.): *Aged in India: Socio-demographic Dimensions*, New Delhi: Ashish Publishing House.

Jamuna, D. (1994): A Psychological and Social Correlates of Successful Aging among Elderly Indian Women, *Indian Journal of Gerontology*, Vol. 8, Nos. 1 and 2, pp. 18-23.

Jamuna, D. (1995): Ageing Women in India: A profile, *Research and Development Journal*, Vol. 1(3), pp. 3-14.

Jamuna, D. and Reddy, N.K.L. (1991): The Widowed Rural Elderly: Status of Mental Health and Adjustment, *The Creative Psychologist*, Vol. 3 (1), pp. 45-50.

Jarvik, L.F. and Small, G.W. (1995): Geriatric Psychiatry: Introduction and Overview. In Kaplan, H.I. and Sadock, B.I. (Eds.): *Comprehensive Textbook of Psychiatry* (VI Ed.) Baltimore: Williams and Willikins.

Jeffers, Frances C., Nichols, Claude R. and Eisdorfer, Carl (1962): Attitudes of Older Persons Towards Death: A Preliminary Study. In Tibbits, Clark and Donahue, Wilina (Eds.): *Social and Psychological Aspects of Ageing,* New York: Columbia University Press.

Joseph, James (1991): *Aged in India: Problems and Personality.* Allahabad: Chugh Publications.

Joshi, P.C. and Sengupta, S.N. (2000): Health Issues, *Seminar,* Vol.488, April, pp. 40-43.

Kailash, R.A. (1976): Death and Dying in Social Context. In Robert, B. and Shanas, Ethal, (Eds.): *Handbook of Aging and Social Sciences,* New York: Behavioural Publications, Inc.

Kakkar, Sudhir (1981): *The Inner World,* Delhi: Oxford University Press.

Kakkar, Sudhir (1982): *Identity and Adulthood,* Delhi: Oxford University Press.

Kamalamma, N. and Selsa, S. (2000): Urban Elderly Women: Problems and Solutions, *Social Welfare,* Vol. 47, June, pp. 30-33.

Kant, Anita and Sharma, Kavita (1996): Well-being and Aging: An Empirical Analysis, *Disabilities and Impairments,* 10 (2), pp. 101-110.

Kapur, Promila, (1997): Elderly Abuse: Some Counselling Tips. *Research and Development Journal,* Vol.3, No.3. pp. 13-23.

Khan, M. Z. (1997): *Elderly in Metropolis.* New Delhi: Inter-India Publications.

Khan, M.Z. and Bagley, N. (1989): Services for the Aged in India, In, Siddiqui, H.Y. (Ed.), *Social Welfare in India,* New Delhi: Harnam Publications.

Khan, M.Z. and Kaushik, Archana (1999): Where do the elderly stand in the changing economic scenario? *Social Welfare,* Vol. 46, No.1, April, pp. 35-39.

Khan, M.Z. and Krishna, K.P. (1983): *Attitudes of Adolescents towards Police,* New Delhi: Institute of Criminology and Forensic Sciences.

Khan, M.Z. and Qamar, Furqan (1996): *Scheduled Castes: Their Socio-economic Background and Development Aspirations,* New Delhi: Inter-India Publications.

Khan, Sakina Yusuf (1998): No Dawn on Sunset Boulevard, *The Sunday Times of India,* November 1, pp. 6, Col. 1-7.

Kincade, Jean E., Rabinder, Donna J., Bernard, Shulamit L. and Woomert, Alison (1996): Older Adults as a Community Resource: Results from the National Survey of Self-care and Aging, *The Gerontologist,* Vol. 36 (4), pp. 474-482.

Kirkwood, T.B.L. (1988): *The Nature and Cause of Aging. In Research and the Aging Population,* MS, CIBA Foundation Symposium, 134 Chichester: Wiley. pp. 193-207.

Klinger, E. (1977): *Meaning and Void: Inner Experience and the Incentives in Public Life,* Minneapolis: University of Minnesota Press.

Kohli, A.S. (1996): *Social Situation of the Aged in India,* New Delhi: Anmol Publications.

Krause, Neal (1993): Neighbourhood Deterioration and Social Isolation in Later Life, *International Journal of Aging and Human Development,* Vol. 36 (1), pp. 9-38.

Krause, Neal (1997): Anticipated Support, Received Support and Economic Stress among Older Adults, *Journal of Gerontology – Psychological Sciences,* Vol. 52B, No. 6, pp. 284-P293.

Kumar, K. (1988): *Concept and Criteria of Adjustment,* MS, NCERT, New Delhi.

Kumar, S. Vijaya (1991): *Family Life and Socio-economic Problems of the Aged,* New Delhi: Ashish Publishing House.

Kumar, S. Vijaya (1995): Ageing in India: An Anthropological outlook, *Research and Development Journal,* Vol. 2, No. 1, pp. 41-45.

Kumar, Vinod, Khetarpal, K., and Soneja, S. (1996): Geriatric Assessment Screening: Further Observations on the AIIMS Experience. In Kumar, Vinod (Ed.): *Aging: Indian Perspective and Global Scenario,* New Delhi: All India Institute of Medical Sciences, pp. 106-107.

Lassonde, Louise (1997): *Coping with Population Challenges,* London: Earthscan Publications Ltd.

Lee, Mee Sook, Crittender, Kathleen S. and Yu, Elena (1996): Social Support and Depression among Elderly Korean Immigrants in the United States, *International Journal of Aging and Human Development,* Vol. 42 (4), pp. 313-327.

Leibenstein (1951): *Economic Backwardness and Economic Growth*, New York: John Wiley and Sons, Inc.

Lin, N., Simeone, R.S., Ensel, W.M. and Kuo, W. (1979): Social Support, Stressful Life Events and Illness: A Model and an Empirical Test, *Journal of Health and Social Behaviour*, Vol. 20, No.1, pp. 108-119.

Liveson, Richard and Peterson, P. (1962): *Aging and Personality*, John Wiley and Sons, Inc., New York.

Lopata, H.Z. (1978): Contributions of Extended Families to the Support System of Metropolitan Area Widows—Limitations of the Modified Network, *Journal of Marriage and Family*, Vol. 40(1), pp. 355-364.

Lopata, H.Z. (1979): *Women as Widows: Support Systems*, North Holland, New York: Elsevier.

Luthra, Prem Nath, (1991): Do not Segregate the Aged from the Mainstream, *Social Welfare*, Vol. 38(3), June, pp. 35-36.

Lynch, J.J. (1977): *The Broken Heart: Medical Consequences of Loneliness*, New York: Basic Books.

Machin, Linda and Davies, V.H. (2000): Women Ageing: Changing Identities, Challenging Myths. In Bernard, M., Phillips, J., Machin, L. and Davies, V.H. (Eds.): *Women Ageing: Changing Identities, Challenging Myths*, London: Routledge.

MacIver, R.M. (1937): *Society: A Textbook of Sociology*, New York: Farrar and Rinehart.

Maddox, George L. (1962): Some Correlates of Differences in Self-assessment of Health Status among the Elderly, *Journal of Gerontology – Psychological Sciences*, Vol. 17, pp. 180-185.

Maddox, George L. (1963): Activity and Morale: A Longitudinal Study of Selected Elderly Subjects. In Riley, M.W. and Foner, A. (Eds.): *Aging and Society*, (Vol.1), New York: Russell Sage Foundation.

Majumdar, Vandana, (1985): The End of the Road, *Hindustan Times* (Magazine), October, 6, p. 1, col.1-8.

Maslow, A.H. (1954): *Motivation and Personality*, New York: Harper.

McDonald, J. (1973): Religious Needs of Older Americans. In John, G. Cull and Richard, E. Hardy (Eds.): *The Neglected Older Americans*, Springfield: Charles C. Thomas.

McKinney, J.C. and Devyver, F.T. (1966): *Aging and Social Policy*, New York: Appleton Century-Craft.

Mcintosh, A.W., Kaplan, H.B., Kubena, K.S., Landmann, W.A. (1993): Life-events, Social Support and Immune Response in Elderly Individuals, *International Journal of Ageing and Human Development*, Vol. 37 (1), pp. 23-36.

Mead, George H., (1937): *Mind, Self and Society*, Chicago: University of Chicago Press.

Mechanic, D. (1980): The Experience and Reporting of Common Physical Complaints, *Journal of Health Social Behaviour*, Vol. 21, pp. 146-155.

Menachery, G. (1987): *Retirement in India: A Psycho-social Study*, Ranchi: Vianney Publications.

Minkler, Meredith, Field, Dorothy, Falk, R. Frank, and Leino, E. Victor (1993): The Influence of Health on Family Contacts and Family Feelings in Advanced Old Age: A Longitudinal Study, *Journal of Gerontology- Social Sciences*, Vol. 48, No. 1, pp. S18-S28.

Mishra, Saraswati (1987): *Social Adjustment in Old Age*. Delhi: B.R. Publishing Corporation.

Mishra, Saraswati. (1996): Coping with Aging at Individual and Societal Levels. In Kumar, Vinod (Ed.): *Aging: Indian Perspective and Global Scenario*, New Delhi: All India Institute of Medical Sciences, pp. 223-225.

Monge, R. and Haltsch, D. (1971): Paired Associate Learning as a Function of Adult Age and the Length of the Anticipation and Inspection Interval, *Journal of Gerontology—Psychological Sciences*, Vol. 26, pp. P157-P162.

Monk, A. (1979): Family Supports in Old Age, *Social Work*, Vol. 24(6), pp. 533-538.

Natrajan, V.S. (1987): Geriatrics: A New Discipline in India, *Indian Journal of Community Guidance Service*, Vol. 4(1), pp. 63-70.

Neugarten, B.L. (1971): *The Awareness of Middle-age and Aging*, Chicago: University of Chicago Press.

Neugarten, B.L., Havighurst, R.J. and Tobin, S.S. (1961): The Measurement of Life-satisfaction, *Journal of Gerontology – Psychological Sciences*, Vol. 16(11B), pp. P134-P143.

O'Brien, Sandra J. and Vertinsky, Patricia A. (1991): Unfit Survivers: Exercise as a Resource for Ageing Women, *The Gerontologist*, Vol. 31 (3), pp. 347-357.

Oberoi, K., and Dey, Seema (1991): A Study of the Physical, Economic, Social and Psychological Problems of Old People, *Indian Psychological Review*, Vol. 36, Nos. 1-2, Jan-Feb., pp. 11-21.

Olteanu, Tatiana, State, Doina and Bodoa, Victoria Negoeseu (1994): Psycho-social and Bio-medical Factors in Human Longevity. In Kumar, Vinod (Ed.): *Aging: Indian Perspective and Global Scenario*, New Delhi: All India Institute of Medical Sciences, pp. 67-70.

Operation Research Group (1990): Family Planning Practices in India, *Third All India Survey*, Vol. II, Monograph, Baroda: ORG.

Paintal, Harinder K. (1991): Factors Related to Successful Aging in Medical Men, *Indian Journal of Gerontology*, Vol. 5, Nos. 3 and 4, pp. 85-91.

Palmore, E., and Cleveland, W. (1976): Aging, Terminal Decline and Terminal Drop, *Journal of Gerontology – Psychological Sciences*, Vol. 31, pp. 76-81.

Palmore, E.B. (1969): Physical, Mental and Social Factors in Predicting Longevity, *The Gerontologist*, Vol. 9(2), pp. 103-108.

Palmore, E.B. and Luikart, C. (1972): Health and Social Factors Related to Life-satisfaction, *Journal of Health and Social Behaviour*, Vol. 13(1), pp. 68-80.

Parbhu, Pradeepa (1997): Geriatric Nutrition, *Research and Development Journal*, Vol. 4, No. 1, pp. 3-8.

Park, J.E. and Park, K. (1970): *Textbook of Preventive and Social Medicine*, (13th Edn.), Jabalpur: Banarsidas Bhanot Publishers.

Patel, Hitesh N. (1997): Mental Problems of Aged and Care of Them by their Family, *Research and Development Journal*, Vol. 4, No. 1, pp. 27-30.

Pati, R.N. and Jena, B. (1989): *Aged in India*, New Delhi: Ashish Publishing House.

Peck, R.C. (1968): Psychological Developments in Second Half of Life, In Neugarten, B.L. (ed.): *Middle Age and Aging: A Reader in Social Psychology*, Chicago: University of Chicago Press.

Pellman, Julie (1992): Widowhood in Elderly Women: Exploring its Relationship to Community Integration, Hassles, Stress, Social Support and Social Support Seeking, *International Journal of Ageing and Human Development*, Vol. 35(4), pp. 253-264.

Peretti, Linda, and Tero, Peter O. (1991): Self-Perceived Variable Patterns in the Closest Friendship Relational Network of Both, or Either Sex among Non-confined Elderly Males, *Indian Journal of Gerontology*, Vol. 5, Nos. 3 and 4, pp. 77-84.

Perlman, D. and Peplau, L. (1982): *Loneliness: A Source Book of Current Theory, Research and Therapy*, New York: John Wiley.

Prakash, Indira Jai (1994): Aging Indian Women. In Ramchandran, C.R. and Shah, Bela (Eds.): *Public Health Implications of Aging in India*, New Delhi: Indian Council of Medical Research, pp. 187-191.

Prakash, Indira Jai (1994): Gender Aging: Psychosocial Issues. In Ramchandran, C.R. and Shah, Bela (Eds.): *Public Health Implications of Aging in India*, New Delhi: Indian Council of Medical Research, pp. 99-105.

Prakash, Indira Jai (1996): Aging Women—A Liability or an Asset? *Research and Development Journal*, Vol. 2, No. 3, pp. 28-32.

Prakash, Indira Jai (1996): Coping with Aging: Psycho-social Situation of Older Indian Women. In Kumar, Vinod (Ed.): *Aging: Indian Perspective and Global Scenario*, New Delhi: All India Institute of Medical Sciences, pp. 291-293.

Prakash, Indira Jai. (1989): *Life-cycle Changes in Aging Indian Women*, MS, Report submitted to UGC, New Delhi.

Prasad, P.H. (1990): Reservation and Class Structure of Castes, *Economic and Political Weekly*, Vol. 25, p. 2.

Puri, Seema and Khanna, Kumud (1999): Health and Nutrition Profile of Middle Class Elderly Women Living in New Delhi, *Research and Development Journal*, Vol. 5, No. 3. pp. 18-26.

R., Kamala and Bhingradiya, Punita (1997): An Intergenerational Study on the Situation of the Elderly in Rural Saurashtra, *Indian Journal of Gerontology*, Vol. 11, Nos. 3 and 4, pp. 78-84.

Raj, B. and Prasad, B.G., (1971): A Study of Rural Aged Persons in Social Profile, *Indian Journal of Social Work*, Vol. 32, No. 2, pp. 23-35.

Ramachandran, C.R. (1994): Introduction: The Emerging Problem of Old Age. In Ramchandran, C.R. and Shah, Bela (Eds.): *Public Health Implications of Aging in India*, New Delhi: Indian Council of Medical Research, pp. 2-3.

Ramamurti, P.V. (1970): Life-satisfaction in the Older Years, *Indian Journal of Gerontology*, Vol. 2, (3-4), pp. 68-70.

Ramamurti, P.V. (1972): *A Study of Role-availability, Role Utilization and Problems of Adjustment of Middle-aged and Older Individuals*, MS, Project Report, ICSSR, New Delhi.

Ramamurti, P.V. (1978): *The Sixth Decade and After*, Tirupati: S.V. University Press.

Ramamurti, P.V. (1989): *An Empirical Study of Needs and Psychosocial Status of Widows of Weaker and Other Sections*, MS, Project Report, ICSSR, New Delhi.

Ramamurti, P.V. (1991): Aging and Society, *Indian Journal of Gerontology*, Vol. 1(1-2), pp. 1-7.

Ramamurti, P.V. (1995): *Health Awareness, Attitudes and Practices among Middle Aged and Elderly Men and Women*, MS, ICMR Project, New Delhi.

Ramamurti, P.V. and Jamuna, D. (1992): Markers of Successful Aging in an Indian Sample, Sandoz Project Report, Basle: Switzerland.

Ramamurti, P.V. and Jamuna, D. (1986): *Self-other Perceptions of Issues and Problems of Aged Women in Andhra Pradesh, India,*

MS, Abstracts of proceedings of IX World Congress of Sociology, ISA, New Delhi.

Ramamurti, P.V. and Jamuna, D. (1987): Psychological Research on the Aged in India. In Biswas, S.K. (Ed.): *Aging in Contemporary India*, Indian Anthropological Society, Calcutta.

Ramamurti, P.V. and Jamuna, D. (1993): Some Predictors of Satisfaction with Present Life in an Indian Sample, *Indian Journal of Gerontology*, Vol. 3, Nos. 3 and 4, pp. 96-103.

Ramamurti, P.V. and Jamuna, D. (1993a): Psychological Dimensions of Aging in India, *Indian Journal of Social Science*, Vol. 6(4), pp. 309-332.

Ramamurti, P.V., Jamuna, D. and Reddy, L.K. (1992b): Improving Human Resources among the Elderly—Effect of an Intervention, *Journal of Personality and Clinical Studies*, Vol. 8(1), pp. 77-79.

Randhawa, Maninder Singh, (1991): *The Rural and Urban Aged: A Sociological Perspective*, Patiala: National Book Organization.

Rao, P. Venkata (1994): Aging in Rural Society, *ICSSR Research Abstract Journal Quarterly*, Vol. XXIII, No. 1-2, Jan.-June.

Rathore, Saroj. (1992): Subjective well-being in Old Age, *Indian Journal of Gerontology*, Vol. 6, Nos. 1 and 2. pp. 37-43.

Reddy, L. K. (1996): Health and Attitude Towards Health among Elderly. In Kumar, Vinod (Ed.): *Aging: Indian Perspective and Global Scenario*, New Delhi: All India Institute of Medical Sciences, pp. 231-234.

Registrar General, India (1997): *Census of India 1991, B series Economic Tables and C series Social and Cultural Tables*, New Delhi: Office of Registrar General of India.

Richard, S., Livson, F. and Petersen, P.G. (1962): *Aging and Personality: A Study of 87 Older Men*, New York: John Wiley and Sons.

Roberto, Karen A. and Stroes, Johanna (1992): Grandchildren and Grandparents: Roles, Influences and Relationships, *International Journal of Aging and Human Development*, Vol. 34, No. 3, pp. 227-239.

Roberts, Beverly L., Dunkle, Ruth and Haug, Marie, (1994): Physical, Psychological and Social Resources as Moderators on the Relationship of Stress to Mental Health of the Very Old, *Journal of Gerontology – Social Sciences*, Vol. 49, No. 1, pp. S35-S43.

Rogers, R.W. (1983): Preventive Health Psychology: An Interface of Social and Clinical Psychology, *Journal of Social and Clinical Psychology*, Vol. 1(1), pp. 120-127.

Rogers, Tommy W., (1991): Correlates of Orientation towards Death, *Indian Journal of Gerontology*, Vol. 5, Nos. 3-4, pp. 102-110.

Rook, K.S. (1990): Stressful Aspects of Older Adults' Social Relationships: An Overview of Current Theory and Research. In Stephens, M.A.P., Crowther, J.H., Hobfall, S.E. and Tennenbaum, D.L. (Eds.): *Stress and Coping in Later Life Families*, Washington, DC: Hemisphere.

Rosow, I. (1967): *Social Integration of the Aged*. New York: Free Press.

Rubinstein, C. and Shaver, P. (1980): Loneliness in Two Northern Cities. In Hartog, J.R. and Cohan, Y.A. (Eds.): *The Anatomy of Loneliness*, New York: International University Press.

Sahayam, M. Deva (1988): Aged Females: The Most Deprived Among the Deprived, *Indian Journal of Social Work*, Vol. 3, No. VIII, pp. 261-670.

Saroja, K. and Badiger, M.S.(1999): Case Study Approach for Research of Divorce, *Social Welfare*, Vol. 45, No.11, pp. 26-29.

Sati, P.N. (1987): *Needs and Problems of The aged (A Study for Social Intervention)*, Udaipur: Himanshu Publications.

Sati, P.N. (1988): *Retired and Aging People*, New Delhi: Mittal Publications.

Schmale, A.H. (1958): The Relationship of Separation and Depression to Disease, *Psychosomatic Medicine* (20), pp. 259-275.

Sen, Kasturi (1994): Women and Aging. In Ramchandran, C.R. and Shah, Bela (Eds.): *Public Health Implications of Aging in India*, New Delhi: Indian Council of Medical Research, pp. 183-186.

Shanas, Ethel (1961): *Family Relationship of Older People*, New York: Health Information Foundation.

Sharma, S.P. (1994): Ageing in India: Some Facts Brought out by Census Data. In Ramchandran, C.R. and Shah, Bela (Eds.): *Public Health Implications of Aging in India*, New Delhi: Indian Council of Medical Research, pp. 36-52.

Sharma, S.P. and Peter Xenos (1992): *Occasional Papers No. 2, Aging in India, Demographic Background and Analysis based on Census Material*, Office of the Registrar General of India and Census Commissioner, India, pp. 38 and 43.

Shaw and Wright (1967): *Scales for the Measurement of Attitudes*. McGraw-Hill, Series in Psychology, San Francisco: St. Louis.

Shock, Nathan W. (1960): Aging: Some Social and Biological Aspects, Symposia presented at the Chicago meeting of the American Association for the Advancement of Science, Dec. 29-30, 1959. Washington: The Association.

Shuval, J.T. (1981): The Contribution of Psychological and Social Phenomenon to an Understanding of the Etiology of Disease and Illness, *Social Science and Medicine*, Vol. 15A, pp. 337-342.

Shuval, J.T., Antonovsky, A. and Davies, A.M. (1973): Illness: A Mechanism for Coping with Failure, *Social Science and Medicine*, Vol. 1(7), pp. 259-265.

Singh, Umesh Kumar (1996): The Health Problems of Aged Persons and the Declining Family Support System. In Kumar, Vinod (Ed.) *Aging: Indian Perspective and Global Scenario*, New Delhi: All India Institute of Medical Sciences, pp. 182-185.

Singh, Vir (1987): Where Women Work More than Bullocks, *Himalaya: Man and Nature*, November.

Singh, Yogendra (1995): Changing Trends in the Indian Family and the Adjustment of the Aged, *Research and Development Journal*, Vol. 3, No. 2, pp. 31-42.

Sinha, R. (1994): The Greying Pains, *The Times of India*, New Delhi, May 28, 1994, Saturday Times, p. 1.

Soodan, K.S. (1975): *Aging in India*, Calcutta: Minerva.

Srinivasan, K. and Shariff, Abusaleh (1997): *Towards Population and Development Goals* (UNFPA), New Delhi: Oxford University Press.

Stevens, Ellen S. (1992): Reciprocity in Social Support: An Advantage for the Aging Female. *Family in Society*, Vol. 73 (9), pp. 533-541.

Stolar, G.E., MacEntee, M.I. and Hill, P. (1993): The Elderly: Their Perceived Support and Reciprocal Behaviours, *Journal of Gerontological Social Work*, Vol. 19, 15-33.

Strehler, B.L. (1976): Introduction: Aging and Human Brain. In Terry, R.D. and Gershon, S. (Eds.): *Neurobiology of Aging*, New York: Raven Press.

Streib, Gorden, (1956): Morale of the Retired, *Social Problems*, Vol. 3(1), pp. 270-276.

Sugisawa, Hidehiro, Jersey, Liang and Liu, Xian (1994): Social Networks, Social Support and Mortality among Older People in Japan, *Journal of Gerontology: Social Sciences*, Vol. 49, No. 1, pp. S3-S13.

The Hindu (2002): *India: Book of the Year*, New Delhi: Encyclopeadia Britannica.

Thomas E.L., Digiulio, R. and Sheehan, N.W. (1988): Identity Loss and Psychological Crisis in Widowhood—A Re-evaluation, *International Journal of Aging and Human Development*, Vol. 26(3), pp. 225-238.

Thurstone, L.L., (1947): *Multiple Factor Analysis*. Chicago: University of Chicago Press.

Thursz, Daniel (1990): The Unfinished Agenda for Coping with an Ageing Society: A Perspective for Washington, *The Journal of Ageing and Judaism*, Vol. 5, No. 1, pp. 41-46.

Tibbitts, Chark (1960): *Handbook of Social Gerontology: Societal Aspects of Aging*, New York: Columbia University Press.

Times of India (2000): India Greying at an Alarming Rate, *TOI*, July 3, Monday, pp. 3, col.4-5.

UNDP, (1999): *World Population Prospects: Revised*, United Nations, Population Division New York: UNDP, 1999.

UNDP (2001): *Human Development Report*, Delhi: Oxford University Press.

UNFPA (1998): *The State of World Population (The New Generation)*, New York: United Nations Population Fund.

United Nations (1989): *United Nations Demographic Yearbook 1989*, New York: United Nations, pp. 106-220.

United Nations (1991): *World Population Prospects*, New York: United Nations.

United Nations (1998): *International Plan of Action on Ageing and United Nations Principles for Older Persons*, New York: United Nations.

United Nations (1999): *World Population Prospects*, New York: United Nations.

United Nations (2002): *International Plan of Action on Ageing 2002*, New York: United Nations.

Verzar, Frigyes (1963): *Lectures on Experimental Gerontology*, Springfield, Ill: Charles C. Thomas.

Vijayanunni, M. (1997): The Graying Population in India: 1991 Census Results, *Research and Development Journal*, Vol. 3, No. 3, pp. 3-12.

Wallace, Paul (1999): Age Quake: Riding the Demographic Roller-coaster Shaking Business, *Finance and Our World*, London: Nicholas Brealey Publishing.

Warren, H.C. (1962): *Dictionary of Psychology*. Massachusetts: Houghton Mifflin Company.

Weiss, C.H. (1972): *Evaluation Research*. Englewood Cliffs, New Jersy: Prentice-Hall.

WHO, (1996): Global Burden of Disease and Injury. In Khan, Sameera's Article, Your Life-style is Killing You, *The Sunday Times of India, Review*, December 22.

WHO, (1999): Ageing: Exploding the Myths. In The Art of Growing Old Healthfully: *The Times of India*, 23rd, March.

Wolff, K. (1959): Group Psychotherapy with Geriatric Patients in a State Hospital Setting: Results of a Three Year Study, *Group Psychotherapy*, Vol. 12, pp. 218-222.

Wolinsky, Fredric D. and Johnson, Robert J. (1992): Widowhood, Health Status and Use of Health Services by Older Adults: A Cross Sectional and Perspective Approach, *Journal of Gerontology – Social Sciences*, Vol. 47, No. 1, pp. S8-S16.

INDEX

Abrams, Robert C. 48
Active Ageing Life-style 231
Activity Theory 79
Adaptation 226, 230
Adelmann, Pamela K. 103
Adjustment 76–77
  Abilities 226
  and Security 209
Age Distribution 46
Age-Care India 35
Ageing
  Concept of 4
  Index of 12
Age-Quake 40
Age-Related Ailments 115–16
Aggression 96
Agrarian Economy 184
Agricultural Economy 1
Aiken, L.R. 113
Alienation and Depression 103
All India Family Planning Survey 186
Alzheimer's Disease 128
Anabolic Reduction 15
Andhra Pradesh 28
Annan, Kofi 4
Annaprassana (Rice-Eating Ceremony) 148
Anxiety 26, 71, 98, 103, 105, 128, 131, 139–40, 146, 171, 175, 178, 206, 218, 222, 229–31
Aoki, R. 69
Ardelt, Monika 143
Aristotle 124
Asha, C.B. 153
Attitudinal Adjustment 85–88, 109, 160, 164
Australia 28
Awareness-Generation Programmes 24

Bagchi, Kalyan 115
Balanced Diet 147, 231
Bali, Arun P. 29
Barer, Barbara M. 83
Barge, S. 67, 201
Basu, Sanjay 124
Bhatia, H.S. 86
Bihar 42
Binstock, R.H. 152
Bio-Chemistry of the Body 15
Biological Age 5, 76
Bio-Psychological Aspects 15
Birren, J.E. 6, 15, 16
Blau, Zena Smith 171
Bodily Ailments 116
Bond, M.J. 103
Boredom 85
Bose, Ashish 26
Breaking-Down Reactions 15
'Building-Up' Reactions 15
Butler, R.N. 17, 116

Cannon, W.B. 76
Capella, J.N. 81
Caring and Adjustment of the Aged 28
Caste-System 57
Cattell, Maria G. 150

Central Public Works Department 33, 46
CGHS Dispensaries 45
Chadha, N.K. 22, 27, 51, 63, 132, 135, 143, 151
Chakravarty, Indrani 124
Child-Care Activities 103, 165
China 39, 213
Chopra, Deepak 76, 123
Chowdhry, D.P. 98
Chronic Illnesses 24, 43
Chronological Age 5–7, 31, 46, 48, 119, 216
Cleanliness 112
Cochran, C.D. 83
Cole, H. 76
Collective Discrimination 50
Commercialization 43, 149
Communication-Skills 82
Compromise 109
Compulsory Retirement 11, 20, 214
Conflict
  Adjustment 85, 92–96, 98, 109, 155, 160, 165
  Conflicting Situations, Effects of 92, 109
  in Relationship 224
Confrontation 85
Constitution of India 151
Cooley, C.H. 147
Coping-Patterns 109
Cost-Reward Aspects 80
Counselling 223
Courtenay, Bradley C. 54
Covey, Herbert C. 115
Crime against Elderly 45, 150
Criminal Procedure Code 151, 187
Criminal Victimization 234
Criterion of 'Being Healthy' 112
Crystallized Personality Patterns 22
Cultural Constraints 70
Cumming, E. 79

D'Souza, Alfred 7
D'Souza, Victor, S. 48, 201
Daily-Life Activities 81, 120–21
Daily-Living Scale 122
Dak, T.M. 195
Dandekar, Kumudini 63
Daniel, Robert 26
Das, Nimai Charam 109
Day-Care Centres 222, 233
Dayton, B.I. 92
De Alvarez, Julia 41
Death-Cum-Retirement-Gratuity 187
Death-Fear 71, 137–38, 141, 146, 218, 222
Delhi Cantonment Board 43
Delhi Development Authority (DDA) 33
Delhi Vidyut Board 46
Dementia 16, 128, 231
Demographic Transition 2–3, 40, 213
Dependency Ratio 13, 28
Depression 16, 26, 103, 231
Desai, H.M. 19, 20, 116, 177, 184
Detachment 79
Dhillon, Paramjeet Kaur 25, 48, 79, 80, 83, 87, 157, 188
Dignity of Older Persons 230
Dimension of Personality Trait 135
Directive Principles of State Policy 186
Discriminal Power 86
Disease Prevention 231
Disengagement Theory 79–80
District Election Office 33
Domains of Social Adjustment Scale 84
Dowd, J.J. 80
Duck, Steve 82
Dunkle, Ruth 120

Economic and Social Dependence 214, 219
Economic Condition of Elderly Females 187

Economic Dependency 41
Economic Development 201
Economic Employment 72, 103
Economic Independence 192
Economic Security 25, 31, 86, 100, 196, 197, 201, 204, 220, 228–29
Economic Self-Reliance 213, 221
Educational and Health-Care Facilities 42
Educational Status 49, 69, 144
Edwards, Allen L. 85
Ego-Differentiation 114
Ego-Preoccupation 114
Ego-Transcendence 114
Emotional Adjustment 48
Emotional and Spiritual Maturity 79
Emotional Distress 83, 92
Empathy 230
Erickson, E.H. 132
Everson, T.C. 76
Ewart, C.K. 83
Extended Families 64
Extrinsic and Intrinsic Factors 108
Eysenck, H.J. 113

Facilitators and Inhibitors of Social Adjustment 81
Fairchild, Henry Pratt 77, 79
Familial Issues 183
Family Composition 63
Feeling of
  Dependency 26
  Guilt 128
  Loneliness 53, 229
  Security 206, 212
  Uselessness 26
Female Fœticide 11
Female Life-Expectancy 28
Financial Insecurity 201
Financial Stringency 20, 201
Fisherman, Sarah 138
France 8
Frustrations 109

Ganesh, Kamla 16, 117
Gangrade, K.D. 54, 63
Gautam, Shiv 128
Gender Issue 143, 185
Generation Gap 92
Germany 7
Getzen, Thomas, E. 186
Grandparents Role 162
Grewal, Hirdaipal 26
Grey World 39, 75
'Grey-Revolution' 213
Greying of Nations 2, 40
Gupta, P. 16, 124
Gynæcological Complications 115, 118

Hall, G. Stanley 16
Hamilton, Iran Sturat 113, 116
Harmonious Social Interactions 109, 147
Haryana 42
Haug, Marie 120
Havighurst, R.J. 17, 79, 83, 144
Health
  -Care, Lack of 41
  Condition of Elderly Females 116, 221
  Degeneration of 222
  Insurance 233
Hearing Impairment 116
Helpage India 35
Helplessness 26
Herzog, A.R. 22
Heyns, Roger W. 22
High Economic Dependency Project 29
Hill, P. 92
Himachal Pradesh 42
Hindu Adoption and Maintenance Act, 187
Hobfoll, S.E. 139, 140
Hobman, David 128
Home Management 103, 157
Home-Like Environment 65

Hopelessness 51
Hot Arguments, Exchanging of 92
Housing Accommodation, Lack of 29
Human Development Report 10
Hurlock, Elizabeth B. 113

Illiteracy 29, 41, 214
Ill-Treatment by Family 131
Inability to Adjust 128
In-built Programme 113
Indian Council of Social Science Research 35
Indicators of Psychological Well-Being 71
Indonesia 213
Industrialization 1, 43, 149, 158, 184, 214
Insomnia 122, 125
Intergenerational Relationship 40
International Action Programme for the Aged 4
International Plan of Action on Ageing 183, 229–30
Interpersonal Relationship 147
Irritability 96, 128
Isolation and Meaninglessness 80
Italy 7

Jamia Millia Islamia University 35
Jamuna, D. 19, 23, 24, 28, 50, 83, 87, 98, 103, 139, 143, 149, 152, 179, 186
Japan 2, 7
Jarvik, L.F. 122
Jawaharlal Nehru University 35
Jealousy 85
Jeffers, Frances C. 137
Johnson, Robert J. 124
Joint Family System 1, 64, 148, 155, 184, 217
Joseph, James 128
Joshi, P.C. 16

Kailash, R.A. 137
Kakkar, Sudhir 17, 18, 149
Kamalamma, N. 20
Kant, Anita 144
Kapur, Promila 21, 23
Karma Philosophy 81
Kaushik, Archana 43, 187
Kedia, Satish 27
Kerala 7, 42
Khan, M.Z. 5, 15, 21, 24, 26, 27, 28, 34, 43, 57, 63, 82, 187
Kincade, Jean E. 152
Kirkwood, T.B.L. 113
Klinger, E. 81
Krause, Neal 92, 151
Kumar, K. 27, 69

Lee, Mee Sook 152
Leibenstein 186
Lewis, M.I. 17, 116
Liberal Attitudes 226
Life Expectancy 9
Life Expectations 106
Life Satisfaction 55, 96, 106, 143–46, 160, 212
  Index 144
Likert Scale 85
Limited Living Space 20
Lin, N. 152
Liveson, Richard 109
Loneliness 26, 55, 71, 105, 129–30, 139, 146, 170, 175, 178, 206, 216–18, 222, 230
Lopata, H.Z. 25, 53
Loss of Recent Memory 26
Luikart, C. 143
Luthra, Prem Nath 173
Lynch, J.J. 114, 125

MacEntee, M.I. 92
Machin, Linda 83, 85
Maciver, R.M. 53
Maddox, George L. 157
Majumdar, Vandana 109
Mal-Adjustment 223

Malnutrition 29, 214
Marital
  Conflicts 131
  Relationship 49, 144–45, 153
Maslow, A.H. 98
Mcdonald, J. 55
Mcintosh, A.W. 114
Mckinney, J.C. 109
Mead, George H. 80, 147
Mechanic, D. 125
Menopause 6
Mental Health Problems 16, 25–26, 49, 115, 122, 231
Migration 19
Ministry of Social Justice and Empowerment 151
Minkler, Meredith 24
Mishra, Saraswati 19, 24, 34, 83, 85
Modernization 19, 158
Monk, A. 188
Morgan, D. 92
Mother-Tongue 60
Motivation 109
Multiple Pregnancies 115, 214
Municipal Corporation of Delhi 44

Naik, R.D. 177
National Council of Educational Research and Training (NCERT) 35
National Policy for Older Persons 7, 151, 187, 229–31
National Sample Survey (NSS) 50–51
Natrajan, V.S. 83
Need Adjustment 85, 100–01, 109, 160
Negative Self-Perception 132
Neugarten, B.L. 48, 144
Nigeria 8
Non-Governmental Organizations (NGOs) 232–33
Non-Traditional Economic Activities 80
Nuclear Family System 20, 155
Nutritional Deficiencies 115

O'Brien 116
Oberoi, K. 153
Occupational
  Patterns 49, 73, 139
  Status 72, 75, 218–19
Old Age
  Economic Stringency 201
  Homes 63
  Pension 7, 42, 187, 220
  Security 67, 186, 201
Older Person's Disengagement 80
Olteanu, Tatiana 24
Optimism 55, 71, 134, 230
Orissa 36
Overlapping Perspectives 5

Paintal, Harinder K. 25, 125, 201, 209
Palmore, E. 23, 143
Pant, Anshuman 128
Parbhu, Pradeepa 15
Patel, Hitesh N. 26
Patriarchal Social Structure 1, 216
Pellman, Julie 156
Peplau, L. 129
Peretti, Linda 27
Perlman, D. 129
Personal
  Autonomy 120
  Problems 183
Pessimism 134–135, 139, 146, 218, 222
Phenomenological Theory 80
Physical
  Health 112
  Independence 184
  Proximity 172
Physiological Deterioration 94
Possessiveness 85
Post-Menopausal Problems 115, 117
Poverty 41

Power Politics in the Family 97
Powerlessness 80
Prakash, Indira Jai 7, 24, 25, 73, 143
Prasad, P.H. 59, 132
Preference for Male-Child 115
Primary Degenerative Dementia 128
Print and Electronic Media 234
Problems of Mobility 24
Productive Activity 98
Product-Moment Correlation 100, 109–10, 147
Property Conflicts 149
Protection of Income-Security 147
Psychological
- Problems 103, 218, 222
- State of Happiness 81, 221
- Support 184
- Well-Being 113

Psycho-Social Integration 217
Psychosocial Theory of Development 132
Psycho-Therapy 223
Punjab 42

Qamar, Furqan 57
Quality of
- Quality of Social Interaction 114, 226
- Relationship 218, 226

Raj, B. 132
Rajasthan 42
Ramachandran, C.R. 40
Ramamurti, P.V. 19, 23, 24, 34, 50, 81, 83, 98, 112, 139, 143, 152
Randhawa, Mahinder Singh 85
Rank Correlation 100
Rao, P. Venkata 27
Rathore, Saroj 132
Realistic Expectations 109, 230
Reddy, L.K. 24, 72
Relational Difficulties 114
Reliability-Coefficient 86
Religious Affiliations 53, 55
Religious Organization 147
Reservation in Jobs 59
Resident Welfare Associations (RWAs) 35, 234
Retirement Benefits 187, 205, 220
Richard, S. 109, 139
Roberto, Karen A. 162
Roberts, Beverly L. 120
Rogers, R.W. 115, 137
Role Adjustment 85, 102, 105–06, 108–09, 160, 165
Role Theory 80
Role-Less Status 80
Rook, K.S. 83, 92
Rosow, I. 80, 147
Rubenstein, C. 129

Sahayam, M. Deva 72
Sanitation and Health Facilities 2
Saroja, K. 50
Sati, P.N. 98, 162
Schmale, A.H. 114
Seclusion 85
Security for Elderly 186
Self-Dependence 120
Self-Evaluation of Health 111, 123, 143
Self-Help Groups of Older Females 232
Selsa, S. 20
Sen, Kasturi 19
Sengupta, S.N.16
Senior Citizens, Needs of 43
Sense of Security 228–29
Sex Ratio 11
Shanas, Ethel 80, 152
Shariff, Abusaleh 185
Sharma, S.P. 11, 144, 195
Shaver, P. 129
Sheehan, N.W. 50
Shock, Nathan W. 5
Short-Term Care 222
Shuval, J.T. 112

Sociability 27
Social Acceptance of Elders 31, 147, 151, 165, 171–72
Social Adjustment 21, 31, 75, 78, 83, 93, 108–111, 114, 121, 139–43, 156, 160, 165–67, 172–73, 175, 179, 183, 199, 217, 221, 223
Social Adjustment Scale 87, 99, 104, 109, 215
Social Age 7
Social Assistance for the Senior Citizens 41
Social Behaviours 15
Social Dependency 41
Social Exchange Theory 80
Social Insurance 41
Social Integration 108, 183
Social Maturity 48
Social Relationships 26, 114
Social Security Systems 40, 187
Social Skills of Elderly Females 219
Social Support
  Absence of 152
  Network 98
Social Welfare Schemes 41–42
Socialization 83
Socially Well-Adjusted People 140
Socio-Cultural Characteristics 17, 42, 115
Socio-Economic Factors 139, 144, 219
Soodan, K.S. 132
Spearman-Brown Formula 86
Special Population Group 4
Spiritual Dimension 54
Split-Half Method 86
Srinivasan, K. 185
Stevens, Ellen S. 147
Stolar, G.E. 92
Strehler, B.L. 5
Streib, Gorden 212
Subjective
  Health Evaluation 116
  Well-Being 132
Submissiveness 83
Subrahmanian, K.A. 153
Sugisawa, Hidehiro 151
Sweden 2, 7–8

Technological Advancement 20
Telephone Helplines 234
Tension 71, 105, 131, 139–40, 146, 171, 175, 178, 206, 216, 218, 222, 230
Third World Countries 6
Thomas, E.L. 50
Thurstone, L.L. 84
Thursz, Daniel 122
Tibbitts, Chark 6
Tobin, S.S. 144
Tolerance 83
'Trait-Lonely' People 223

United Kingdom 2, 8
United Nations 4, 9, 29, 39, 40, 42
United States 2–3, 122
Urbanization 19, 43, 149, 214
  of Leisure Time 124

Value-Development 162
Verbal or Non-Verbal Expression 83
Verification of Domestic Help 234
Verzar, Frigyes 5
Vijayanunni, M. 43
Vohra, A.K. 16

Wallace, Paul 40
Weiss, C.H. 114, 127
Well-Being of Elderly Females 128
West Bengal 42
Widowhood 29, 43, 50, 127, 156, 214, 216
Willigen, John Van 27
Wolff, K. 54
Wolinsky, Fredric D. 124
Work Force Participation Rate (WFPR) 11–12, 29

World Assembly on Ageing 4
World Health Organization (WHO)
31, 115, 131, 147, 218
World's Health Day 115
Worldly Affairs Renouncement 79

Yoga and Meditation 231
Young-Old 47